AWS
Certified Machine Learning
Study Guide
Specialty (MLS-C01) Exam

AWS
Certified Machine Learning
Study Guide
Specialty (MLS-C01) Exam

Shreyas Subramanian

Stefan Natu

SYBEX
A Wiley Brand

To our parents.

Acknowledgments

Although this book bears our names as authors, many other people contributed to its creation. Without their help, this book wouldn't exist, or at best would exist in a lesser form. Kenyon Brown was the acquisitions editor and so helped get the book started. Christine O'Connor, the managing editor, and Caroline Define, project manager, oversaw the book as it progressed through all its stages. Sonam Mishra was the technical editor, who checked the text for technical errors and omissions—but any mistakes that remain are our own. We would also like to thank Matt Wagner from FreshBooks, who helped connect us with Wiley to write this book. Finally, we would like to thank our wives for their patience as we spent many weekend hours researching the content and writing this book over the past 8 months.

About the Authors

About the Technical

Shreyas Subramanian has a PhD in multilevel systems optimization and application of machine learning to large-scale optimization. He is currently a principal machine learning specialist at Amazon Web Services, and he has worked with several large-scale companies on their business-critical machine learning and optimization problems. Subramanian is passionate about simplifying difficult concepts within optimization, and he holds two patents in areas connected to aviation-related tools and techniques for improving efficiency and security of the airspace. He has also published over 20 conference and journal papers on the topics of aircraft design, evolutionary optimization, distributed optimization, and multi-level systems or systems optimization. He has several years of experience building machine learning and optimization models for customers in large enterprises to small startups, while taking part in and winning hackathons on the side. Subramanian is passionate about teaching practical machine learning to citizen data scientists and has trained hundreds of customers in private, hands-on environments and has helped customers build proofs-of-concept that are now in production today, providing millions of dollars' worth of revenue to the AWS business as well as customers.

Stefan Natu is a principal machine learning (ML) architect at Alexa AI, where he is building an ML platform for Alexa scientists and engineers. Prior to that, Natu was the lead ML architect at Amazon Web Services, where he focused on financial services and helped major investment banking, asset management, and insurance customers build and operationalize ML use cases on AWS, with an emphasis on security, enterprise data, and model governance. Natu has developed and evangelized common ML architecture and infrastructure patterns globally across AWS highly regulated customers, leading to numerous production ML deployments and millions of dollars in AWS cloud revenue. He has authored over 25 AWS machine learning blogs, code samples. and whitepapers, and is a frequent speaker at conferences such as AWS re:Invent. He completed his PhD in atomic and condensed matter physics from Cornell University, and he worked as a research physicist at ExxonMobil, submitting two patents and over 25 peer-reviewed publications. Natu is passionate about mentorship and has served as a technical adviser at Insight Data Science, where he guided students in their transition from careers in academia to industry.

About the Technical Editor

Sonam Mishra is an IT consultant with several years of experience in diverse roles ranging from software development, to application testing, to technical content creation. She is passionate about new and emerging technologies, particularly in the area of cloud computing. She lives in the United Kingdom with her family.

Contents at a Glance

Contents

Introduction

Machine learning (ML) is one of the most popular and rapidly growing fields in the technology industry today, with far-reaching business implications. The market for ML solutions and products is expected to grow annually by tens of billions of dollars, and with it, the demand for professionals who understand how to analyze data and build ML solutions is expected to grow as well.

ML is a highly technical field, and successful ML professionals need a foundation in mathematics, statistics, and data analysis. They must be able to code and have a fundamental understanding of infrastructure and software development best practices. In the past, the practitioners of machine learning were academics and PhDs, but the industry demand for ML is much larger than the supply of new PhDs emerging from academic institutions.

The purpose of this book is for you to understand the concepts and principles behind ML, with the practical goal of passing the AWS Certified Machine Learning Specialty exam. As practicing ML solution architects, we go well beyond the scope of the test in this book and incorporate architecture patterns and best practices that we have seen employed in the industry today. Reading this book will also give you an understanding of what is required to be a successful machine learning architect.

This is not a book on ML foundations. That is simply too vast a field for us to do it justice in this book and also is not our intention. There are a number of excellent textbooks and online resources you can use to develop a foundation on ML algorithms, deep learning, and similar topics. However, we will cover the concepts that you will need for the test.

Finally, one of our favorite leadership principles here at Amazon that widely applies to the solution architect role is *learn and be curious*. We have found that the best way to learn a topic is to get hands-on, and we highly recommend that you go beyond this book and get hands-on experience in ML. Download and explore some public datasets, and train some simple predictive models. Build a neural network from scratch using TensorFlow/PyTorch or just native Python. Explore AWS services such as Amazon SageMaker by running some of the sample Jupyter Notebooks. We highly recommend getting some hands-on knowledge before taking the test. Check out the AWS Training and Certification web page for helpful courses: www.aws.training.

Don't just study the questions and answers! The questions on the actual exam will be different from the practice questions included in this book. The exam is designed to test your knowledge of a concept or objective, so use this book to learn the objectives behind the questions.

The ML space is maturing and growing very quickly; what this means is that our book is just a snapshot in time of our understanding of the industry and certification requirements. We highly recommend that you read the SageMaker home page to review the latest releases that may appear on the test.

The AWS Certified Machine Learning Specialty Exam

The AWS Certified Machine Learning Specialty exam is intended for professionals who perform a data science, machine learning engineer role. The official details of the test can be found here: https://aws.amazon.com/certification/certified-machine-learning-specialty.

The focus of the test is to validate your understanding of foundational ML concepts, foundations of statistics, data analysis, exploration, feature engineering, and common ML algorithms. This is required knowledge for anyone performing this role in industry today. However, in addition to this, this certification focuses on your ability to deploy those solutions on AWS and to be able to architect an end-to-end solution on AWS from data ingestion to model deployment and monitoring using a host of relevant AWS services for a given business use case.

Why Become AWS Machine Learning Specialty Certified?

There are several good reasons to get your AWS Certified Machine Learning certification:

It provides proof of professional achievement.   Certifications are quickly becoming status symbols in the computer service industry. Organizations, including members of the computer service industry, are recognizing the benefits of cloud certification such as the AWS Solution Architect Professional, Certified Security, and Advanced Networking Specialty. As ML becomes increasingly popular, these certifications provide proof of your understanding of ML and your ability to practically deploy ML solutions on AWS.

It provides an opportunity for advancement.   The solution architect role is one of the most coveted roles in the tech industry today due to the breadth and depth of the knowledge you gain, while having an outsized impact on customers' business. The Machine Learning Specialty Certification could provide you with an opportunity to specialize in ML and become a practicing ML architect, a unique role that many employers are looking to hire.

It helps you develop an industry understanding of ML.   ML education is rapidly becoming a crowded space with blogs, textbooks, online courses that cover the foundations of ML, statistics and data science, and even ML tooling. However, there is no substitute for experience, and there isn't much material on actual industry use cases with solutions and best practices (with the exception of some fantastic tech blogs published by companies like Uber, Google, Netflix, Lyft, Airbnb, and many others). This book aims to cover some of that gap by providing you with a practical understanding of building real-life ML solutions on AWS.

It will satisfy your curiosity. As technologists and technology enthusiasts, we are constantly learning new areas and expanding our knowledge. One of the best and most fulfilling reasons to take this certification is simply to satiate your curiosity to learn how to build ML solutions on AWS.

How to Become AWS Machine Learning Specialty Certified

The AWS Certified Machine Learning Specialty exam is available to anyone and does not require other AWS certifications as prerequisites. It is recommended, however, that you have 1–2 years of experience developing and architecting ML and deep learning workloads on AWS prior to taking the test. Because it is a specialty certification, it also assumes prior foundational understanding of AWS services for storage, networking, security, databases, and so forth; however, these are not tested in detail.

The exam is administered by Pearson VUE and PSI. To register for the test with PSI, you can register online at https://awsavailability.psiexams.com. To register with Pearson VUE, you can register online using https://home.pearsonvue.com/Clients/Amazon-Web-Services.aspx.

> Exam policies can change from time to time. We highly recommend that you check both the PSI and Pearson VUE sites for the most up-to-date information when you begin preparing, when you register, and again a few days before your scheduled exam date.

Who Should Buy This Book

Anybody who wants to pass the AWS Certified Machine Learning Specialty exam may benefit from this book. This book is also helpful for business and IT professionals who want to learn how ML is practically used in the industry and pivot their careers toward an ML-centric role such as a data scientist or ML engineer working on AWS. We include a number of practical case studies, industry best practices, and architecture patterns that we have seen used in industry today from our engagements with hundreds of AWS customers. This book is also essential for data scientists, engineers, and other data professionals who are curious about how you can build, train, and deploy models at scale on AWS.

This book assumes some familiarity with ML and with AWS. If you are completely new to machine learning, we recommend that you first learn some basic ML concepts since this book is mainly focused on the practical aspects of building ML solutions. There are several great resources that cover ML foundations, particularly for building statistical models and for deep learning. Two of our favorites are Aurélion Géron's Hands-on Machine Learning with Scikit-learn and TensorFlow (O'Reilly Publishing) and Francois Chollet's *Deep Learning with Python* (Manning, 2017). There are also several awesome blogs on Medium .com and TowardsDataScience.com. Finally, we also recommend a number of industry blogs from leading tech companies like Uber, Google, Facebook, Amazon, Airbnb, and others on how they deploy large-scale ML solutions to have a holistic understanding of the industry landscape in this space.

As a practical matter, you'll need a laptop or desktop with which to practice and learn in a hands-on way. This book does not cover labs, and there is no substitute for hands-on experience. Go get familiar with AWS ML services such as SageMaker, as well as the AI services, before taking the test. We also recommend that you explore some public datasets, engineer features, and train simple models as well as some deep learning models.

Study Guide Features

This study guide uses a number of common elements to help you prepare. These include the following:

Summaries   The summary section of each chapter briefly explains the chapter, allowing you to easily understand what it covers.

Exam Essentials   The Exam Essentials focus on major exam topics and critical knowledge that you should take into the test. They focus on the exam objectives provided by AWS.

Chapter Review Questions   A set of questions at the end of each chapter will help you assess your knowledge and if you are ready to take the exam based on your knowledge of that chapter's topics.

The review questions, assessment test, and other testing elements included in this book are *not* derived from the actual exam questions, so don't memorize the answers to these questions and assume that doing so will enable you to pass the exam. You should learn the underlying topic, as described in the text of the book. This will let you answer the questions provided with this book *and* pass the exam. Learning the underlying topic is also the approach that will serve you best in the workplace—the ultimate goal of a certification.

Interactive Online Learning Environment and Test Bank

We've worked hard to provide some really great tools to help you with your certification process. The interactive online learning environment that accompanies the AWS Certified Machine Learning Study Guide: Specialty (MLS-C01) Exam provides a test bank with study tools to help you prepare for the certification exam—and increase your chances of passing it the first time! The test bank includes the following:

Sample Tests: All the questions in this book are provided, including the assessment test at the end of this introduction and the review questions at the end of each chapter. In addition, there is a practice exam with 76 questions. Use these questions to test your knowledge of the study guide material. The online test bank runs on multiple devices.

Flashcards: The online text bank includes flashcards specifically written to challenge you, so don't get discouraged if you don't ace your way through them at first. They're there to ensure that you're really ready for the exam. And no worries—armed with the book, reference material, review questions, practice exams, and flashcards, you'll be more than prepared when exam day comes. Questions are provided in digital flashcard format (a question followed by a single correct answer). You can use the flashcards to reinforce your learning and provide last-minute test prep before the exam.

Glossary: A glossary of key terms from this book is available as a fully searchable PDF.

> Go to www.wiley.com/go/sybextestprep, register your book to receive your unique PIN, and then once you have the PIN, return to www.wiley.com/go/sybextestprep and register a new account or add this book to an existing account.

Conventions Used in This Book

This book uses certain typographic styles in order to help you quickly identify important information and to avoid confusion over the meaning of words such as on-screen prompts. In particular, look for the following styles:

- *Italicized text* indicates key terms that are described at length for the first time in a chapter. (Italics are also used for emphasis.)

- A `monospaced` font indicates the contents of configuration files, messages displayed at a text-mode Linux shell prompt, filenames, text-mode command names, and Internet URLs.

- *Italicized monospaced text* indicates a variable—information that differs from one system or command run to another, such as the name of a client computer or a process ID number.

- **Bold monospaced text** is information that you're to type into the computer, such as at a shell prompt. This text can also be italicized to indicate that you should substitute an appropriate value for your system.

In addition to these text conventions, which can apply to individual words or entire paragraphs, a few conventions highlight segments of text:

A note indicates information that's useful or interesting but that's somewhat peripheral to the main text. A note might be relevant to a small number of networks, for instance, or it may refer to an outdated feature.

A tip provides information that can save you time or frustration and that may not be entirely obvious. A tip might describe how to get around a limitation or how to use a feature to perform an unusual task.

Warnings describe potential pitfalls or dangers. If you fail to heed a warning, you may end up spending a lot of time recovering from a bug, or you may even end up restoring your entire system from scratch.

 **Real World Scenario**

Real-World Scenario

A real-world scenario is a type of sidebar that describes a task or an example that's particularly grounded in the real world. This may be a situation we or somebody we know has encountered, or it may be advice on how to work around problems that are common in real, working ML environments.

AWS Certified Machine Learning Specialty Exam Objectives

AWS Certified Machine Learning Study Guide has been written to cover every AWS exam objective at a level appropriate to its exam weighting. The following table provides a breakdown of this book's exam coverage, showing you the weight of each section and the chapter where each objective or subobjective is covered:

Subject Area	% of Exam
Domain 1: Data Engineering	20%
Domain 2: Exploratory Data Analysis	24%
Domain 3: Modeling	36%
Domain 4: Machine Learning Implementation and Operations	20%
Total	100%

Domain 1: Data Engineering

Subdomain 1.1: Create Data Repositories for Machine Learning

Exam Objective	Chapter
1.1-1. Create data repositories for machine learning	5
▪ Identify data sources	5
▪ Determine storage mediums	2, 5

Subdomain 1.2: Identify and Implement a Data Ingestion Solution

Exam Objective	Chapter
1.2-1. Data job styles/types (batch load/streaming)	6, 7
1.2-2. Data ingestion pipelines	7
▪ Kinesis	7
▪ Kinesis Analytics	7
▪ Kinesis Firehose	7

Subdomain 1.3: Identify and Implement a Data Transformation Solution

Domain 2: Exploratory Data Analysis

Subdomain 2.1: Sanitize and Prepare Data for Modeling

Subdomain 2.2: Perform Feature Engineering

Exam Objective	Chapter
2.2-2. Analyze/evaluate feature engineering concepts (binning, tokenization, outliers, synthetic features, One-hot encoding, reducing dimensionality of data)	7

Subdomain 2.3: Analyze and Visualize Data for Machine Learning

Exam Objective	Chapter
2.3-1. Graphing (scatter plot, time series, histogram, box plot)	9
2.3-2. Interpreting descriptive statistics (correlation, summary statistics, p value)	9
2.3-3. Clustering (hierarchical, diagnosing, elbow plot, cluster size)	9

Domain 3: Modeling

Subdomain 3.1: Frame Business Problems as Machine Learning Problems

Exam Objective	Chapter
3.1-1. Determine when to use/when not to use ML	3
3.1-2. Know the difference between supervised and unsupervised learning	4
3.1-3. Selecting from among classification, regression, forecasting, clustering, recommendation, etc.	4

Subdomain 3.2: Select the Appropriate Model(s) for a Given Machine Learning Problem

Exam Objective	Chapter
3.2-1. XGBoost, logistic regression, K-means, linear regression, decision trees, random forests, RNN, CNN, Ensemble, Transfer learning	8
3.2-2. Express intuition behind models	8

Subdomain 3.3: Train Machine Learning Models

Subdomain 3.4: Perform Hyperparameter Optimization

Subdomain 3.5: Evaluate machine learning models

Domain 4: Machine Learning Implementation and Operations

Subdomain 4.1: Frame Build Machine Learning Solutions for Performance, Availability, Scalability, Resiliency, and Fault Tolerance

Subdomain 4.2: Recommend and Implement the Appropriate Machine Learning Services and Features for a Given Problem

Subdomain 4.3: Apply Basic AWS Security Practices to Machine Learning Solutions

Exam Objective	Chapter
4.3-1. IAM	2, 13
4.3-2. S3 Bucket Policies	2, 13
4.3-3. Security groups	2, 13
4.3-4. VPC	2, 13
4.3-5. Encryption/anonymization	13

Subdomain 4.4: Deploy and Operationalize Machine Learning Solutions

Exam Objective	Chapter
4.4-1. Exposing endpoints and interacting with them	10, 11
4.4-2. ML model versioning	8, 12
4.4-3. A/B testing	10
4.4-4. Retrain pipelines	15
4.4-5. ML debugging/troubleshooting	12
▪ Detect and mitigate drop in performance	15
▪ Monitor performance of the model	15

Exam domains and objectives are subject to change at any time without prior notice and at AWS's sole discretion. Please visit their website (https://aws.amazon.com/certification/certified-machine-learning-specialty) for the most current information.

Assessment Test

1. You are building a supervised ML model for predicting housing prices in the United States. However, you notice that your dataset has a lot of highly correlated features. What are some methods you can use to reduce the number of features in your dataset? (Choose all that apply.)

    A. Use principal component analysis to perform dimensionality reduction.

    B. Add an L2 regularization term to your loss function.

    C. Add an L1 regularization term to your loss function.

    D. Add an L3 regularization term to your loss function.

2. Which of the following is an unsupervised learning algorithm useful with tabular data?

    A. K-nearest neighbors

    B. K-means clustering

    C. Latent Dirichlet Allocation (LDA)

    D. Random forest

3. Which of the following ML instance types is ideally suited for deep learning training?

    A. EC2 M family instances

    B. EC2 Inf1 instances powered by AWS Inferentia

    C. EC2 G4 family of instances

    D. EC2 P3 family of instances

4. Your company has a vast number of documents that contain some personally identifiable information (PII). The company is looking for a solution where the documents can be uploaded to the cloud and for a service that will extract the text from the documents and redact the PII. The company is concerned about the costs to train deep learning models for text and entity extraction. What solution would you recommend for this use case?

    A. Upload the data to S3. Train a custom SageMaker model for text extraction from raw documents, followed by an entity extraction algorithm to extract the PII entities.

    B. Use an off-the-shelf optical character recognition (OCR) tool to extract the text. Then use an entity detection algorithm to extract PII entities.

    C. Use Amazon Textract to extract text from documents and Amazon Comprehend PII detection to detect PII entities.

    D. Use Amazon Textract to extract text from documents and Amazon Rekognition PII detection to detect PII entities.

5. You have written some algorithm code on a local IDE like PyCharm and uploaded that script to your SageMaker environment. The code is the entry point to a training container, which contains all the relevant packages you need for training. However, before kicking off a full training job, you want to quickly and interactively test whether the code is working as expected. What can you do to achieve this?

    A. Kick off a SageMaker processing job to test your code. Once it is working, then kick off a SageMaker training job.

    B. Kick off a SageMaker training job on a t3.medium. Once you are convinced it is working, then switch to a larger instance type.

    C. Use SageMaker local mode to kick off a job locally on your SageMaker notebook instance. Debug your scripts, and once they are working, start a SageMaker training job.

    D. Kick off a SageMaker Batch Transform job to test your code. Once it is working, then kick off a SageMaker training job.

6. You are building a supervised ML model for forecasting average sales for your products based on product metadata and prior month sales. The data is arranged in a tabular format, where each row corresponds to a different product. Which machine learning algorithms might you choose for this task? (Choose all that apply.)

    A. Random forest classifier

    B. DeepAR forecasting

    C. Random forest regressor

    D. Linear regression

7. A business stakeholder from a solar energy company comes to you with a business problem to identify solar panels on roofs from aerial footage data. Currently, the business stakeholder does not have much labeled data available. What advice would you give them to proceed with this use case?

    A. Semantic segmentation is an unsupervised ML problem that doesn't require labeled data. You can use a clustering algorithm to discover the roofs.

    B. Semantic segmentation requires labels. Since this use case is very domain specific, you will need to train a custom model to detect them. For this, you will need to first develop a strategy to acquire labels. Advise the business stakeholder that you will need to factor in data labeling as part of this project.

    C. Semantic segmentation requires labels. Simply pick up an off-the-shelf object detection model that is trained on ImageNet corpus for detecting the roofs.

    D. Semantic segmentation is not an ML problem. Advise them to write a set of rules to detect solar panels on roofs based on the geometry of the solar panels.

8. Consider the same problem as the use case in Question 7. What AWS solution would you recommend to the stakeholder for generating labeled data?

    A. Use Amazon Rekognition custom labels to label the rooftops.

    B. Use SageMaker Data Wrangler.

    C. Use Amazon Augmented AI.

    D. Use SageMaker Ground Truth.

9. Which AWS service would you use to optimize your ML models to run on a specific hardware platforms or edge devices with processors from ARM, NVIDIA, Xilinx, and Texas Instruments?

   A. Amazon CodeGuru

   B. Amazon DevOps Guru

   C. SageMaker Neuron SDK

   D. SageMaker Neo

10. Which AWS AI/ML service would you use to detect anomalies in retail transaction data? (Choose all that apply.)

    A. Amazon SageMaker Random Cut Forest

    B. Amazon SageMaker DeepAR

    C. Amazon Lookout for Metrics

    D. Amazon Forecast

11. You have set up your S3 buckets in such a way that they cannot be accessed outside of your VPC using an S3 bucket policy. You are now passing the S3 prefix for your training dataset to SageMaker's training estimator to kick off training but find that SageMaker is unable to access your S3 buckets and give a Permission Denied Error. How can you resolve this issue?

    A. Remove the bucket policy to allow the bucket to be accessed by SageMaker from outside of your VPC.

    B. Modify the IAM role passed to SageMaker training estimator to make sure it has access to the S3 bucket.

    C. Provide your network settings using the `security_group_ids` and `subnets` parameters for the VPC. Make sure to create an S3 VPC endpoint.

    D. Migrate your dataset over to EFS and try again.

12. Which of the following is the customer's responsibility when it comes to security of Amazon Comprehend? (Choose all that apply.)

    A. Patching of the instances used to run Comprehend custom entity detection jobs

    B. Maintaining the availability of Comprehend Detect Entities endpoints

    C. Creating an IAM role that provides permissions for the user to call Amazon Comprehend's APIs

    D. Setting up a Comprehend VPC endpoint to ensure that network traffic flows through your VPC

13. Your team uses Amazon S3 for storing input datasets and would like to use PySpark code to preprocess the raw data before training. Which of the following solutions will require the least amount of setup and maintenance?

    A. Create an EMR cluster with Spark installed. Then use a notebook to prepare data.

    B. Use SageMaker Processing for Spark preprocessing.

    C. Create a Glue crawler to populate a Glue data catalog, then write an ETL script in PySpark to be run in Glue.

    D. Use AWS Data Pipeline with an Apache Hive Metastore for preprocessing.

14. A classification model has the following confusion matrix: true positives (tp) = 90, false positives (fp) = 4, true negatives (tn) = 96, false negatives (fn) = 10, as shown below. What is the recall for this model?

Predicted/Actuals	Positive	Negative
Positive	90	4
Negative	10	96

    A. 0.9

    B. 0.85

    C. 0.8

    D. 0.95

15. What methods of hyperparameter optimization does Amazon SageMaker provide? (Choose all that apply.)

    A. Grid Search

    B. Random Search

    C. Matrix Search

    D. Bayesian Optimization

16. You are helping a company that uses segmentation models in PyTorch to identify ships from high-resolution satellite images. The customer feels that the average IoU across all classes of ships is low and would like to explore hyperparameter optimization. What is the easiest way to set this up on SageMaker?

    A. Use a custom container in SageMaker that explores multiple hyperparameters within a single training job.

    B. Use SageMaker's built-in HPO functionality with PyTorch.

    C. Implement your own HPO code since SageMaker's built-in HPO functionality does not work with PyTorch.

    D. Use Ray Tune along with PyTorch with SageMaker in Script mode.

17. A financial services customer holds 20 years of stock market data in Amazon Redshift. They have a suite of ML-based algorithms trained on SageMaker and would like to back test these algorithms using 20 years of data. Which of the following services or features can be used? (Choose all that apply.)

    A. SageMaker Processing

    B. SageMaker Backtest

    C. SageMaker Batch Transform

    D. SageMaker Feature Store

18. You are helping a customer set up an update to their existing machine learning API. Their new model has a higher accuracy than the existing model but has not been tested with live traffic yet. What advice will you have for the customer for next steps?

    A. Perform canary testing

    B. Perform blue/green testing

    C. Perform shadow testing

    D. Perform A/B testing

19. A logistics company would like to group similar invoices together using an API call. An upstream process processes raw invoices and creates metadata in a tabular format. Which of the following built-in algorithms in SageMaker can help this customer?

    A. DeepAR

    B. K-means

    C. Neural topic model

    D. Sequence to sequence

20. You are writing code for a regression model using decision trees. Which of the following metrics will you use to evaluate your model?

    A. RMSE close to 0

    B. RMSE close to 1

    C. AuC close to 1

    D. F1 score close to 1

21. Your customer primarily uses Scikit Learn and XGBoost for developing ensemble models. In many cases, the selected ensemble models involve both XGBoost and Scikit Learn models working together. What is the easiest way to implement this using features available in SageMaker?

    A. Build and use a container that includes both XGBoost and Scikit Learn for Inference.

    B. Use Scikit Learn script mode and include XGBoost as a dependency to use both types of models in the ensemble.

    C. Deploy two separate endpoints, one for all Scikit Learn models and another for XGBoost. Use a Lambda function to obtain results from both endpoints and collate the results.

    D. Use multimodel endpoints.

22. Your company released a product 6 months ago and has been collecting customer reviews. Which of the following services can help with detecting sentiment in these reviews? (Choose all that apply.)

    A. Amazon Sentiment

    B. Amazon Comprehend

    C. Amazon SageMaker BlazingText

    D. Amazon Connect

xxxiv   Assessment Test

23. A healthcare customer of yours has developed a model to detect skin cancers but is confused as to which metric to use for evaluating these models. What will your advice to them be?

   A. Use Recall.

   B. Use Precision.

   C. Use Accuracy.

   D. Use F1 score.

24. You and your teammates use the PyCharm IDE on your laptop to develop models. Management has now asked you to figure out how to deploy these models on the cloud using Amazon SageMaker. Which of the following options will you test before going back with an answer to your management?

   A. Use the PyCharm SageMaker plug-in.

   B. Upload the models to Amazon S3, and then use SageMaker for model hosting.

   C. Deploy the models locally using PyCharm and provide credentials to SageMaker.

   D. None of the above options are correct.

Answers to Assessment Test

1. A, C. Options B and D are valid regularization terms, but they will not penalize small weights as much as the L1 penalty.

2. B. Option C is also unsupervised, but LDA is not used on tabular datasets but rather on textual data. Options A and D are supervised learning algorithms.

3. D. Deep learning training often requires GPU instances, so option A is wrong. Option B is a custom Amazon chip designed for inference, and G4 instances, while of GPU type, are more suited for inference than training. Option D is the right answer.

4. C. Options A and B are complex solutions requiring a lot of custom development. Rekognition does not detect PII, so only option C is correct.

5. C. SageMaker Processing and Batch Transform jobs are not used for debugging code. Option B will only help you lower cost, but that is not what the question is asking. Only option C is the right response.

6. C, D. This is a regression problem, so options C and D are correct. The data is not contained in a time series, so DeepAR forecasting will not apply.

7. B. Object detection is an ML problem that requires labels, so options A and D are incorrect. Option C is incorrect because the use case is very domain specific. You will need to factor in data labeling as part of the solution.

8. D. Rekognition custom labels builds image classification algorithms on *already* labeled data. Data Wrangler and Augmented AI are not data labeling solutions. SageMaker Ground Truth is the right answer.

9. D. SageMaker Neo automatically optimizes machine learning models to run on supported edge devices and processors. CodeGuru and DevOps Guru are services to improve code quality and identify bottlenecks in code and application availability, respectively. The Neuron SDK is an SDK for deep learning inference. So only option D is correct.

10. A, C. Both Random Cut Forest and Lookout for Metrics can be used for anomaly detection. The other two are used for time series forecasting.

11. C. Options A and D are incorrect, and though option B is a requirement, by itself it will not ensure that SageMaker accesses your data only via your VPC.

12. C, D. Since Comprehend is an AI service, AWS will take care of ensuring that the instances are patched and maintain the availability of the comprehend API endpoints.

13. B, C. Both SageMaker Processing and Glue can be used with PySpark scripts for preparing your data for training.

14. A. Recall = TP / (TP + FN) = 90 / (90 + 10) = 0.9.

15. B, D. Options A and C are not available in SageMaker.

16. B. SageMaker HPO can be used with your own code written in PyTorch.

17. A, C. Both SageMaker Batch Transform and Processing can be used once the data is offloaded from Redshift to S3.

18. D. Options B and C are deployment strategies. A/B testing can be used to compare real-world performance of the two models before deciding to update the endpoint.

19. B. K-means is an unsupervised learning algorithm. It attempts to find discrete groupings within data, where members of a group are as similar as possible to one another and as different as possible from members of other groups.

20. A. Minimize root mean squared error (RMSE) for regression problems.

21. B. The easiest way is to use script mode; both options A and C involve more effort. For option D, multimodel endpoints let you query different individual models behind the same endpoint but not an ensemble model. For ensemble models in option D, you may still need to bring your own container to accept both types of models.

22. B, C. Option A does not exist, and option D can be used to analyze sentiment in voice calls along with Comprehend but not with recorded text data.

23. A. Use Recall, since in this case false negatives should be 0, because predicting an actual cancer as benign may be risky for the patient. False positives may lead to more screenings but are less risky.

24. B. Once your model is in S3, it is easy to use the SageMaker APIs to host the same.

Introduction

Chapter 1

AWS AI ML Stack

THE AWS CERTIFIED MACHINE LEARNING (ML) SPECIALTY EXAM OBJECTIVES COVERED IN THIS CHAPTER INCLUDE BUT ARE NOT LIMITED TO THE FOLLOWING:

✓ **Domain 3.0: Modeling**

- 3.1 Frame business problems as machine learning problems

- 3.2 Select the appropriate model(s) for a given machine learning problem

    - Sample ML architectures for common business workflows such as video analysis, text mining, and others

    - Details about some common algorithms used in solving complex problems involving unstructured data like text and image

✓ **Domain 4.0: Machine Learning Implementation and Operations**

- 4.2 Recommend and implement the appropriate machine learning services and features for a given problem

    - Details about algorithms for different ML use cases

    - Details about when to use the proper AWS AI/ML Service

In this chapter, you will learn about different AWS Services for Machine Learning, starting with the artificial intelligence (AI) services for common machine learning (ML) tasks such as image and video analysis, natural language processing, text-to-speech conversion or vice versa, or building recommendation systems or time-series forecasting into your applications. These services make it easy for you to build ML-powered applications without machine learning experience. You will then learn about Amazon SageMaker, which is a fully managed service for data scientists and machine learning developers to build, train, and deploy ML models in the AWS cloud for various business applications. For reference, the exam guide can be found at https://d1.awsstatic.com/training-and-certification/docs-ml/AWS-Certified-Machine-Learning-Specialty_Exam-Guide.pdf.

Amazon Rekognition

Amazon Rekognition is an AI service that makes it easy for users to implement image or video analysis workflows into their applications. Amazon Rekognition aims to leverage Amazon's vast experience in using deep learning for various image-based workloads such as image classification, object detection, detection of text in image, facial recognition, sentiment, and most recently, public safety.

Although there is a vast amount of deep learning research behind developing models for image analytics, training these deep learning models is often computationally expensive and can take several cycles of data scientist or developer time. That's where Amazon Rekognition comes in. With Amazon Rekognition, developers can simply leverage pretrained models or train custom machine learning models without having to worry about writing the algorithm code, or about setting up or managing the infrastructure to train and deploy a deep learning model. More importantly, you don't require any prior machine learning or deep learning knowledge to use this service.

Before diving into Amazon Rekognition, let's quickly grasp the lay of the land on the subject of images and videos in deep learning. Image recognition typically relies on convolutional neural network (CNN) architectures. CNNs are deep learning algorithms consisting of alternating convolutional layers, which apply various filters on the input data to capture different information at different scales, followed by pooling layers, which reduce the number of parameters in the network and also the spatial size of the representation. The initial layers capture low-level features like edges and curves, whereas latter layers build up to higher-level ones to eventually identify the object. There are many popular architectures for CNNs such as ResNet or Inception V4, but it is important to understand the basic concept.

It is also useful to understand the concept of *transfer learning*. Transfer learning refers to taking a model that was pretrained on one dataset, freezing the initial layers, and letting it relearn the last few layers of the model on a different dataset. The benefits of this are that:

- It is computationally less expensive than training a full neural network from scratch.
- When you don't have a lot of data or data labeling is expensive, using a pretrained model can provide better model performance than training a model from scratch.

Both Inception V4 and ResNet models are popular algorithms for transfer learning in the image classification space. Transfer learning can be used in many deep learning applications—not just image or video data use cases, but also in natural language processing (NLP).

For object detection, the fundamental architecture is similar, but instead of detecting objects such as a cat versus a dog (fixed label), the model aims to detect a bounding box encapsulating the object of interest. Common algorithms used include single-shot detector (SSD), R-CNN or Faster R-CNN, and YOLO v4.

Finally, semantic segmentation actually segments the object of interest in an image by classifying whether or not an object belongs in a given pixel. An example is detecting a tumor in a human tissue. In order to be useful for doctors, it is not just sufficient to draw a bounding box, but you also need to accurately isolate the tumor from healthy tissue.

You can use Amazon Rekognition with the following key use cases:

Image Labeling   This refers to labeling whether an image consists of certain objects (popular objects in nature), events (party, graduation, etc.), concepts (landscape, nature, evening), or activities.

Custom Image Labeling   Imagine that you are a manufacturer and you need to detect whether or not parts on your assembly line are defective. Since your parts do not correspond to common objects found in nature, you may need to train a custom model. We will discuss this in more detail later, but Amazon Rekognition allows you to train a custom model for use cases of this kind.

Face Detection and Search   Amazon Rekognition can not only detect faces in images but also search for faces from an existing collection. Imagine you are a company that wants to implement face detection for your employees to access your corporate buildings. You can store pictures of your employees in a collection, and call Amazon Rekognition APIs to recognize employees from that collection.

People Paths   Amazon Rekognition can track the movement of people in a video. For example, you may want to track the movement of players on a field during a game for postprocessing, stats, and analytics for fans.

Text Detection   Amazon Rekognition can detect text in images and convert it to machine-readable text that you can use for downstream actions.

Celebrity Detection   Amazon Rekognition recognizes celebrities from images and stored videos.

Personal Protective Equipment (PPE)   Amazon Rekognition can now detect PPE on persons in an image.

- Look out for key phrases like "without any prior machine learning/deep learning knowledge" or "cost effective" or any of the use cases just described to think of Amazon Rekognition as the solution.

- If the question contains a phrase like "custom model," unless it has to do with image labeling, usually Amazon Rekognition is not the answer.

Image and Video Operations

Amazon Rekognition operates on both static images and stored videos. Image operations are synchronous whereas video operations are asynchronous. This means that when you ask Amazon Rekognition to process a video, once the job is completed, Amazon Rekognition will notify you using Amazon SNS by publishing to an SNS topic. You then have to call a `Get*` API to access the outputs. For synchronous API calls, you will get the answer right away.

Amazon Rekognition does not support video for all operations; for example, the PPE detection APIs only support images. Likewise, the people pathing use case is only available for video and not for images.

Let's take a concrete use case example to illustrate this further, such as detecting objects in an image or video.

For object detection in an image, you simply need to pass in the location of the image (in JPEG or PNG) in Amazon S3 or a byte-encoded image input. If you are using `boto3`, which is Amazon's Python SDK, then you need to make the following API call, reproduced from the AWS developer guide at https://docs.aws.amazon.com/rekognition/latest/dg/labels-detect-labels-image.html:

```
import boto3
def detect_labels(photo, bucket):
    client=boto3.client('rekognition')
    response =
client.detect_labels(Image={'S3Object':{'Bucket':bucket,'Name':photo}},MaxL
abels=10)
```

The sample output may look like this:

```
{

    {
    "Labels": [
        {
```

```
    "Name": "Vehicle",
    "Confidence": 99.15271759033203,
    "Instances": [],
    "Parents": [
        {
            "Name": "Transportation"
        }
    ]
},
{
    "Name": "Transportation",
    "Confidence": 99.15271759033203,
    "Instances": [],
    "Parents": []
},
{
    "Name": "Automobile",
    "Confidence": 99.15271759033203,
    "Instances": [],
    "Parents": [
        {
            "Name": "Vehicle"
        },
        {
            "Name": "Transportation"
        }
    ]
},
{
    "Name": "Car",
    "Confidence": 99.15271759033203,
    "Instances": [
        {
            "BoundingBox": {
                "Width": 0.10616336017847061,
                "Height": 0.18528179824352264,
                "Left": 0.0037978808395564556,
                "Top": 0.5039216876029968
            },
            "Confidence": 99.15271759033203
        },
```

```
        {
            "BoundingBox": {
                "Width": 0.2429988533258438,
                "Height": 0.21577216684818268,
                "Left": 0.7309805154800415,
                "Top": 0.5251884460449219
            },
            "Confidence": 99.1286392211914
        },
    ],
    "Parents": [
        {
            "Name": "Vehicle"
        },
        {
            "Name": "Transportation"
        }
    ]
    },
    "LabelModelVersion": "2.0"
}


}
```

By specifying MaxLabels, you can limit how many responses you receive and Amazon Rekognition will synchronously return a response showing the bounding boxes and confidence scores of the various objects detected in the image, as shown in the previous example. The confidence score can be used for downstream actions.

By contrast, for a video job, you cannot pass in bytes but must pass in the location of a video stored in Amazon S3. The API is StartLabelDetection and you also need to pass in an SNS topic for Amazon Rekognition to push a notification to, once it completes the video labeling task. You can then call a GetLabelDetection API to access the outputs.

 The quality of Rekognition's output strongly depends on the quality of your image. Refer to the best practices documentation (https://docs. aws.amazon.com/rekognition/latest/dg/best-practices.html) for more on this subject. In particular, for object detection, the object must be at least 5 percent in size of the shorter pixel dimension.

A key benefit of Amazon Rekognition Video is that you can work with streaming videos. Amazon Rekognition can ingest streaming videos directly from Amazon Kinesis Video streams, process the videos, and publish the outputs to Amazon Kinesis Data Streams for stream processing.

If you are looking to build a scalable image or video analytics workflow, consider using tools like the AWS Lambda function to make Amazon Rekognition API calls in a serverless manner. You may also consider using Amazon SQS to queue your incoming data to prevent throttling of Amazon Rekognition APIs. See a detailed architecture pattern here: https://github.com/aws-samples/amazon-rekognition-large-scale-processing.

 Real World Scenario

Facial Recognition in Video

Imagine you are a solutions architect at a media company who wants to ingest streaming video content as it is aired and detect faces of known people in the videos. However, your executives are concerned that building, training, and maintaining these ML models could be time intensive and challenging given the deep learning expertise required. They want you to design an architecture that can address this use case but also keep costs low.

The key to a scenario like this is to understand that the executives are concerned about the lack of deep learning expertise in their organization being a barrier to developing this use case. Amazon Rekognition Video is ideally suited for this.

First, create a collection of faces using Rekognition Image or Video by detecting faces from an existing database of images or stored video. Once your collection is created, consider using a tool like Kinesis Video Streams to first ingest the video stream and a Kinesis Data Stream as the output data stream. Rekognition Video can then process the incoming video stream using the `CreateStreamProcessor` API, passing the Kinesis Video stream as input. The outputs of the analysis will be published to Kinesis Data Streams. From Kinesis Data Streams you can use AWS Lambda as a consumer to publish the outputs to S3 or to a key-value store such as Amazon DynamoDB. The following graphic illustrates the high-level architectural flow.

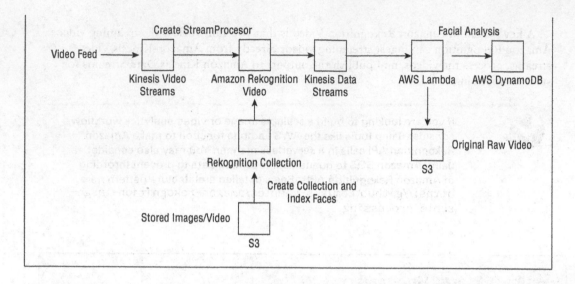

- While the machine learning specialty will generally not test your ability to memorize service limits, know that to avoid throttling APIs, you can use SQS to queue jobs.

- Similarly, make sure to read the Rekognition FAQs: https://aws .amazon.com/rekognition/faqs.

Amazon Textract

Amazon Textract is an AI service that allows you to quickly extract intelligence from documents such as financial reports, medical records, tax forms, and university application forms beyond simple optical character recognition (OCR). With Textract, you don't have to build deep learning computer vision models to extract text, forms, or tables from PDF documents; Amazon Textract will do that for you, so you can focus on using the extracted information for downstream business tasks.

More importantly, Amazon Textract allows you to quickly build automated document processing workflows, which are largely manual today. Most large organizations such as financial institutions have huge amounts of unstructured and semi-structured text data stored in documents as free-form text, tables, or forms. Companies are only now beginning to realize the power of using machine learning to process these documents and derive insights from them.

■ Note that Textract is used for extracting forms, tables, and text from PDFs or images. It does not do document classification, sentiment analysis, or entity recognition on those documents themselves. That is done by a different service called Amazon Comprehend, which we will cover later in this chapter.

■ For the exam, know the differences between Textract and Comprehend and also how they can work together.

Common use cases for Amazon Textract include the following:

■ Creating a search index by storing the outputs of Textract document analysis in a key-value store like DynamoDB.

■ Mining text from documents for natural language processing (NLP): Textract can extract words, lines, and tables that you can subsequently use in NLP-based workflows.

■ Automating data capture from forms: Textract can extract information from structured documents such as tax forms or application forms.

■ Cost effective: As with most AWS services, you pay for what you use, or what documents you analyze in Textract's case.

Sync and Async APIs

Documents can come in many different sizes, varying lengths, scanned images in PNG or JPEG format, or multipage PDFs.

For the synchronous APIs, you have the option of passing a document to Textract for processing either as a byte array or as an Amazon S3 object. You can use a synchronous API such as `DetectDocumentText` or `AnalyzeDocument` to return a JSON output containing the detected or analyzed text. The Analyze API also recognizes the hierarchy in a document such as form data, tables, and lines and words of text. The Detect API only detects text.

Although documents are generally considered unstructured data, there is often a hierarchy in document structure. For example, consider a form such as an application that contains a Name field, with the name John Smith. Now, if the service simply returned the outputs as Name, John Smith, that would not be very useful to someone trying to parse the document downstream.

Amazon Textract instead returns the text as a key-value pair, allowing the user to seamlessly ingest these outputs into a key-value database store that you may use to query later. Similarly, tables and table data are returned as Block and Cell objects, respectively, providing the bounding box information about the table location in the document, followed by information about underlying cells in the table.

For documents in PDF form or documents that are larger than a single page, use the async APIs `StartDocumentAnalysis` and `StartDocumentTextDetection`. Since detecting text in large documents can take some time, Amazon Textract will process your documents behind the scenes and publish the Completion status to an SNS topic. A subscriber to this topic will be subsequently notified that the job is complete and can view the outputs by calling the GetDocumentAnalysis or GetDocumentTextDetection API. The outputs of the job can then be stored in a DynamoDB table, an Amazon S3 bucket, or another data store.

> **NOTE** Repeatedly calling Textract APIs can result in a throttling exception called ProvisionedThroughputExceededException if the transactions per second (TPS) exceed the maximally allowed value. In that case, specify an automatic retry using the Config utility with the AWS SDK. Amazon Textract will automatically retry jobs a certain number of times before failing. Generally, you can set this value to 5. For more information on the AWS service limits for Textract, refer to the documentation here: https://docs.aws.amazon.com/general/latest/gr/aws_service_limits.html#limits_textract.

Before concluding our discussion of Textract, let's consider a use case where a medical company wants to extract text from patient forms for downstream processing such as improving the overall patient experience using machine learning. The company has millions of PDF documents currently stored in Amazon S3. Since this is a medical company, protecting patient data is a paramount concern and Health Insurance Portability and Accountability Act (HIPAA) eligibility is a requirement for any cloud service. Finally, the company executives don't trust entirely ML-based solutions and want humans to review some of the ML outputs. The company has reached out to AWS to see if they can help develop a cost-effective solution for them.

First, Amazon Textract can be a potential solution here since it is HIPAA eligible and has async APIs to extract text from large numbers of PDF documents with a pay-as-you-go pricing model. Furthermore, Amazon has a service called Amazon Augmented AI (Amazon A2I) that can directly integrate with the Textract document analysis API to send documents for human review based on a particular threshold condition such as low confidence on the detected text (Figure 1.1). We will discuss A2I in more detail later in this chapter.

FIGURE 1.1 Document analysis with human review flow

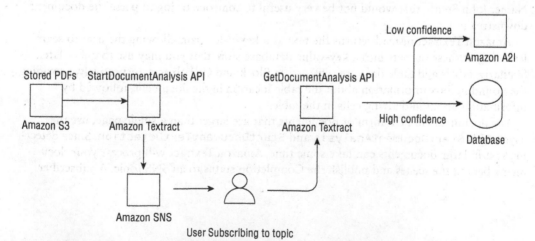

Amazon Transcribe

Imagine that you work for a global hotel chain that has a large volume of incoming customer call voice data that needs both real-time/streaming and batch transcription. Due to your global brand, the calls take place in multiple languages such as Arabic, Mandarin, English, French, Spanish, Japanese, Korean, German, and some others. Your manager has asked you to find a solution that leverages machine learning but is both scalable and cost-effective and does not require significant setup.

Traditionally, human speech recordings were stored simply as waveforms. By matching these waveforms with those of common sounds, a computer could transcribe speech to text.

The modern approach for this is called Automatic Speech Recognition (ASR) and powers technologies such as Amazon Alexa. These technologies use neural networks to take an input audio sequence as input and produce an output sequence consisting of text, using models known as sequence-to-sequence models. However, building these models accurately requires massive amounts of data that not all companies have.

Enter Amazon Transcribe. Amazon Transcribe leverages the same technologies powering Amazon Alexa but is available as a transcription service that allows you to transcribe your voice data without any prior machine learning knowledge. Let's dive into some of the features.

Transcribe Features

Here is a list of some the features provided by Transcribe:

Stream and Batch Mode   Transcribe supports both streaming and batch transcription modes. For streaming transcription, audio is directly streamed via the HTTP/2 protocol. Transcribe provides a streaming client, or you have the option to use your own client with the WebSocket protocol. For existing audio files stored in S3, you can run a batch transcription job using the `StartTranscriptionJob` API.

Multiple Language Support   You can transcribe speech in an ever-growing list of languages. Although the exam will not test you on specific languages, it is helpful to know that many of the popular ones are supported.

Multiple Language Transcription   Transcribe does not require your audio to contain a single language. If you know whether your audio will include additional languages, you can pass the language code as part of your API call by specifying `LanguageOptions`. See `https://docs.aws.amazon.com/transcribe/latest/dg/transcribe-lang-id.html` for the full list of supported languages.

Job Queuing   Transcribe provides options for you to send jobs to a queue so that you don't have to build custom logic to prevent API throttling.

Custom Vocabulary and Filtering   Transcribe provides a custom vocabulary that includes a list of words you want Transcribe to recognize, such as proper nouns or domain-specific language. Additionally, you can filter unwanted words such as any profane or offensive language.

Automatic Content Redaction   If your audio includes personally identifiable information (PII), Transcribe gives you the option to redact it from the transcribed output or provide both unredacted and redacted scripts. This information may include entities such as account numbers, credit card numbers, names, U.S. phone numbers, and U.S. Social Security numbers. Note that this feature is only available in English.

Language Identification   Transcribe will identify the dominant language in your transcription.

Speaker Identification   This feature allows you to identify different speakers in a transcription for English audio.

Going back to the hotel chain scenario, you have researched the aforementioned options and have secured buy-in from your management to develop a proof-of-concept (POC) with Amazon Transcribe to transcribe audio output. Since customer data security is extremely important, your manager has asked whether the service can be used to remove PII to be stored separately. On researching, you learn that you can use the PII detection capability within Transcribe to produce an output transcription with the original and the redacted versions of the transcript.

Having started your POC, you notice that although Transcribe is doing well overall, there are some domain-specific situations where the transcriptions are not as accurate. Furthermore, this domain has highly specialized vocabulary that exceeds the 50 KB limit for custom vocabulary. Your AWS Solutions Architect recommends that you build a custom model to improve the transcription accuracy.

Amazon Transcribe now lets you build a custom language model simply by providing your text as an input. Transcribe will build the model, and then you can use this model instead for your domain-specific transcriptions. Furthermore, you can provide a training dataset consisting of your text, and a test dataset containing a sample of audio transcripts.

Know the difference between a custom model with Amazon Comprehend (which we will cover later) versus Amazon Transcribe. The Transcribe custom language model is only applicable for audio transcription use cases. Comprehend Custom is for document classification and entity extraction, among other uses.

Transcribe Medical

The medical domain is highly specialized with a vast vocabulary. As a result, most common deep learning transcription models do not work well in this field, unless they have been specifically trained on medical data. Amazon Transcribe Medical is an ASR service that enables you to transcribe medical audio such as physician dictation, patient-to-physician conversations, and telemedicine. Transcribe Medical is available both in streaming and batch mode (only for Primary Care) and allows you to build custom vocabularies and redact personal health information (PHI) from your streaming transcriptions. For more information on Transcribe Medical, see the following document: `https://docs.aws.amazon.com/transcribe/latest/dg/transcribe-medical.html`.

- Remember, not all AI services have a medical specialty. Among the ones that do are Comprehend and Transcribe. You may get a question on the test that requires custom transcription but the answers may include non-existent services like Translate Medical or Textract Medical. Those are immediately incorrect, allowing you to narrow down your answers.

- Know that the batch transcriptions for Transcribe Medical is only available with Primary Care use cases. For medical use cases in cardiology, neurology, oncology, urology, and radiology, only streaming transcriptions are supported.

Amazon Translate

Once again, you work for a global hotel chain that operates in several different countries all over the world and you want to aggregate and collect customer service chat data in order to improve customer experience. The only problem is, the calls happen in different languages, and you know that building neural-network-based translation models in different languages is hard and expensive. You are also concerned with the quality of existing third-party translation tools and prefer a pay-as-you-go pricing model without any vendor lock-in.

Enter Amazon Translate, a text translation service that uses advanced state-of-the-art deep learning to provide high-quality translations to customers without any deep learning experience, with a pay-for-what-you-use pricing structure. As the name suggests, the main use case for Amazon Translate is to translate text from various languages such as Spanish, Arabic, Hindi, Greek, German, French, Chinese, and many others.

As always, know what a service is and what it is not. Amazon Translate does not translate directly from voice, such as calls. You can, however, chain Amazon Transcribe with Amazon Translate to make this flow work.

Having told your boss about Amazon Translate, you have secured their buy-in to experiment with this new tool. Next, you meet with the teams that have been storing all the chat data, and they have posed two problems:

- There are a few applications they have built using AWS Lambda that contain small amounts of text to translate, but the bulk of the incoming chat data is stored in S3 buckets and requires asynchronous processing.

- For certain countries where your chain operates, you have some custom terminology, corresponding to your hotel names, that need to be accounted for during translation instead of being translated into the local language.

Amazon Translate Features

Here is a list of features offered by Amazon Translate:

- Sync and Async APIs: Amazon Translate allows customers to asynchronously process large numbers of documents using a batch job (in 5 GB batches) with the StartTextTranslationJob API. This API is helpful when the individual documents comprising the collection are small, such as social media postings or user reviews. For smaller documents you can run a translation operation in real time using the TranslateText API. Please refer to the Developer Guide for more details on this synchronous API: https://docs.aws.amazon.com/translate/latest/dg/sync.html.

  To run a batch job, you need to provide the path to your chat data in Amazon S3, an output location for the translated chats, and the source and target language for translating the chats.

- Custom terminology and parallel data: Furthermore, you can customize the outputs of your translation by supplying a custom terminology as a CSV file, which provides the custom terms in the source language and the target terminology that you want. You can also pass in parallel data that shows the service how you want segments of text to be translated. Note that not all languages are suitable for custom terminologies; you can find the list at the following site: https://docs.aws.amazon.com/translate/latest/dg/permissible-language-pairs.html.

Having reviewed these features, your boss is now super happy as it appears that Amazon Translate will fully meet her requirements. Her final concern is whether Amazon will use any client data to improve its own machine learning algorithms.

Remember that Translate does not let you build your own custom translation models; it uses models trained by Amazon. As a result, Amazon may use customer data to improve the quality of its algorithms and models. To opt out of this for Amazon Translate and other AI services, refer to the following documentation: https://docs.aws.amazon.com/organizations/latest/userguide/orgs_manage_policies_ai-opt-out.html.

- In addition to individual features of a service, understand how services play together to form a coherent end-to-end architecture.

- For example, a text-related service like Translate can be combined with Amazon Transcribe to transcribe calls before translation, Amazon Polly to convert translated text to speech or audio after translation, or even Amazon Comprehend to extract sentiment from translated text.

- You might get a question or two on the exam on combining different services together.

- You don't need to know all the supported languages for Translate, but it is helpful to know the popular ones.

Figure 1.2 shows an entirely batch-based flow to process stored customer service calls from one language to English and then run a custom entity or label detection model using Amazon Comprehend.

FIGURE 1.2 Flow showing how to translate customer service calls followed by entity or label detection.

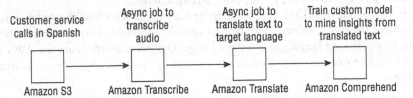

Amazon Polly

Amazon Transcribe converts speech to text, whereas Amazon Polly does the opposite—converts text to speech (TTS). How it works is that a user provides some text either as plain text or using a syntax called Speech Synthesis Markup Language (SSML). Polly reads this syntax and generates a lifelike voice using one of the prebuilt voices in different languages such as English, Arabic, Danish, Mandarin, Spanish, or Russian.

The exam will not test on different languages supported by Polly, but it will often contrast Polly with Transcribe, so it is important to remember the difference.

So how does speech synthesis work? Standard speech synthesis TTS works by stringing together basic speech units called *phonemes* into a natural-sounding synthesized speech.

More recently, artificial intelligence techniques such as deep learning have been applied to this problem to produce neural TTS (NTTS). A neural TTS model consists of what is called a sequence-to-sequence model, which takes an input sequence (in this case a line of text) and generates an output sequence (a spectrogram consisting of frequency bands that mimic the acoustic features used by the brain while processing speech). The output of this model then passes to a neural vocoder. A *vocoder* is the voice equivalent of the phoneme that converts the spectrogram to speech.

So when would you use TTS versus NTTS?

Training NTTS models to be accurate requires a lot of data, so naturally they are not available in all languages yet. So first, you want to check whether NTTS is available for the language you are interested in translating into. If you are looking for Newscaster speaking style, you have to use NTTS. Generally, if you have the option, NTTS generates more superior speech compared to standard TTS.

What if you want to have control of how the speech output is produced, such as slowing down or increasing the speed or controlling pitch or speaking style? This is where SSML tags come in. Think of SSML as a language similar to HTML that allows you to use tags to define how particular objects will be rendered. For more information on SSML tags and supported tags with Amazon Polly, refer to the documentation here: `https://docs.aws.amazon.com/polly/latest/dg/supportedtags.html`.

SSML is analogous to HTML for voice. By specifying tags such as the `<prosody>` tag, you can control the pitch, volume, and rate of speech. Similarly, if you want a word to be spelled out in a different language, use the `<lang>` tag. An example from the AWS documentation (`https://docs.aws.amazon.com/polly/latest/dg/supportedtags.html`) follows:

```
<speak>
    Sometimes it can be useful to <prosody volume="loud"> increase the volume
    for a specific speech.</prosody>
</speak>
```

By specifying **volume="loud"**, you can make the volume louder based on the applied tag. To make the volume softer, you would use **volume="soft"**.

Optionally, Amazon Polly also returns the metadata associated with the generated speech in the form of *speech marks*. These can tell you at what timestamp a particular audio started, the type of speech mark (sentence, word, SSML, etc.), the start and end offsets, which of the available Polly voice IDs is speaking, and so on. For more information on speech marks, refer to the documentation here: `https://docs.aws.amazon.com/polly/latest/dg/SynthesizeSpeechMarksSample.html`.

- A typical exam question might be as follows: "A mobile app company wants to develop a chatbot with a voice output to respond to the user's query. What service would you use to generate the voice portion of the output?" Be careful of such questions because the "chatbot" may immediately make you think of Amazon Lex (a service we will cover next). But in reality, the question is asking about how to convert text to speech and that is Amazon Polly.

- Alternatively, the question may ask you about a service that can generate speech from text that can be stored in MP3 or OGG formats that can be played later, such as in an IoT (Internet of Things) device. Amazon Polly is again the answer.

Amazon Lex

In many applications today, customers interact with the application using chatbots, and the application understands the user's intent and provides responses. Common examples include using e-commerce applications that provide customer support, booking doctor's appointments, and making hotel or airline reservations.

Amazon Lex is an AWS service, powered by natural language understanding (NLU) and automatic speech recognition (ASR), that allows users to build and deploy conversational interfaces for their applications. With Amazon Lex, you can build a tailored and personalized experience for your customers to engage with your platform without any deep learning expertise.

- As with all these AI services, the key is that these services allow you to build applications without expert deep learning knowledge.
- Also, do not confuse Lex with Polly. Although Polly also employs ASR, Polly converts text to speech. Amazon Lex is used to build and deploy the chat interface and responds to user intents. We explain intents in more detail in the following section.

The core steps behind developing an application are as follows:

1. Create a bot in a desired language or languages. You want to configure the bot to understand the user's goal and engage in conversation to fulfill the user's intent.

2. Test the bot.

3. Publish the bot as a version so that you can roll back to a prior version if needed.

4. Deploy the bot to an end application such as Facebook Messenger, Slack, or Twilio.

To execute these steps, you first need to understand some key concepts.

Lex Concepts

Let's start with a bot. A *bot* is the entity that will perform the desired action. For an e-commerce application, this action could be fulfilling a customer order, connecting the customer to a human representative, or providing the customer with information by performing a lookup in a database.

With Amazon Lex, the backend actions can be performed by using an AWS Lambda function. For example, if your bot is designed to make an appointment at your local doctor's office, you could have the Lambda function write to Amazon Relational Database Service (RDS) or Amazon Aurora or even a DynamoDB Appointments table. Likewise, if a customer wanted a reminder of their appointment, the bot could call a Lambda function to read from the table and return the appointment details.

On the front end, the bot needs to understand the user's intent. This requires that the user type in one of the supported languages. A full list of them can be found here: `https://docs.aws.amazon.com/lex/latest/dg/how-it-works-language.html`. You will not be required to memorize this list.

An intent is the action you want the bot to perform. An utterance is what the user actually asks for. For example, if you are ordering a pizza, the utterance could be "I would like a pizza" and the intent is "OrderPizza."

This is where the NLU and deep learning comes in. Amazon Lex needs to take a few sample intents provided by the user to build a model that can generalize to the myriad of ways in which a user can ask for something.

Let's think about how this would work prior to deep learning. A developer would either need to first provide an ontology of all the ways in which a particular request can be made and then build a set of rules to react to the intents in certain ways or prompt the user to ask a question differently if the user's utterance was not part of the bot's vocabulary.

With deep learning, the model can generalize to new utterances without requiring a predefined set of rules. You can provide a few sample utterances such as "I want a pizza," "Can I order a pizza," and "I want to get a pizza," and Lex will build a model to generalize to other intents.

A *slot* is a set of parameters that define the user's ask and a *slot type* is a characterization of that slot. The slot can be used to make the chatbot conversational. For example, if a user wants to order a pizza, the slot type can be size, and the slots can be small, medium, and large. The bot can ask the user to provide a size, or a list of toppings. Once the required slots are provided, the chatbot can connect with the backend Lambda function, which will then call an API to place the order or write the order to an Orders table. To simplify building the chatbot application, Lex provides a set of built-in slots and slot types for common items like Date, Name, Number, Email, Address, and Time.

If you are building a bot using Lex, and if your bot is not performing well, try increasing the number of sample utterances. The more examples you provide, the better the model will be able to generalize to unseen utterances.

What if the bot does not understand the user? Amazon Lex automatically includes a fallback intent, so you don't have to build one yourself. This intent is invoked when the bot does not recognize the user after a configured number of retries, or an intent does not recognize the user's input as a slot value or a response to a confirmation prompt.

Generally, if the fallback intent is invoked, you can have your Lambda function perform some predefined action such as connecting to a human representative. In this way, the dialogue flow feels conversational and natural.

Alternatively, if your bot cannot understand a user's request, it can trigger a document search to provide an answer. To do this, you can use the `KendraSearchIntent` API, which leverages Amazon Kendra behind the scenes. We will dive into Kendra next.

Figure 1.3 shows how you can integrate Lex on the back end with different AWS services using Lambda functions. In this case, `AppointmentBot` uses both relational and nonrelational databases to surface relevant information to the end user.

FIGURE 1.3 The `AppointmentBot` can be built using Amazon Lex and backend AWS Services.

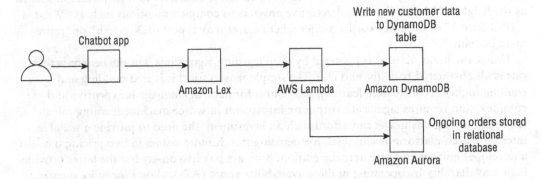

Chatbot app — Amazon Lex — AWS Lambda — Amazon DynamoDB (Write new customer data to DynamoDB table)

Ongoing orders stored in relational database — Amazon Aurora

- Understand the differences between slots, utterances, and intents. Slots are configuration parameters, utterances are the actual sentences, and intents are the meanings behind them. In the pizza example, slots can be pizza size or individual toppings, the intent is to order a pizza, and utterances may be, "I want olives on my pizza," "I want a small pizza," or "Can I order a pizza."
- Know which external tools Lex can integrate with, namely Facebook Messenger, Slack, and Twilio Short Message Service (SMS).

Amazon Kendra

A global bank contains internal information that needs to be shared among employees. Furthermore, this information is often contained in unstructured textual format across disparate data sources from Microsoft Word documents, Microsoft PowerPoint presentations, PDF documents, and even third-party tools such as Confluence, Salesforce, ServiceNow Microsoft OneDrive, and Microsoft SharePoint.

The CIO of the bank wants to build an application that allows users to query and search this unstructured text and mine it for insights as well as provide users with quick and relevant responses to their search queries to improve knowledge sharing and user productivity. What AWS service will allow you to build such an application?

At first, you might think this is asking you to extract text from documents and you might think Textract is the correct service, but there are two key points here: (1) The CIO is not asking you to simply extract the text; she is asking you to search text and build an application that provides intelligent answers. (2) The data sources go beyond simple PDFs. Both of these will tell you that Textract is not the solution here but rather Amazon Kendra.

Amazon Kendra allows you to build your own search application using natural language that provides highly relevant responses to user queries as you would get from a human expert within your organization. With Kendra, you can get answers to facts or factoids (such as the height of Mount Everest), descriptive answers to complex questions such as "What is a 10-K form?" or even keyword searches where a user may type "401K match" or "retirement benefits."

Under the hood, Kendra is powered by deep learning algorithms, but the benefit is that this is all abstracted from the end user. The simple reason for this is that building and training highly accurate deep learning algorithms for natural language is expensive and complex, and requires significant corporate investment in scarce machine learning talent. Although not all businesses can afford such an investment, the need to provide a scalable, internal search platform is universal. Recognizing this, Kendra comes in two pricing models: a developer edition and an enterprise edition. Both are pay-as-you-go, but the latter provides higher availability by operating in three availability zones (AZs), allows for more queries, and can ingest more documents and text.

How Kendra Works

So how do you get started with Kendra? The following key concepts are essential:

1. Index: In order to search documents, first you need to index them. An index is an object that is managed by Kendra that carries some metadata about that document, such as when it was created and updated, the version, and custom fields such as date and number that you can modify as a user.

2. Documents: These include the actual documents that Kendra will index. They may include frequently asked questions (FAQs) or purely unstructured documents such as HTML files, PDFs, plain-text or Microsoft Word documents, or Microsoft PowerPoint presentations.

3. Data sources: You may be wondering if you need to manually index documents. The answer is no; you simply provide Kendra with a data source such as a Confluence server, Microsoft SharePoint, Salesforce sites, ServiceNow instances, or an Amazon S3 bucket, and Kendra will index your documents as well as synchronize the data source with the index to keep it relevant and updated. For a full list of the supported data sources for Amazon Kendra, refer to the following document: https://docs.aws.amazon.com/kendra/latest/dg/hiw-data-source.html.

Once your index is ready, you can write queries to the index and it will use all the information provided about the documents to return the most relevant items. Additionally, you can filter your search queries by context or categories such as documents authored by a certain person. You can also sort responses based on a custom attribute. The default sort order is specified by the relevance of the response based on your search query according to Kendra.

Often when you search for an item, you may not use the exact name. Examples include if you are searching for Amazon Web Services; you may wish to use "AWS" instead, or Kendra instead of Amazon Kendra. You can provide a list of synonyms to Kendra in a thesaurus file, which may include internal company acronyms or domain-specific common phrases.

Later on, we will cover Amazon Comprehend, which is a general-purpose natural language processing (NLP) tool that allows you to train your own or use pretrained NLP models for sentiment analysis, document classification, and entity recognition. Know the difference between Comprehend and Kendra. Kendra also uses NLP behind the scenes, but it is aimed at document search and question and answering (Q&A) as opposed to a general-purpose tool for NLP.

Recall that in the previous section on Amazon Lex, we covered how you can build a chatbot application on AWS without any ML knowledge. You can now build an end-to-end FAQ chatbot using Lex and Kendra. Lex provides the front end to identify the user intent based on utterances, and it can call Kendra using KendraSearchIntent by passing in the intent as the input. Kendra can then search and return the most relevant results that are surfaced by the chatbot.

Amazon Personalize

Personalization has rapidly become a ubiquitous use case across a broad set of verticals such as the following examples:

Financial Services   A bank providing its customers with a personalized experience of credit card offers

An E-commerce Platform   A company providing its customers with recommendations on purchases or next-best actions and offers based on a customer's search history

A Travel Company   A company providing its customers with recommendations on where to travel, activities to do, or places to stay

A Media and Entertainment Business   A company recommending what to watch next based on customer preferences and history

Amazon Personalize is a machine learning service that allows businesses to rapidly develop personalized recommendation systems to provide a better customer experience to their end customers.

From a machine learning perspective, all these diverse business problems share some common aspects. They all rely on three forms of data:

User Data   This may include data about user's age, location, income, gender, personal preferences, and other demographic information.

Item Data   This is data about the actual products a company sells or is trying to recommend.

User-Item Interaction Data   This is data about how the set of users have interacted with these items, such as whether they have purchased the items in the past, do they like or dislike these items, or have they provided reviews or ratings for these items.

The goal of any personalization service is to take this data and extract meaningful insights that can lead to a customer purchasing a product or an item or simply spending more time on the digital platform.

Traditionally, this was done in a couple of ways: using only user data, companies would cluster users into similar groups and recommend items others in that cluster had purchased, or they would cluster the items into similar groups and recommend similar items to what a user had purchased or based on user feedback. This is often known as *clustering* and *content-based filtering*, respectively.

More recently, a method called *collaborative filtering* has emerged wherein the user-item interactions data is often used to recommend items. This user-item interaction data is often a very large sparse matrix (proportional to the number of users and number of items). For example, imagine a company like Netflix, with millions of subscribers (users) and hundreds of thousands of movies and shows (items). Collaborative filtering decomposes large sparse matrices into smaller matrices (matrix factorization) to extract hidden or latent vectors for each user and each item. The dot product of these gives the final score, which determines whether or not to recommend an item.

Although this is a highly popular technique, if you don't have a lot of items, matrix factorization can often not work as well. In that case, you can consider other approaches such as supervised learning using models like XGBoost and Factorization machines (which we will cover in depth in more detail in Chapter 8, "Model Training"). Here you predict a probability that a user will purchase an item based on the model and recommend the highest probability items.

One of the drawbacks of collaborative filtering is that it is time invariant; it doesn't take into account a user's purchase or session history. For example, if you were in the market for shoes a month ago, purchased them, and now are interested in a watch, a good recommender should probably not recommend shoes to you.

For this reason, scientists began to use recurrent neural networks (RNNs), which have the ability to retain a user's session history information as part of the model training. If you want to dive deep into the RNN architecture, there are a number of great references and articles (see, for example, "Session-Based Recommendations with Recurrent Neural Networks," by Balázs Hidasi, Alexandros Karatzoglou, Linas Baltrunas, and Domonkos Tikk, available at `https://arxiv.org/pdf/1511.06939.pdf`).

Scientists at Amazon extended this even further to a model called *HRNN-Metadata*, which uses an RNN to store user histories but also has the ability to incorporate user and item metadata (remember the user data we mentioned earlier?) as part of the training. This allows them to solve not only the temporal history problem, but simultaneously the cold start problem, which is the inability of a recommender to recommend products to completely new users (see `https://openreview.net/pdf?id=ByzxsrrkJ4`).

Finally, most recently the use of so-called multiarmed bandits (MABs) has become popular in personalization. The topic of MABs goes beyond the scope of this book, but at a high level, a MAB uses the concept of exploration-exploitation trade-off. The goal is to maximize the total reward after a fixed number of steps. In the exploration phase, the algorithms explore different possible combinations that could maximize the gain, recording the rewards at each step to build up a reward distribution. In the exploitation phase, it selects a known option that is known to increase the overall gain. The trade-off arises when exploration may reduce the gain as compared to the current choice. However, unless you explore, you will not know if there are other options that beat your current choice. For more details on MABs, see the following site: `https://en.wikipedia.org/wiki/Multi-armed_bandit`.

So as you can see, personalization has a long history in machine learning, in particular, at Amazon itself. Although we can by no means do the topic justice, setting the context is important in order to understand the benefits provided by Amazon Personalize.

Amazon Personalize is an AI service that takes this domain knowledge of personalization into a web service that allows customers to build recommendation systems into their applications.

Amazon Personalize employs the concept of recipes, grouped into three types for a given use case. Recipes allow you to build recommender systems without any prior ML knowledge:

User Personalization Recipes   These recipes come in three flavors. First, user-personalization uses the user-item interaction data and tests different recommendation scenarios. It is the recommended personalization recipe and built using the exploration-exploitation trade-off we discussed earlier. Second, popularity count recommends the most popular item among all your users and is a good baseline to compare other recipes against. Finally, there are legacy recipes that involve the HRNN and HRNN-meta models we discussed earlier.

Ranking-Based Recipes   This recipe also uses an HRNN but it also ranks the recommendations.

Related Item Recipe   This is the collaborative filtering algorithm we described earlier.

In addition to recipes, Amazon Personalize recognizes three kinds of datasets: user data, item data, and interaction data, which we described earlier. The user and item datasets are metadata types and only used by certain recipes. For more information on this, refer to the following document: https://docs.aws.amazon.com/personalize/latest/dg/ how-it-works-dataset-schema.html.

When Amazon Personalize uses the HRNN recipe, the interaction data needs to include a timestamp to pass in the history of the interaction. The exam will generally not test you on the specifics of the data, but this is good to know for your own use. The user-personalization recipe requires interaction data.

Creating a personalization model using Amazon Personalize is called a *solution*. Once you upload the data, the first step to creating a solution is to pick a recipe. Amazon Personalize will create a solution version based on the provided data and will automatically split your data into data for training versus testing. Amazon Personalize will use 90 percent of your data for training and the remaining 10 percent for testing. You can also tune the algorithm's hyperparameters or have Personalize do that on your behalf. It will then evaluate the solution version on the evaluation or test datasets but feeding it the oldest 90 percent of the test data as input. It will then evaluate the recommendations on the latest 10 percent of the test data.

The performance of the model is based on evaluation metrics such as Precision at K and Mean Reciprocal Rank at K. It is important to know what these metrics mean to be able to judge the quality of your model:

- Precision at K: Of the K items recommended, how many were actually relevant, divided by K.

- Mean Reciprocal Rank at K: The mean of the reciprocal rank of the first recommendation out of K, where the mean is taken over all queries.

For more details on other metrics used by Amazon Personalize, refer to the following document: https://docs.aws.amazon.com/personalize/latest/dg/ working-with-training-metrics.html.

Once your solution version is created, you can create a campaign to score your items in real time or in batch. A *campaign* is used to make recommendations for your users. Personalize provides a SQL-like interface to filter the recommendations based on queries both in real time and in batch use cases. For more information on campaigns, visit https://docs .aws.amazon.com/personalize/latest/dg/campaigns.html.

A common question that you may ask is how often you need to retrain your models as new user-item data comes in. For certain recipes, Personalize allows you to include real-time events data in your recommendations without having to retrain a model each time, by adding the new data to your user history and automatically updating the model with the new data. For more information on making recommendations based on real-time events data, see the following document: https://docs.aws.amazon.com/personalize/latest/dg/ recording-events.html.

That said, many customers will retrain their models at a certain fixed cadence (nightly, weekly) depending on the freshness (or relevance) of their recommendations. This is often a business-driven question—in some industries, a customer's preferences may change much more quickly than others. Generally, when building any ML use case, you will want to work with the relevant business stakeholders to answer these questions.

Amazon Personalize uses some unique terminology, and it is useful to map this to the typical data scientist workflow (Figure 1.4).

FIGURE 1.4 The end-to-end flow with Amazon Personalize (text on top) and how it maps to the common machine learning terminology (text on bottom)

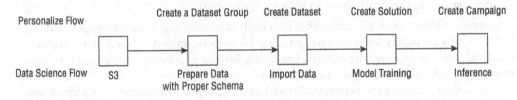

- Generally, on the test, if you see a question about recommender systems or real-time personalization, think Amazon Personalize.
- The test may also give you a personalization question and ask you to recommend real-time or batch depending on the use case. Remember that Personalize supports both modalities.
- Later in this chapter, we will cover Amazon SageMaker, which has a built-in algorithm called Factorization Machine. Understand that this is a supervised learning algorithm that works well when you have a small number of items compared to algorithms like HRNN that are ideally suited for large numbers of items (>100). In the test, if the question asks about Personalization on SageMaker, think Factorization Machine.

For the test, it may be important to understand the distinction between Personalize and what is provided with SageMaker. Remember that as an AI service, the key benefit of Personalize is that it handles the heavy lifting of the underlying algorithm code, training the models, deploying the models for both batch and real time with little to no code. Although you can do all of this with SageMaker, you will have to train the models yourself and deploy the model endpoints using code on your own. However, SageMaker gives you the flexibility of trying out any algorithm, whereas Personalize offers a limited set of algorithms.

Amazon Forecast

Like Personalization, forecasting is another problem that affects nearly all industries:

- A shipping company needs to forecast the demand for its ships at various ports to schedule shipping routes accordingly.
- A health care company needs to forecast the demand of medical supplies at different hospitals.

- A major retailer needs to forecast product demand to determine the inventory to keep in their warehouse.

- A cloud computing provider needs to forecast infrastructure and compute demand from their customers to plan capacity for their data centers.

- A customer service agency needs to forecast the volume and duration of calls during various periods in their call center to plan for hiring staff.

Amazon Forecast is an AI service that uses both statistical and deep learning–based algorithms to provide highly accurate forecasts. Similar to personalization, as a major retailer and cloud services provider, forecasting has a long history at Amazon as well, and Amazon Forecast provides that experience to customers.

From a data science perspective, traditional approaches to forecasting were autoregressive in nature, one of the most popular algorithms being the autoregressive integrated moving average (ARIMA). ARIMA is a statistical algorithm where past values are used to make predictions about future values. The ARIMA model predicts the value of a time series at time t, based on the historical value at times $t - 1 \ldots t - p$ plus some error terms. The moving average is the regression error and the autoregressive part is the lagged temporal features. The integrated part is to add a differencing component (taking the difference of the time series value at adjacent points) in order to make the time series stationary.

The key benefit of this model is its simplicity, and there are many packages in different languages (Python, R, etc.) to use ARIMA to forecast a time series. Over the years, the ARIMA approach has been improved upon in many ways—for example, S-ARIMA or seasonal-ARIMA, which includes seasonality, and more recently Prophet, which was introduced by a team at Facebook (https://research.fb.com/prophet-forecasting-at-scale).

Unlike ARIMA, which assumes a mathematical form for the time series, Prophet attempts to fit a time series to the data by detecting trends at different intervals such as seasonality; daily, weekly, and yearly trends; and even holiday effects. This has led to Prophet becoming one of the most popular models in use for forecasting today. But remember that this also adds complexity; the ARIMA model is easy to explain as it has a simple, linear mathematical form. More recently Facebook released a neural network version of Prophet, called Neural Prophet (https://m.facebook.com/FacebookAI/photos/a.360372474139712/1710 575115786101/?type=3).

With the advent of deep learning, in particular the ability of deep learning models to learn sequences, it is natural that these methods also be applied to time series forecasting, which can be viewed as a sequence. Amazon scientists developed an algorithm called Deep-AR (https://arxiv.org/abs/1704.04110) that uses a long short-term memory (LSTM)–based model and a probabilistic sampling technique to generate a probabilistic forecast. We will not cover LSTM architectures in detail in this book, but there are many excellent books and courses on machine learning for time series (see https://www.oreilly.com/library/view/hands-on-machine-learning/9781492032632 and https://www.manning.com/books/deep-learning-with-python).

Like Amazon Personalize, Amazon Forecast aims to combine the externally used popular forecasting algorithms and algorithms researched within Amazon into a service that makes it easy for customers to build accurate forecasts without prior machine learning knowledge.

You provide your data in a specific schema, and either let Amazon Forecast choose an algorithm for you or pick one of the many algorithms available within Forecast such as ARIMA, DeepAR+, and Prophet.

Let's cover some of the algorithms available in Forecast (also known as predictors):

- DeepAR+: This is an extension of DeepAR we discussed earlier and trains a single model on many similar time series (>100s). It works by splitting your time series randomly into fixed-length "windows" called context length and aims to predict the future up to a length called the *forecast horizon*. By doing this over many epochs and different time series, DeepAR can learn common patterns across different time series to generate an accurate global model. DeepAR+ treats the context length as a hyperparameter in your model, allowing you to tune them to get better performance. Additionally, DeepAR accepts metadata about the item in the form of related time series or simply item metadata. So if you are forecasting sales, a related time series could be a time series of weather data or foot traffic data to your store. Although DeepAR+ can handle missing values in your data, if your data has many missing values, then your forecasts may suffer because the model is not able to learn useful patterns.

- ETS: ETS, or exponential smoothing, is a statistical algorithm that is useful for datasets with seasonality. It works by computing a weighted average of prior features, but instead of a constant weight, it applies an exponentially decaying function as the weighting parameter. ETS does not accept any metadata or related time series.

- Prophet: Prophet is useful when your time series has strong seasonal variations over many months/years and if you have detailed time series information. It is also useful when your data contains irregularities (such as spikes during holidays) or has missing values.

- CNN-QR: The convolutional neural network quantile regression algorithm also uses deep learning, but this time uses convolutional neural networks (CNN) over recurrent neural nets like DeepAR. It uses a concept called sequence-to-sequence learning, where a model is fed an input sequence and it generates a hidden representation of that sequence. This is called an encoder. That representation is then used to predict the output sequence using another network called the decoder. We don't cover sequence-to-sequence models in great depth here, but it is useful to understand the distinction between this and DeepAR. DeepAR uses LSTMs whereas CNN-QR uses causal convolutional networks. To learn more about CNNs, we refer you to the many courses and textbooks on this subject (see https://www.oreilly.com/library/view/hands-on-machine-learning/9781492032632/ and https://www.manning.com/books/deep-learning-with-python).

- Nonparametric time series (NPTS): Unlike ARIMA or ETS, which use a formal mathematical form to fit the time series, NPTS is nonparametric. It is useful when you have seasonal data or bursty data, or data with a lot of intermittent values. In practice, however, NPTS is often outperformed by Prophet.

If you only have a handful of time series, consider algorithms like ARIMA, ETS, or Prophet. Once you have hundreds of time series, only then consider DeepAR+ or CNN-QR.

When should you use CNN-QR versus DeepAR+?

Both these models accept metadata and related time series inputs. However, CNN-QR does not require the related time series to extend to the forecast horizon, but DeepAR does. Imagine you have a time series of item sales up to time t and you are trying to predict sales from time $t + 1$ to $t + n$ into the future. If you are using weather data as your related time series, DeepAR requires you to have a weather forecast handy from time $t + 1$ to $t + n$ in order to predict your future sales. CNN-QR does not have that requirement.

One of the other benefits of Amazon Forecast is that in addition to algorithms, it allows you to include weather information as well as holiday information in your time series.

Forecasting Metrics

One of the complications of time series algorithms is how to measure model performance. Unlike a typical classification problem where you can randomly split data into train/test, that is no longer possible with time series as different rows of data in a time series are related to one another temporally.

Instead, time series use a concept called *backtesting*, where a model is tested against historical data where you have ground truth. For example, say you are an intrepid and avid fan of the markets and are trying to predict a stock price. You have trained a model to take historical stock data and predict future values. How will you test your model quality?

In this case, you can backtest your model on historical stock prices where you know exactly how the market behaved. Generally it is a good practice to conduct multiple backtests each with a little more training data (expanding window), but the fixed-length test horizon or fixed but sliding training data (sliding window) and fixed test horizon.

In each case, a good metric to evaluate your model is the mean-squared error (MSE), often reported as a root mean-squared error (RMSE). This is encapsulated in the following formula:

$$RMSE = \sqrt{\frac{1}{NT} \sum_{i,t} \left(y'_{i,t} - y_{i,t}\right)^2}$$

where $y'_{i,t}$ is the predicted value for time series i and time t; $y_{i,t}$ denotes the actual/observed value of the time series; and the sum is over all time series and times, normalized by NT: the number of points in the backtest window.

This metric amplifies outlier values whereas another metric called the weighted absolute percentage error (WAPE) is more robust against outliers since it does not take the square. WAPE is also sometimes known as mean absolute percentage error (MAPE).

$$WAPE = \sqrt{\frac{\sum_{i,t} |y'_{i,t} - y_{i,t}|}{\sum_{i,t} |y_{i,t}|}}$$

Which metric to rely on for your forecast depends on the use case: if an outlier might have an outsized business impact and a few large mispredictions can be expensive, you may consider RMSE over WAPE.

In both these forecasts, the model does not care if you underpredict versus overpredict. However, in many business problems, the cost of underpredicting can be very different from that of overpredicting. For example, in retail, you may want to be overstocked versus understocked. Similarly, if you are a cloud computing provider like AWS, you want your data centers to be overstocked versus understocked.

Amazon Forecast also provides a probabilistic forecast by providing you with quantiles such as p10, p50, or p90. It is useful to understand what these quantiles mean:

- p10 means that your model predicts that the true value will be less than this value only 10 percent of the time.
- p90 means that your model predicts that the true value will be less than this value 90 percent of the time.

As a retail firm, if the value of being understocked exceeds the cost of being overstocked, a p75 or p90 forecast may be more useful to you as a business, as you prefer to be overstocked rather than understocked.

In this case, you can choose a weighted quantile loss (wQL), which allows you to set a quantile, which can take values from 0.01 to 0.99. You may want to set this to 0.75, and your model will incorporate automatically different penalties for underfitting versus overfitting. We will not show the weighted quantile loss formula here, but for the test, it suffices to understand that this loss distinguishes between under- and overpredicting, unlike RMSE or WAPE.

When should you use WAPE versus RMSE versus wQL loss? If your business will have an outsized impact for a few large mispredictions, then consider RMSE. If your business costs change based on whether your forecast under- or overpredicts, consider wQL loss. Otherwise, consider WAPE. In general, it is a good practice to look at your model performance against multiple metrics and visualize your predictions with different quantiles, such as p10, p50, and p90.

Note that the p50 quantile is identical to the WAPE forecast. The WAPE forecast is often known as mean absolute percentage error (MAPE) or median forecasting.

Amazon Comprehend

Amazon Comprehend provides a set of natural language processing–based APIs to pre-trained and custom models that can extract insights from text. Amazon Comprehend can analyze a document for the following characteristics:

1. *Entities*—Date, location, organization, persons, quantity, title, event, commercial item, and other entities.

2. *Key phrases*—A noun phrase that describes a particular thing; for example, the sentence "Your latest statement was mailed to 100 Main Street, Anytown, WA 98121." has a key phrase: "Your latest statement."

3. *Personally identifiable information (PII)*—Data that could be used to identify an individual such as a name, address, or bank account number. In the previous example, "100 Main Street, Anytown, WA 98121" is PII data.

4. *Language*—Amazon Comprehend can be used to identify what the dominant language is in the text. This can be one of 100 recognized languages.

5. *Sentiment*—Amazon Comprehend can determine the sentiment of the text provided; this can be positive, negative, mixed, or neutral.

6. *Syntax*—This is used to extract the part of speech for each word in the document.

Apart from these API calls to pretrained models, you can also train custom models on Amazon Comprehend using your own data. Training these custom models is a synchronous process—the customer prepares a set of documents, trains a model, and then uses these trained models to predict with a new set of documents. Three types of custom models you can train with Amazon Comprehend are as follows:

1. *Custom document classification*—For this, you provide a set of documents that are each associated with a label. Once your custom model is trained, you can pass in a new document to get a predicted label with a confidence value.

2. *Custom entity detection*—This can be used to extract custom entity types. As you can imagine, custom terms like policy numbers or part numbers are not included in the default entity detection on Comprehend. Custom entity detection can be trained with a list of entities and a set of documents that contain them. Once the model is trained, you can use this custom model to extract entities custom to your use case.

3. *Document topic modeling*—Topic modeling on Comprehend uses an unsupervised learning technique called Latent Dirichlet Allocation. A set of words that frequently show up in the same context across many documents form a topic. The same word can be associated with different topics.

Some overall guidelines that apply to Amazon Comprehend that are worth remembering are that the character encoding used in all text documents is UTF-8, and the size of each document must be less than 5,000 bytes. If you plan to send more than 25 documents per second, you should use batch detect operations. For example, you can use the

`DetectDominantLanguage` API if you are sending 20 documents per second, but using the `BatchRequestDominantLanguage` API, you can send up to 250 documents per second, but since it's a batch job, it may take more time for you to receive final results for all the documents in Amazon S3. The maximum quotas for asynchronous operations such as `StartEntitiesDetectionJob` or `StartSentimentDetectionJob` include a maximum document size of 1 MB, a maximum size of a batch of documents of 5 GB, and less than a million documents in a batch operation. For other guidelines and limits, visit this documentation page on Amazon Comprehend: `https://docs.aws.amazon.com/comprehend/latest/dg/guidelines-and-limits.html`.

 Real World Scenario

Email Parsing Model

A customer collects incoming email in a JSON document and wants to use the subject line to redirect emails to the right department. The customer first organizes their data into a set of two-column CSV files; the first column is the department label, and the second column is the subject line. They can then use the console or the `CreateDocumentClassifier` API to start a custom training job. Amazon Comprehend uses between 10 and 20 percent of the training data for testing the final trained model and provides a classifier performance metric to help you determine if the model is trained well enough for your purposes. The customer can then analyze incoming emails by passing in the subject line to the hosted model endpoint and routing the email using the results obtained from this API call.

Amazon CodeGuru

Amazon CodeGuru uses program analysis and machine learning built from millions of lines of Java and Python code from the Amazon codebase to provide intelligent recommendations for improving code performance and quality. CodeGuru consists of two main services: Reviewer and Profiler.

Amazon CodeGuru Reviewer proactively detects potential code defects and offers suggestions for improving your Java or Python code. CodeGuru Reviewer does not identify syntax errors (an IDE is a better way to do this), but it does suggest improvements related to AWS best practices, resource leak prevention, concurrency, sensitive information leak prevention, refactoring, input validation, and security analysis. CodeGuru Reviewer can analyze code in AWS CodeCommit, Bitbucket, GitHub, or Amazon S3.

Amazon CodeGuru Profiler collects runtime performance data from your live applications and provides recommendations on how to fine-tune performance. Using machine learning,

CodeGuru Profiler helps find the most expensive lines of code, provides visualizations of profiling data, and suggests ways to reduce CPU bottlenecks. CodeGuru Profiler provides a single dashboard to understand application performance issues and can also be used to profile code running in AWS Lambda and other AWS compute services. On AWS Lambda, the easiest way to add `codeguru_profiler_agent` if you are using Python is by first adding a Lambda layer containing the package, and then using a function decorator as follows:

```
from codeguru_profiler_agent import with_lambda_profiler

@with_lambda_profiler(profiling_group_name="MyGroupName")
def handler_name(event, context):
    return "Profiler is active"
```

Amazon Augmented AI

Amazon Augmented AI (or A2I) is used to get a secondary human review of a low-confidence prediction from machine learning models. A2I works out of the box with Amazon Rekognition and Textract, but you can also use A2I with your own custom ML models. A2I is usually used when you want to review low-confidence predictions or to audit a random sample of predictions regardless of confidence levels. The first thing you need to do is define a human review workflow.

A human review workflow involves (1) defining a *work team* that will review predictions, and (2) using a UI template for providing instructions and the interface for humans to provide feedback (called the *worker task template*). A work team can be made up of a public workforce (powered by Amazon Mechanical Turk), a vendor-managed workforce, or your own private workforce. The worker task template displays your input data such as images or documents, and provides interactive tools to allow human reviewers to complete their task of reviewing the machine learning model's prediction.

For the two built-in task types with Amazon Rekognition and Textract, the corresponding AWS service will automatically trigger a human review loop. Conditions for when to trigger a human review loop are defined in a JSON document. For example, if you are using Amazon Textract to extract a specific key from submitted forms, you can use the *ImportantFormKey* parameter along with the *KeyValueBlockConfidenceLessThan* parameter to trigger a human review job when the confidence associated with a specific key is less than a particular threshold. When using a custom machine learning model, you can use the Amazon A2I Runtime API to start a human loop by calling the *StartHumanLoop* API.

Real World Scenario

Detecting Loan Application Fraud

A financial services company has a machine learning model that predicts whether a loan application is fraudulent or not. A recent mandate states that this company must review predictions of fraudulent loan applications by humans before making a decision on the loan. The company uses A2I to support automated machine learning by first calling the machine learning model endpoint and analyzing the confidence score. If the confidence score is less than 90 percent, the client triggers a human review loop in A2I and later analyze these results from humans from output files stored in Amazon S3 (see the following graphic).

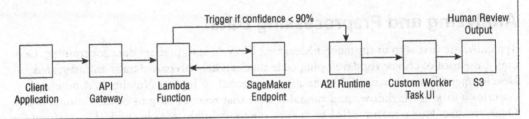

Amazon SageMaker

Amazon SageMaker is an end-to-end machine learning platform that lets you build, train, tune, and deploy models at scale. SageMaker provides features through every step in the typical machine learning lifecycle. Here, we discuss each major step in this lifecycle and provide details about features that SageMaker provides. Note that we will not be discussing every single feature of SageMaker here but will focus on the features that support the most important phases of a typical machine learning lifecycle. For your reference, please see Table 1.1 for features of SageMaker that are relevant to the different phases of machine learning (for the latest set of features, please refer to the developer guide: https://docs.aws.amazon.com/sagemaker/latest/dg/whatis.html).

TABLE 1.1   Various features of SageMaker corresponding to the different phases in typical machine learning workflows

Prepare	Build	Train and tune	Deploy
GroundTruth	Notebooks	Managed Training	Managed Endpoints
Data Wrangler	Studio	Experiments	Model Monitor
Processing	Autopilot	Tuning	Pipelines
Feature Store	Jumpstart	Debugger	
Clarify		Spot Training	

Analyzing and Preprocessing Data

Typically, the first step in the machine learning lifecycle is to prepare data for training. Generally, the tool of choice for developing code that can help prepare data is an Integrated Development Environment (IDE), and more commonly a Jupyter Notebook. A notebook contains a mix of Markdown and runnable code that records outputs of each runnable cell. Once you are done experimenting with code on a notebook, it is also typical to perform the same preprocessing in stand-alone Python code. SageMaker provides the following components that helps with this phase in the ML lifecycle:

1. SageMaker notebook instance
2. SageMaker Studio
3. SageMaker Data Wrangler
4. SageMaker Processing
5. SageMaker GroundTruth

We will discuss all these components in detail next.

SageMaker Notebook Instance

A SageMaker notebook instance is a managed ML compute instance running the Jupyter server. Users can create a notebook instance from the SageMaker console or using the *CreateNotebookInstance* API. When creating the notebook instance, SageMaker first creates a network interface in the chosen VPC and associates the security group that you provide in your request with the subnet in a particular availability zone. SageMaker then launches an instance in the service VPC and enables traffic between your VPC and the notebook instance. SageMaker then installs common packages and ML frameworks and additionally runs any lifecycle configuration scripts that you define; these scripts can be used to pull the latest updates from a Git repository, mount a shared drive, or download data and packages. SageMaker then attaches an EBS storage volume (you can choose a size between 5 GB and

16 TB). Files stored inside the /home/ec2-user/SageMaker directory persist between notebook sessions (that is, when you turn the notebook instance off and on again). Note that scheduling a notebook to be turned off during idle times is important to reduce costs; this can be done using lifecycle configuration scripts or via Lambda functions. For more details on this, please read the following document: https://aws.amazon.com/blogs/machine-learning/right-sizing-resources-and-avoiding-unnecessary-costs-in-amazon-sagemaker.

From the AWS Console, SageMaker displays a list of notebook instances that are in your account as well as ones that are stopped or running. When you access your notebook instance, the console uses the credentials you used to sign in to get a presigned URL by calling the *CreatePresignedNotebookInstanceUrl* API call. If you are signing in through your company's single sign-on, Active Directory, or another identity provider like Google or Facebook, identity federation using identity and access management (IAM) roles are already set up, and this lets you assume a role indirectly that allows access to SageMaker resources, such as a notebook instance. Lastly, SageMaker uses the nbexamples Jupyter extension to provide over 200 examples showcasing various use cases and SageMaker features. SageMaker also lets you associate your notebook instance with a project Git repository that automatically gets cloned to your instance on startup.

When using a SageMaker notebook instance, you can edit the notebook execution role to access other AWS services. For example, you can use the notebook instance to manage large-scale data preprocessing by making API calls to AWS Glue or connect your notebook to Amazon EMR to run a PySpark kernel. You can also query an Amazon Redshift data warehouse for data that you need to prepare for training.

SageMaker Studio

SageMaker Studio is a web-based IDE for machine learning and is based on a highly customized JupyterLab environment. In a single visual interface, you can write and maintain notebooks, track experiments, deploy and monitor models, and more. Compared to notebook instances, SageMaker Studio launches containerized images that are used to run kernels for your notebooks. This lets you have multiple back-end compute instances run your notebooks. For example, one notebook tab on Studio could be running a general-purpose m4 instance, while another notebook may run a GPU instance for local training. SageMaker Studio lets you share a snapshot of your notebook with your teammates, which other users who share the same domain can copy and use in their own personal workspace. The workspace setup is a folder in an Amazon EFS drive that can elastically scale in size as your local data grows.

SageMaker Studio also provides a visual interface to many other SageMaker features, such as the following:

- Visual Git workflow
- Experiment tracking
- SageMaker Autopilot for AutoML on tabular datasets
- Curated one-click solutions for applications on SageMaker Jumpstart

- Pretrained and fine-tunable models for typical vision and NLP jobs through Sage-Maker Jumpstart
- Model-building pipelines using SageMaker pipelines
- SageMaker Clarify for detecting pretraining bias
- SageMaker Feature store for creating, sharing, and managing curated data for ML development
- SageMaker Data Wrangler for preparing data (we will discuss this next)

SageMaker Data Wrangler

SageMaker Data Wrangler lets you import, transform and analyze data through a visual workflow, and then export that workflow. Data Wrangler allows you to import data from Amazon S3, Athena, and Redshift. A data preparation pipeline on SageMaker Data Wrangler is called a *data flow*.

SageMaker Data Wrangler automatically creates a new intermediate data frame when you add a new step to the data flow. You can add four different types of steps:

Data Transform Step   Data Wrangler provides over 300 built-in transforms to normalize, transform, and combine columns without writing any code. You can also create your own custom steps using Python or PySpark code.

Data Analysis Step   This step uses 100,000 rows of your dataset to provide built-in or custom visualizations, a quick machine learning model to assess feature importance scores, statistical summaries of your columns, and a correlation or target leakage report.

Join   This step joins two datasets and produces one data frame, including left joins, right joins, and inner joins.

Concatenate   This step concatenates one dataset to another and adds the result to your data flow.

SageMaker Data Wrangler steps can be exported to a Data Wrangler job, a notebook with all the steps, a feature store, or stand-alone Python code. This lets you modularize your preprocessing step and run it on demand, usually with SageMaker Processing, which we will discuss next.

SageMaker Processing

SageMaker Processing is a simple, managed feature on SageMaker that allows you to run common data processing workloads such as preprocessing, feature engineering, and model evaluation. SageMaker takes your Python or PySpark script, copies data from an Amazon S3 location, processes your data, and writes back output data to another Amazon S3 output location in your account. You can also provide a custom container image rather than using one of the built-in images provided by SageMaker Processing. When passing in a Python script, you use SKLearnProcessor, and when passing in a PySpark script, you use the

PySparkProcessor classes in the SageMaker Python SDK. It is common to use multiple instances to process data, in which case you can shard the input objects by S3 key so that each instance receives the same number of input files to process.

SageMaker GroundTruth

SageMaker GroundTruth provides an important functionality in this preprocessing phase of the ML lifecycle. To train an ML model using a supervised training algorithm, you need high-quality, labeled data. GroundTruth provides built-in labeling functionality for common task types (like image classification or document classification), and also allows completely customized workflows. With GroundTruth, you can use a public workforce (Amazon Mechanical Turk), a private workforce, or a vendor company. You can optionally use automated data labeling for some task types, which uses active learning to train a model in parallel and decide which samples of data to send to human labelers. Built-in task types involving images, video frames, text data, and LiDAR data have managed UIs that are surfaced to workers in a secure way. You can also provide custom UIs for your data labeling jobs. For more information about SageMaker GroundTruth, visit https://docs.aws .amazon.com/sagemaker/latest/dg/data-label.html.

Training

Once you have prepared your training data, you can train your models using one of the following training modes on Amazon SageMaker:

- Amazon SageMaker provides 17 built-in algorithms for typical use cases. These include binary or multiclass classification, regression, time series forecasting, anomaly detection, IP address anomalies, embedding generation, clustering, topic modeling, text classification and summarization, image classification, object detection, and semantic segmentation. We cover these in more detail in Chapter 8, "Model Training."

Read up on the typical use cases and algorithm mappings at the following documentation site: https://docs.aws.amazon.com/sagemaker/ latest/dg/algos.html.

- When using a popular ML framework like TensorFlow, PyTorch, or MXNet, you can submit a script to SageMaker. SageMaker will provide a managed container that can run several versions of these popular frameworks. This is useful when you want to bring your own algorithm without the additional heavy lifting of managing a custom container.

- Lastly, you can create a completely custom container for your training job. SageMaker will simply run your container in a managed training instance of your choice with the entry point that you provide. For example, your entry point in the Dockerfile could look like: ENTRYPOINT ["python", "train.py"].

Some additional training features provided by Amazon SageMaker are as follows:

Distributed Training   SageMaker provides both model parallel and data parallel distributed training strategies. Let's briefly discuss what these strategies are. Data parallel strategy in distributed training is where the dataset is split up across multiple processing nodes. Each node runs an epoch of training and shares results with other nodes before moving on to the next epoch. In model parallel training, the model is split up across multiple processing nodes. Each node carries a subset of the models and is responsible to run a subset of the transformations as decided by a pipeline execution schedule so that performance losses due to sequential computations are minimized.

Managed Spot Training   You can use managed spot instances instead of on-demand instances to reduce the cost of training by up to 90 percent. Spot instance interruptions are handled by SageMaker, but you are responsible for creating your own checkpoints to allow the training to continue post any disruptions.

Automatic Model Tuning   SageMaker's Automatic model tuning, also known as hyperparameter optimization, can be used to search for the optimal set of hyperparameters using either a random search or Bayesian optimization. You can use the hyperparameters that result in the best version of your model, measured by a metric that you choose (for example, validation accuracy).

Monitoring Training Jobs   SageMaker training job logs can be viewed in Amazon CloudWatch. Additionally, training job metrics such as training error that are emitted can be viewed as graphs in the console. After the training job has ended, you can also view final metrics using the *DescribeTrainingJob* API call.

SageMaker Debugger   SageMaker Debugger can be used to profile and debug your training jobs to improve the performance of ML model training by eliminating bottlenecks and detecting nonconverging conditions. Debugger stores instance-level metrics, framework-level metrics, and custom tensors that you define from within your training code. You can use either various built-in rules (like loss not decreasing or overtraining), or your own custom rules to analyze tensors emitted by your training code. Debugger also provides profiler rules such as CPU bottleneck threshold and I/O bottleneck threshold. When a rule is activated, you can trigger an Amazon SNS notification or Lambda function to take further action, such as stopping a training job.

Model Inference

Training a model on SageMaker results in a trained model artifact on Amazon S3 (usually in the format of a `model.tar.gz` file). To get predictions from this model, you can either host a persistent endpoint for real-time predictions or use the SageMaker batch transform APIs to apply model predictions to an entire test dataset.

For real-time predictions, SageMaker provides fully managed model hosting services and generates a private HTTPS endpoint where your model can return prediction outputs. You can deploy multiple production variants of the model to divert different percentages of traffic to different versions of your model. You can host multiple models and target these models from your client application calling the endpoint. And finally, after you deploy your model into production, you can use SageMaker's Model Monitor to continuously monitor model quality metrics in real time and provide you with a notification when deviations such as data drift are detected.

For batch predictions, SageMaker initializes the requested number of compute instances and distributes inference workload involving getting predictions for a large test dataset between these instances. Batch transform jobs create the same number of output files as input files, with an additional .out extension. You can reduce the time it takes to do large-scale batch transform jobs by tuning parameters that control the maximum payload accepted, the maximum number of concurrent transforms, or the batch strategy used.

Additional features of model deployment that become important in production are as follows:

Endpoint Autoscaling   Dynamically adjust the number of instances used to host your model based on changes in your workload.

Model Compilation   SageMaker Neo automatically optimizes your models to run more effectively on cloud or edge hardware.

Elastic Inference (EI)   EI lets you add GPU-based accelerators to your hosting instances at a fraction of the cost of using a full GPU instance and supports any TensorFlow, MXNet, PyTorch, or ONNX model.

Inference Pipelines   This lets you deploy a linear sequence of up to five containers that perform steps on your incoming data. Typically this sequence may involve a preprocessing step, a model prediction step, and a post-processing step done in real time.

SageMaker Model Registry   SageMaker Model Registry lets you catalog models for production, manage versions, add and manage manual approval steps for the model, and automate model deployment using continuous integration/continuous delivery (CI/CD).

 Real World Scenario

A/B Testing Deployment

A customer who already has a hosted model would like to test a new version with production traffic. To do this, the customer updates the endpoint configuration and diverts 10 percent of the traffic to a new production variant (see the following graphic).

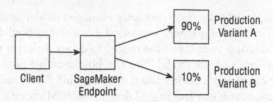

An exhaustive list of features related to SageMaker are discussed in the AWS documentation section here: https://docs.aws.amazon.com/ sagemaker/index.html. Please take note of the Exam Essentials section at the end of this chapter.

AWS Machine Learning Devices

In this brief section, we describe devices that belong to the machine learning stack:

AWS DeepLens   The DeepLens ecosystem lets you learn about vision systems and deep learning by providing you with a fully programmable video camera and several pre-trained models and examples.

AWS DeepRacer   The DeepRacer ecosystem lets you learn about reinforcement learning using a fully managed simulation and training environment, as well as a 1/18 scale RC (race car) car that can run your trained model.

AWS DeepComposer   DeepComposer is a fully programmable MIDI keyboard that lets you play, record, train, and generate music using generative adversarial networks (GANs).

AWS Panorama Device and SDK   This allows you to add computer vision–based applications to your IP camera setup. You can analyze video feeds from multiple cameras in parallel generating predictions from models that you trained and compiled on the cloud with SageMaker.

For the exam, it is sufficient to understand at a high level what these device offerings may be used for. For more information about the Machine Learning Stack on AWS, visit the documentation page here: https://aws.amazon.com/machine-learning. To dive deeper on any of these services, follow the detailed documentation pages—for example, https://docs.aws.amazon.com/panorama/latest/dev/panorama-welcome.html and https://docs.aws.amazon.com/deeplens/latest/dg/what-is-deeplens.html. Trying out the getting started guides can help you go beyond just passing the exam.

Summary

As you have seen in this chapter, machine learning has a wide range of applications such as analyzing images and videos for insights, mining text data, translating and transcribing speech, enterprise search, personalization, and others. You have learned that the AI services like Rekognition, Personalize, Forecast, Transcribe, and others make it easy to build these ML applications with little prior ML knowledge or via little code.

That said, sometimes ML developers need the flexibility to train their own algorithms, tune hyperparameters, explore and analyze data for machine learning, and then deploy those models to production. This requires some ML knowledge and writing code to develop algorithms. This is where Amazon SageMaker comes in; SageMaker lets data scientists focus on the data and ML model development while abstracting the underlying infrastructure needs from them.

Finally, you have seen how even once models are deployed, often humans need to review the ML model outputs. A service like Augmented AI can put humans in the loop in the ML workflow to review model performance.

Exam Essentials

Understand the various areas of machine learning that are covered by AI/ML services on AWS.   AI services cover several subdomains of machine learning such as vision (Rekognition, Textract, etc.), speech (Lex, Polly, Transcribe), recommendation systems (Personalize), and forecasting systems (Forecast). For more customer use cases, or for custom implementations of the aforementioned common AI/ML use cases, you can use Amazon SageMaker's built-in algorithms or bring your own algorithm to build, train, tune, and deploy.

Familiarize yourself with the basics of what each service is meant to do and the main features of each service.   Use the descriptions provided here as a starting point, and dive deeper into it using the documentation on AWS (https://docs.aws.amazon.com).

Review Questions

1. You have raw text data stored in S3 and would like to use each document to train a custom text classification model. What is the easiest way to achieve this?

   A. Download all your data and work with an open-source framework on your laptop.

   B. Use Comprehend Custom labels to train a custom document classification model.

   C. First use SageMaker Processing to preprocess your data; then use the SageMaker built-in Blazing text algorithm to train and deploy your model.

   D. None of the options is correct.

2. A customer would like to run computer vision models at a manufacturing facility and already uses IP cameras and custom edge devices for other purposes. The customer is a current user of SageMaker and needs suggestions on how to deploy these models. Which of the following options would you as a solutions architect suggest?

   A. Replace all IP cameras with DeepLens cameras, and use SageMaker models at the edge.

   B. Use outposts and attach cameras directly to Outpost.

   C. Purchase "smart cameras" from a vendor and retrain your models on the vendor-provided software.

   D. Download and use SageMaker trained models on the custom edge devices.

3. A marketing data provider has 50 GB of time series data from various customers and would like to train a forecasting model to predict future sales. The customer uses an open-source algorithm on premises and is exploring ways to build multiple forecasting models based on cohorts of customers. Which of these solutions will work for this company?

   A. Use Amazon Forecast. It automatically recognizes cohorts and can easily handle up to 100 GB of files on premises or on S3.

   B. Use the open-source algorithm on SageMaker either by using Script mode or by bringing in a custom container and pointing the training job to data on S3.

   C. Redshift is the best option to both store and query data. It can also be used to forecast data in this case.

   D. None of the options is correct.

4. A customer using SageMaker Studio has been manually running each step in a complex workflow. What is the easiest way to automate and manage these manual steps?

   A. Use SageMaker Pipelines. It is integrated with Studio, and converting the manual steps to a workflow is easy with the Python SDK.

   B. Move all steps to Step functions. Author the individual steps on Studio, but run pipelines in the Step functions.

   C. Move all steps to Managed Workflows for Apache Airflow. Author the individual steps on Studio, but run pipelines in Airflow.

   D. Move all steps to an EC2 instance, and use a Bash script to run each step in succession.

5. A customer currently uses Spark on premises to transform datasets for machine learning purposes. The customer is new to AWS and is aware of training options that are available on SageMaker. The customer would like to reuse Spark code that they have developed as is but make it part of their machine learning lifecycle on AWS. What solution will require the least amount of maintenance and would integrate well with other steps in the machine learning lifecycle?

   A. Use EMR to run on-demand Spark jobs.

   B. Use the Spark processing container provided by SageMaker and prepare data for training steps that will also use SageMaker.

   C. Use Glue DataBrew to import your Spark code and run as part of a data preparation pipeline.

   D. Set up an EC2 instance that replicates the on-premises setup. Since the setup on AWS now matches the on-premises setup, the customer can easily run Spark jobs without any additional effort.

6. A customer running a streaming service has 10,000 audio files in S3. The customer would like to easily label these audio files and use them in a deep learning algorithm for music genre classification. Which solution will allow the customer to achieve this?

   A. Use a built-in UI template for audio classification on SageMaker GroundTruth, followed by a built-in audio classification algorithm to train the model.

   B. Use a built-in UI template for audio classification on SageMaker GroundTruth, followed by a custom audio classification algorithm to train the model.

   C. Use a custom UI template for audio classification on SageMaker GroundTruth, followed by a built-in audio classification algorithm to train the model.

   D. Use a custom UI template for audio classification on SageMaker GroundTruth, followed by a custom audio classification algorithm to train the model.

7. A media company wants to process image data to detect persons, objects, and text from a database of images, but the company is concerned about their lack of machine learning expertise to build and deploy a custom solution. Which AWS service would you advise them to use to solve this problem?

   A. Amazon Comprehend

   B. Amazon Rekognition

   C. Amazon SageMaker

   D. Amazon Textract

8. An asset management firm would like to build a chatbot-based solution to automate advice given to their clients by their financial advisers. They are concerned that due to their diverse global client base, the chatbot will need to translate incoming text into English before the advice can be rendered. What services would you use to build this solution?

   A. Lex, Translate

   B. Lex, Polly

   C. Translate, Polly

   D. SageMaker, Lex

9. A retail company wants to build a forecasting model to forecast demand for their products. They have thousands of products and related product metadata. Although they have tried a few models like ARIMA on premises, they are concerned with the model performance and are also looking for a solution that can be scaled and deployed easily. Another concern they have is that they do not want to understock their warehouses. What solution would you recommend?

   A. Train DeepAR on Amazon SageMaker for scalability and pick MAPE loss to solve the understocking problem.

   B. Train ARIMA on EC2 and use EC2 AutoScaling to solve the scalability issue.

   C. Use Amazon ETS on Amazon Forecast. Include product information as item metadata. Pick a 0.75 weighted quantile loss metric to solve the understocking problem.

   D. Use DeepAR+ on Amazon Forecast. Include product information as item metadata. Pick a 0.75 weighted quantile loss metric to solve the understocking problem.

10. You are trying to get your organization excited about machine learning. You host a tournament where employees can race a car around a race track that is programmed using reinforcement learning to teach them about applications of ML to real-world scenarios. Which AWS service is suited for this activity?

   A. AWS Deep Lens

   B. AWS Deep Composer

   C. Amazon S3

   D. AWS DeepRacer

11. You have trained an ARIMA-based forecasting model to forecast electricity prices in ZIP codes across the country. You want to use a metric that penalizes the model differently for under- versus overpredicting the price. Which metric would you use?

   A. Weighted quantile error

   B. Root mean squared error (RMSE)

   C. Mean squared error (MSE)

   D. Mean absolute percentage error (MAPE)

12. You want to train a single model across a multitude of time series ranging in the thousands. You also have contextual data associated with the time series as a related time series, but the related time series data does not extend in the prediction interval. Finally, you wish to use a fully managed service to produce the ML model instead of developing your own algorithm code from scratch. What service and algorithm would you use?

   A. Amazon Personalize, multi-arm bandits

   B. Amazon SageMaker, XGBoost

   C. Amazon Forecast, CNN-QR

   D. Amazon Forecast, DeepAR

13. A major sports company wants to detect helmets on players to ensure player safety. The company has terabytes of video, but it is largely unlabeled. What AWS service would you use to label the data?

    A. Amazon Comprehend

    B. Amazon SageMaker Ground Truth

    C. Amazon SageMaker Processing

    D. Amazon Forecast

14. Consider the same use case as in the previous two questions. Having trained the object detection algorithm, you want to deploy it in production. However, the incoming raw video first needs to be processed before it can be sent to the model for inference. This processing code is written in Spark. You want to jointly deploy the Spark-based processing code and the inference code. Which AWS tool lets you do this?

    A. Inferentia

    B. Neuron SDK

    C. Inference Pipelines

    D. SageMaker Model Monitor

15. You work for an insurance firm trying to automate insurance claims processing. As a first step, you want to parse PDF documents and extract relevant entities. What AWS service could you use to get started with entity detection without much ML experience?

    A. AWS SageMaker

    B. Amazon Comprehend

    C. Amazon Kendra

    D. Amazon Personalize

16. You are the head of a law firm trying to modernize your internal document search systems. What AWS service would you use where users can type their questions and the service will parse the question and provide the most relevant collection of documents that may match the response?

    A. Amazon Kendra

    B. Amazon Comprehend

    C. Amazon Forecast

    D. Amazon Rekognition

17. You work for an insurance firm trying to automate insurance claims processing. As a first step, you want to perform optical character recognition (OCR) and extract forms and tables from PDF documents. What AWS service could you use to get started with this use case without having to build your own or use an open-source OCR solution?

    A. AWS SageMaker

    B. Amazon Textract

    C. Amazon Kendra

    D. Amazon Comprehend

18. You have some custom PySpark code that you use to process data prior to training an ML model on that processed data. Which of the following AWS tools can be used to process the data? (Choose all that apply.)

A. SageMaker Clarify

B. AWS Glue

C. SageMaker Processing

D. Amazon TimeStream

19. Which AWS services allow you to build ML Ops pipelines by defining a directed acyclic graph (DAG) that can be executed to process data, train a model, and deploy the model? (Select all that apply.)

A. AWS Step Functions

B. AWS SageMaker Pipelines

C. Amazon CodeCommit

D. Amazon CodeBuild

20. Which AWS service proactively detects bottlenecks and defects in your code and offers suggestions to improve based on AWS code best practices for code in AWS CodeCommit or GitHub?

A. AWS Guru Code

B. AWS Code Guru

C. AWS DevOps Guru

D. AWS Lookout for Code

Chapter 2

Supporting Services from the AWS Stack

THE AWS CERTIFIED MACHINE LEARNING (ML) SPECIALTY EXAM OBJECTIVES COVERED IN THIS CHAPTER INCLUDE BUT ARE NOT LIMITED TO THE FOLLOWING:

✓ **Domain 1.0: Data Engineering**

- 1.1 Create data repositories for machine learning

- 1.2 Identify and implement a data-ingestion solution

    - Storage services to use on AWS for Machine learning including S3, EFS, and FSx

    - Details about some common services that are used alongside machine learning services

✓ **Domain 4.0: Machine Learning Implementation and Operations**

- 4.3 Apply basic AWS security practices to machine learning solutions

- 4.4 Deploy and operationalize machine learning solutions

    - Details about how to orchestrate machine learning work-flows with AWS services

    - Details about when to use a specific service along with an AWS AI/ML Service

This chapter discusses services that support architecting production ML solutions. You must be familiar with these services before we begin discussing some typical architectures.

Let's get started!

Storage

In this section, we cover three main storage services that can be used in ML workflows on AWS—Amazon S3, Amazon EFS and Amazon FSx for Lustre.

Amazon S3

Amazon Simple Storage Service (S3) provides a set of APIs, SDKs, and a user interface that you can use to store, update, version, and retrieve any amount of data from anywhere on the web. When it comes to machine learning, users can store any common training file formats, including, but not limited to, CSV and Parquet tabular data, image data, audio or video data, and any other object data. Amazon S3 was built to focus on simplicity and robustness. Amazon S3 integrates with several data analytics and machine learning services.

Before we look at how Amazon S3 is used in the context of machine learning, here are some key concepts:

- *Buckets*—A bucket is where objects are stored in Amazon S3. Every object is contained in a bucket you own.

- *Objects*—An object that is stored in a bucket consists of the object data and object metadata. Metadata is a set of key-value pairs that describe the object like data modified or standard HTTP metadata such as Content-Type.

- *Keys*—A key is a unique identifier for an object in a bucket.

- *Regions*—A bucket is tied down to the region it is created in. You can choose a region that optimizes latency or that satisfies regulatory requirements.

For example, in the URL https://*mybucket*.s3.amazonaws.com/*mykey*/*myobject*.*docx*, *mybucket* is the bucket name, *mykey*/*myobject*.*docx* is the key, and *myobject*.*docx* is the object name.

Amazon S3 has various features that let you effectively manage your data in a centralized location. A single object in S3 can be up to 5 TB in size, and you can add up to 10 key-value pairs called *S3 object tags* to each object, which can be updated or deleted at a later time. Some important features of S3 are as follows:

- S3 storage is nonhierarchical. Although object keys may look like folder structures, they are just a way to organize your data.

- With S3 batch operations, you can copy large amounts of data between buckets, replace tags, or modify access controls with a simple API or through the console.

- S3 provides data versioning capabilities that can help categorize data or recover from unintended user actions. Furthermore, you can prevent accidental deletions by enabling Multi-factor Authentication (MFA) Delete on an S3 bucket.

- With S3 replication, you can copy objects to multiple locations automatically. These buckets can be in the same or different regions.

- D3 Object Lock lets you implement write-once, read-many (WORM) policy. This lets you retain an object version for a specific period of time.

- S3 Select lets you query data without accessing any other analytics service using SQL statements. For more involved SQL queries, you typically use an analytics service like Amazon Athena or Redshift Spectrum to query data directly on S3.

- S3 offers a range of storage classes that are designed for different use cases: S3 standard, S3 intelligent tiering, S3 Standard Infrequent Access, S3 One Zone Infrequent Access, S3 Glacier, and S3 Glacier Deep Archive. Visit this page to learn more about S3 storage classes: https://aws.amazon.com/s3/storage-classes. Examples and case studies that you will read in this book assume the use of S3 Standard.

- Here are some AWS Security features:

  - You can grant access to users using a combination of AWS Identity and Access Management (IAM) and access control lists (ACLs).

  - Query string authentication can be used to grant access to users for a limited time.

  - AWS Trusted Advisor can check your S3 buckets for logging configurations, open access permissions, and lack of versioning.

  - S3 supports both server-side encryption (SSE-KMS, SSE-C, SSE-S3) and client-side encryption. You can enable default encryption behavior for an S3 bucket so that all new objects are encrypted after they are added to a bucket. See the following document for more information on default encryption: https://docs.aws.amazon.com/AmazonS3/latest/userguide/bucket-encryption.html.

  - You can use VPC endpoints to connect to your S3 resources from entities in your own VPC. Using a VPC endpoint for obtaining data from S3 securely is an important aspect of security-related best practices, which we will cover in Chapter 13, "Security Pillar".

Amazon EFS

Amazon Elastic File System (EFS) provides a fully managed, POSIX-compliant, elastic NFS filesystem that can be shared by multiple instances. EFS is built for petabyte scale, and it grows and shrinks automatically and seamlessly as you add and remove data. AWS manages the infrastructure under the hood, and you just use it in your instances as a local drive. EFS also supports authentication, authorization, encryption at rest, and transit. Typically, these are the steps to get started with EFS:

1. Use the console or APIs to create a filesystem.

2. Create mount targets for your filesystem.

3. Create and configure security groups. You can use the security group that is associated with the mount target to control inbound traffic; best practice is to only allow traffic from security groups associated with specific EC2 instances that need access. For more information on security best practices, see Chapter 13.

EFS filesystems can be mounted inside your VPC by creating a mount target in each availability zone so that all instances in the same availability zone can share the same mount target.

 Real World Scenario

Sharing Data within a Team of Data Scientists

A group of data scientists working on projects together want to be able to easily share data and files, without first copying them into a notebook for preprocessing and then copying them back to S3 for training. They create a common EFS, mount the same EFS on multiple notebook instances, and use the EFS filesystem directly to train SageMaker models without the need to copy files back to S3 (see the following graphic).

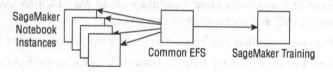

Amazon FSx for Lustre

Amazon FSx is a fully managed, high-performance filesystem that can be used for large-scale machine learning jobs and high-performance computing (HPC) use cases. Amazon FSx provides two types of filesystems: FSx for Windows and FSx for Lustre. Amazon FSx for Lustre is based on the popular Lustre filesystem (www.lustre.org) that is used for distributed computing workloads such as machine learning and HPC. Lustre can support hundreds of petabytes of data storage and hundreds of gigabytes of aggregate throughput. The majority of the top 100 fastest supercomputers in the world use Lustre.

On AWS, it is easy to set up FSx for Lustre and start using this filesystem for machine learning. Let's look at a common pattern (Figure 2.1).

FIGURE 2.1   Pattern for using FSx for Lustre with Amazon SageMaker for training

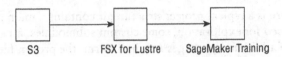

As you can see in Figure 2.1, FSx for Lustre can connect to an existing S3 bucket and can automatically update files and directory listings of changed objects. As a result, FSx acts as a POSIX-compatible front end to all your files in S3, which can then be accessed by any Linux system or container. In this case, SageMaker integrates directly with FSx for training your model.

Training on Terabytes of Data

A customer performing large-scale distributed training has several terabytes of data on S3. Using FSx is a great fit in cases where you have terabytes of data (as with the autonomous vehicle datasets) and you need to train your model without redownloading all your data onto the Sage-Maker training instances.

Data Versioning

Now that we have talked about the different options for storing data for ML applications, let's talk about data versioning. What is data versioning? Why do we need it?

Developers and ML practitioners are well aware of using tools like Git for versioning their code. Typical version control tools like Git, however, are not meant for storing large training datasets or trained ML models. Typically on AWS, your code is versioned using CodeCommit (see https://aws.amazon.com/codecommit), which is a fully managed service for securely hosting Git-based repositories (think of a private version of GitHub) that eliminates the need to host and maintain your own source-control servers. The typical workflow for collaborating on a project with multiple files making up your project code involve adding files that need to be tracked, committing changes to files, and pushing these changes to a central repository, where others can pull changes from, branch out your projects, merge new features, and so forth. Imagine you had a project folder that looked like this:

```
└── Root folder/
    ├── project submodule 1/
    │   └── module1.py
    ├── project submodule 2/
```

```
│         └── module2.py
├── requirements.txt
├── training_script.py
├── training_notebook.ipynb
└── data folder/
    ├── huge_file1
    └── huge_file2
```

What is shown here is a typical project structure; it contains a main training script, a notebook that was used for exploration, some custom submodules, a requirements .txt file that defines additional packages required to run the project files, and a data folder. Notice that the data folder contains two huge input files. It is not good practice to use the same Git-style versioning to upload these data files; in fact, CodeCommit has a limit of 6 MB per file, so it may be impossible to version these large files. This is where data versioning tools like DVC (https://dvc.org) come to the rescue! DVC is used to track, version, back up, and restore snapshots of datasets by using familiar tools and AWS back-end storage services like S3 and EFS (which we discussed earlier). DVC uses local caches that can also be shared across users using services like EFS and can use S3 as a persistent store. It is considered best practice to version your datasets, although other factors such as restrictions of your current stack or lack of appropriate training might prevent you from incorporating a tool like DVC into your workflow. As a curious reader, you may ask why we can't simply use differently named buckets or S3 versioning to obtain the effect of data versioning. This is similar to asking why we can't use differently named folders for code versioning—this does not enforce best practices by design. Versioning systems go beyond this by allowing you to branch, commit, merge, and use datasets using a structured approach.

 Do try out this tutorial (https://dvc.org/doc/command-reference/remote/add) to get started with DVC for data versioning with AWS storage services.

Amazon VPC

Amazon Virtual Private Cloud (VPC) enables you to launch cloud resources into logical virtual networks that you define. We assume that you are aware of what Amazon VPCs are and direct interested readers to the documentation on this topic available here: https://docs.aws.amazon.com/vpc/latest/userguide/what-is-amazon-vpc.html.

You should already know about the basics of VPC, subnets, and security groups. An important concept that we would like to focus on here is *VPC endpoints*. VPC endpoints allow resources in your VPC to privately connect to supported AWS services and VPC endpoint services without using an Internet gateway or a NAT device; this enables more secure communication that limits all traffic to the private AWS network.

Several AI and ML services allow you to perform certain functions from resources in your VPC in a secure manner using an interface VPC endpoint (which is powered by AWS PrivateLink). You first create a VPC endpoint type that is supported by the service and then securely connect to it. This will create an elastic network interface (ENI) in your subnet with a private IP that serves as an entry point to API calls to the AWS service. As an example, you can use an interface endpoint as shown in Figure 2.2 to securely perform API calls to Sage-Maker and other services. Some services, like Amazon Personalize and Amazon Forecast, do not support the S3 VPC gateway, and so pointing to training data in buckets that only allow VPC traffic will result in an *AccessDenied* error.

FIGURE 2.2   Architecture showing the use of VPC endpoints to connect to various services to managed ML services like SageMaker and Rekognition

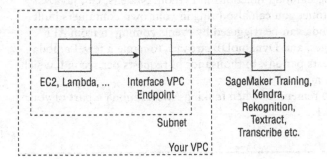

Let's take a look at some more details on how to set up an interface VPC endpoint to access Comprehend APIs. You can do this by entering **create-vpc-endpoint** in the command-line interface (CLI), or by using the AWS Console for Comprehend; in both cases, you will provide your VPC ID, subnets that will use the endpoint, and security groups to associate with the endpoint network interface. To restrict entities in the VPC from calling certain Comprehend APIs, you can add an endpoint policy to your VPC endpoint. The following policy allows all resources in the VPC to access just the DetectEntities API call in Comprehend:

```
{
    "Statement":[
        {
            "Principal":"*",
            "Effect":"Allow",
            "Action":[
                "comprehend:DetectEntities"
            ],
            "Resource":"*"
        }
    ]
}
```

> Remember that when you create an interface endpoint, best practice is to create and associate a custom security group with the endpoint network interface that is created in your VPC; if you do not create a custom security group, the default security group is automatically associated with the endpoint network interface.

AWS Lambda

AWS Lambda is a serverless compute service that lets you run code without configuring any infrastructure. You can write these Lambda functions in Python, Node.js, Go, Java, C#, Ruby, PowerShell, or any custom runtime; you can also bring in your own containers built using Docker to run in Lambda. Lambda can be triggered by events coming in from API Gateway, SNS topics, S3 bucket changes, and DynamoDB streams, to name a few. Lambda scales automatically, from a few requests per day, to thousands of requests per second, which can be done in a concurrent (parallel) manner.

Some important limits or quotas to remember when making AWS Lambda a part of your architecture are mentioned in Table 2.1.

TABLE 2.1   AWS Lambda limits

Resource	Quota
Memory allocation	128 MB to 10,240 MB
Timeout	15 minutes
Number of layers	5
Invocation payload	6 MB
Deployment ZIP file size	50 MB zipped, 250 MB unzipped
Container image size	10 GB

Two types of permissions are commonly used with Lambda functions: execution roles and resource-based policies. Use execution roles to grant your Lambda function permissions to access AWS services and resources; use resource-based policies to give other accounts and AWS services permission to call your Lambda function. Let's clarify this distinction with an example.

The following execution role allows your Lambda function to publish logs to Cloud-Watch (included in the basic execution role when you create your Lambda function) and publish an SNS topic (edit your functions execution role in IAM):

```
{
  "Version": "2012-10-17",
  "Statement": [
    {
      "Effect": "Allow",
      "Action": "logs:CreateLogGroup",
      "Resource": "arn:aws:logs:<region>:<account>:*"
    },
    {
      "Effect": "Allow",
      "Action": [
        "logs:CreateLogStream",
        "logs:PutLogEvents"
      ],
      "Resource": [
        "arn:aws:logs:<region>:<account>:log-group:/aws/lambda/sns-test-func:*"
      ]
    },
    {
      "Effect": "Allow",
      "Action": "sns:Publish",
      "Resource": "arn:aws:sns:<region>:<account>:<topic name>"
    }
  ]
}
```

On the flip side, the following resource-based policy allows Amazon SNS to invoke your function (add an SNS trigger to view this resource-based policy):

```
{
  "Sid": "sns",
  "Effect": "Allow",
  "Principal": {
    "Service": "sns.amazonaws.com"
  },
  "Action": "lambda:InvokeFunction",
  "Resource": "arn:aws:lambda:<region>:<account number>:function:<function name>"
}
```

It is typical for customers in the machine learning space to create Lambda functions in Python or Node.js. As an example, here is how you can invoke a SageMaker endpoint from a Lambda function:

```python
import json
import boto3
import os

def lambda_handler(event, context):

    client = boto3.client('sagemaker-runtime')

    response = client.invoke_endpoint(
        EndpointName=os.environ['endpoint_name'],
        Body=event['body'],
        ContentType=os.environ['content_type'])

    return {
        'statusCode': 200,
        'body': json.loads(response['Body'].read())
    }
```

First, we initialize the SageMaker runtime client in Boto3 (AWS Python SDK). Then we call the `invoke_endpoint` function using three parameters: (1) the endpoint name (picked up from the Lambda environment variables), (2) the prediction input (picked up from the incoming event), and (3) the content type accepted by the endpoint (like `'text/csv'`), again picked up from the environment variables. Finally, we read and return the response.

Finally, AWS Lambda automatically monitors your Lambda function and reports metrics and logs to Amazon CloudWatch. AWS Lambda provides useful graphs in the console to record the number and time of each invocation, and any throttles, delivery failures, and error traces.

For the exam, it is sufficient to understand the basics of how AWS Lambda functions can be used to connect to various AI/ML services on AWS. Typically, a developer may use the Boto3 APIs in Python corresponding to a model hosted behind a managed endpoint for various AI/ML services. The Boto3 APIs enable you to pass a payload to the endpoint and receive a prediction as a JSON response.

Serverless Object Detection

A customer would like to detect objects in an image in a completely serverless way using AWS components. You can set up an architecture as shown in the following graphic, where uploading an image into a specific location in S3 triggers a Python Lambda function that first does some required preprocessing and uses the Boto3 SDK to call the detect_labels API call that returns instances of real-world entities found in the image. The returned labels are hierarchical (e.g., Transportation > Vehicle > Car) and include the confidence score as well as bounding box information. Remember to edit the function's execution role to include the detect_labels actions.

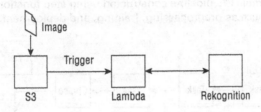

AWS Step Functions

Now that you know the basics of how Lambda works, we can start thinking of how to orchestrate a sequence of Lambda functions that call various services on AWS (or steps involving calls to other services). AWS Step Functions is a serverless function orchestration service that lets you manage complex, distributed applications with built-in operational controls. Step Functions lets you define your state machines with a JSON document using the Amazon states language, where each state can pass output data from the previous step to your own microservices, or AWS service integrations such as DynamoDB, SNS, Athena, Glue, EMR, or SageMaker, to name a few. AWS Step Functions lets you monitor your state machine, has built-in error handling, and saves a history of each execution you have run.

Let's discuss some (not all) of the state types that you can include in your step functions workflow:

- *Task state*—Represents a unit of work done in a state; a task state can invoke a custom Lambda function with specific input parameters, or even call other supported AWS services. Note that custom activities can also run in EC2 instances, on ECS, or even on mobile devices. Tasks can also involve human approval steps, such as emailing links to approve.

- *Choice state*—Used to branch out based on some logic, similar to an `if-then-else` block, with ways to check most string and numeric logical operations (equals, greater than, not, etc.).

- *Wait state*—Used to delay the state machine from continuing for a specified number of seconds.

- *Parallel state*—Can be used to create parallel branches of execution in your state machine. The output of the parallel state is a list containing outputs from all branches.

- *Map state*—Used to iterate through multiple entries of an input array, where you can also process many tasks in parallel, defined by the *MaxConcurrency* value.

Let's take a look at a typical machine learning workflow that can be constructed using step functions, Lambda, and SageMaker components (Figure 2.3).

FIGURE 2.3 An example ML pipeline constructed using step functions that orchestrate various individual steps, such as preprocessing, training, and deployment, in order

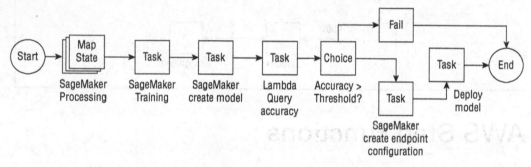

First, we use a Map state to run several SageMaker processing jobs to preprocess data in parallel; we then train the model using SageMaker, and then use the `CreateModel` API to create a model. We use a custom Lambda function to query the accuracy of the training job, and if the (validation) accuracy is greater than a predefined threshold (Choice state), for example 90%, we create a SageMaker endpoint configuration and then deploy the model; if not (Fail state), we don't deploy the model.

AWS RoboMaker

AWS RoboMaker lets you create robotics applications at scale using the Robot Operating System (ROS) framework and extends this to other cloud services like SageMaker for machine learning. RoboMaker provides you with a robot development environment on the cloud, with simulation capabilities to test these robots on the cloud.

What exactly is ROS? ROS is a set of software libraries and tools to help you build robots. The core components of ROS include a communications interface for message passing (pub/sub), robot-specific libraries such as a standard description language, remote procedure calls, mapping, navigation, pose estimation and diagnostics, and a tool for simulating and visualizing robots.

Typically, your own setup of ROS includes installing many packages from source and selecting where on AWS (e.g., an EC2 instance, a container) you would like to run the development environment and the simulations. With AWS RoboMaker, you can make use of a Cloud9 instance that already comes integrated with the tools you need to develop robot applications. The typical steps followed are to create a custom application (including the robot, terrain, and other assets in a scene) within this development environment, develop simulation environments and test in simulation jobs, and finally, if required, deploy these applications using AWS Greengrass to your robot fleets.

Although you can use your simulation environment in a stand-alone way, it is common to also use it in conjunction with SageMaker, for example, with a reinforcement learning job.

 Real World Scenario

Simulating a Real-World Factory Setting

Your customer would like to explore what settings to use in machines within the factory she owns to maximize throughput (units produced per hour). Her data scientist team first creates a simulated version of her factory in ROS and tests out these simulations in AWS RoboMaker. RoboMaker is configured to simulate a fixed number of production hours in the factory. Amazon SageMaker can interface with AWS RoboMaker to train a model policy using reinforcement learning (RL). Once trained, the RL agent can be used to simulate which sequence of actions throughout the day would maximize production throughput.

In the following graphic, SageMaker RL can be used to train an RL agent where a single training instance spawns simulation jobs in multiple simulation instances (called "rollout" instances). Here the type of instance used in the training could be different from the rollout instances. As you can imagine, some types of simulation jobs may require a GPU instance type, whereas the training instance that updates the model after each set of simulations may be a general-purpose instance.

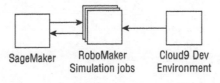

SageMaker   RoboMaker   Cloud9 Dev
                 Simulation jobs   Environment

Summary

In this chapter, we covered services that support ML workflows such as storage services (like Amazon S3, Amazon EFS, and Amazon FSx for Lustre) as well as serverless components (like AWS Lambda and Step Functions). These services are an essential part of production architectures involving ML.

Exam Essentials

Know how different storage services can be used as data sources for ML training.   All AI/ML services connect to Amazon S3 as a data source for preparing datasets and training models. Additionally, Amazon SageMaker lets you connect to Amazon EFS and FSx for Lustre as data sources. Although knowing when exactly to use what is beyond the scope of the exam, you should know that these choices exist today.

Learn how AWS Lambda and Step Functions can be used to orchestrate entire ML pipelines.   Lambda functions can be used to connect to various ML services for training or prediction, and multiple Lambda functions can be used together, in a particular order, using Step Functions. Note also that many services have been directly integrated with Step Functions (such as SageMaker, Glue, Athena, and EMR), so there is no need to use a Lambda function to call these supported APIs.

Read the FAQs for certain key services like Amazon S3, AWS Lambda, and Step Functions.   You will likely not be tested on memorization-related topics (like how many training jobs you can run concurrently), but reading the FAQs for these key services is valuable.

Review Questions

1. A customer who is familiar with Lambda is curious to try training machine learning models on Lambda. The customer says that the data is usually about 100 MB in size, and the generated models are usually less than 10 KB. What will you, as a solutions architect, suggest as next steps for the customer?

   A. Tell the customer that Lambda cannot run machine learning workloads and tell her that she may be thinking of SageMaker when she mentioned Lambda.

   B. Tell the customer that though she can use Lambda for this purpose, the 100 MB dataset may be too large for Lambda to handle.

   C. Tell the customer to explore using a custom container for Lambda that includes the machine learning framework of choice, and read data from S3, and write trained models back to S3.

   D. Tell the customer she can use SageMaker APIs to directly run training on Lambda. SageMaker manages the containers for her, and all she has to do is submit a script containing training code.

2. An ML engineer is trying to figure out a way to connect an EC2 instance that runs a business-critical application to Kendra that contains a trained index with data from some internal websites. The EC2 instance is in a VPC and cannot query the Kendra index. Which solution will enable querying the Kendra index from this EC2 instance?

   A. Since Kendra is a managed service, you cannot access it from your own EC2 instance in a VPC.

   B. Since Kendra is a managed service, you can contact AWS support to place it in your VPC so that you can securely access it.

   C. Since Kendra is a managed service, you can establish a private connection between your VPC and Kendra by creating an interface VPC endpoint and continue to use Kendra APIs.

   D. Since Kendra is a managed service, you can establish a private connection between your VPC and Kendra by creating a Gateway VPC endpoint and continue to use Kendra APIs.

3. A customer is using Step Functions to orchestrate batch transform workloads on Amazon SageMaker. The customer wants to start multiple batch transforms at the same time. What type of state should the customer use?

   A. Parallel state

   B. Map state

   C. Choice state

   D. Task state

4. A company that builds an intelligent search service would like to first call Amazon Textract and then use Amazon Comprehend for each paragraph found as raw text from Textract. What services can be used in this architecture for an end-to-end serverless implementation, assuming that the input files can be stored in S3?

   A. S3

   B. S3 and Lambda

   C. S3 and EC2 instances

   D. S3, Lambda, Step Functions, and DynamoDB

5. Your customer is interested in exploring reinforcement learning for building indoor navigation systems for their fleet of workshop robots. What services on AWS can help them with their product?

   A. AWS Lambda and EC2 instances

   B. Amazon Personalize and DynamoDB

   C. Amazon SageMaker RL and RoboMaker

   D. Deep Graph Library and Neptune

6. You want to train ML models on terabytes of data using SageMaker but are concerned with the time it takes to load such massive datasets into the SageMaker training instance attached storage. What service could you use instead?

   A. Use separate Elastic Block store volumes

   B. Use Amazon S3

   C. Use FSx for Lustre

   D. Use Redshift

7. You are building a Step Functions workflow to compare the outputs of your ML model inference to Ground Truth data. You want to add branching logic that forks the workflow based on the results. Which state would you use?

   A. Task state

   B. Parallel state

   C. Choice state

   D. Pass state

8. What networking construct would you use to ensure that AWS services only access your data in Amazon S3 using AWS PrivateLink?

   A. Security groups

   B. VPC endpoints

   C. AWS Transit Gateway

   D. NAT gateway

9. What resource-based policy can you use to restrict which AWS services can access your S3 buckets?

    A. IAM role

    B. IAM policy

    C. S3 bucket policy

    D. Service control policy

10. You are an MLOps engineer working to deploy ML models built by your data science teams. There is a considerable amount of code and dependencies that can be reused across these models such as ML frameworks, as well as custom libraries developed by scientists. The models are all relatively small and can be deployed using Lambda. What feature of AWS Lambda would you use to promote code reuse and package code into zip files that can be shared across multiple Lambda functions?

    A. Lambda runtime

    B. Lambda layer

    C. Lambda provisioned concurrency

    D. Lambda function

11. You are an MLOps engineer working to deploy ML models built by your data science teams. The models can be deployed using Lambda functions but are subject to a low-latency serving requirement. You are concerned that the cold start problem due to initializing the execution environment will add additional latency during serving. What can you use to mitigate this concern?

    A. Use Amazon SageMaker for inference instead.

    B. Use Lambda provisioned concurrency.

    C. Use EC2 to host your models.

    D. Lambda functions don't suffer from cold start.

12. You have built a Step Functions workflow to retrain your ML models whenever a sufficient amount of new data is stored in your S3 bucket. You want to now automate this to trigger the pipeline in an event-driven manner. What AWS service would you use to start the execution of the Lambda function when new data is added?

    A. AWS EventBridge

    B. Nothing; Step Functions can automatically be triggered by new data in S3

    C. AWS Lambda

    D. AWS CodeCommit

13. You have designed an EKS cluster for training large-scale transformer models of hundreds of millions of parameters for NLP applications. You wish to attach a filesystem to the cluster that allows you to store public datasets used for training, algorithm logs, and so forth. Which service would you use?

    A. AWS FSx for Lustre

    B. Amazon EBS

    C.   Amazon S3

    D.   Amazon Lake Formation

14. A customer would like to use AWS Lambda to do large-scale video processing in a serverless fashion. The processed frames will be used to train downstream computer vision models. However, processing such a large dataset at scale requires several Lambda functions and custom code that cannot fit in the size of a Lambda layer. What storage service would you recommend instead to store the custom code and share video data across all the Lambda functions?

    A.   Amazon EBS

    B.   Amazon EFS

    C.   Amazon S3

    D.   Amazon RDS

Phases of Machine Learning Workloads

PART
II

Chapter

3

Business Understanding

THE AWS CERTIFIED MACHINE LEARNING (ML) SPECIALTY EXAM OBJECTIVES COVERED IN THIS CHAPTER INCLUDE BUT ARE NOT LIMITED TO THE FOLLOWING:

✓ **Domain 3.0: Modeling**

- 3.1 Frame business problems as machine learning problems

Business
Understa

In this chapter you will learn about the phases of machine learning (ML) workloads, starting with the business stakeholders. As an ML practitioner, in order to derive the most value for your organization, you will want to work backward from a business outcome. This will also allow you to set clear standards and goals for your ML models, identify a business budget, and measure success against that desired outcome. Communicating either success or failure against that outcome will help determine next steps such as continuing to invest in ML workloads across different lines of business, whether you need to gather more data in order to obtain a successful outcome, or whether the project is not even suitable for ML.

Phases of ML Workloads

Let's start by reviewing the typical phases for machine learning workloads. You may have heard that machine learning is a complex and iterative process that requires experimentation and diverse skill sets. Studies have indeed shown that, as of this writing, a majority of ML projects do not end up in production—that is, they do not get implemented into an organization's business workflow.

There are a number of reasons for why this may be the case, including the following:

- Business reasons, such as changing business priorities due to market conditions
- People reasons, such as changing senior leadership or lack of data science or engineering talent
- Process reasons, such as a poor understanding of the ML workflow or the company's internal business workflow and how to put the two together

The Cross Industry Standard Process for Data Mining (or CRISP-DM) can be used as a baseline to understand the various phases of the ML workflow. CRISP-DM is application agnostic and can be considered as a general guideline. The phases of the ML workflow are shown in Figure 3.1 (see also https://www.the-modeling-agency.com/crisp-dm.pdf).

For the ML test, you may be asked to name the industry standard for the phases of the ML workloads, namely CRISP-DM.

You may also get a question around the order of the ML lifecycle. Remember, for example, that you first need to collect and ingest data before you can prepare the data for ML or start to engineer features.

FIGURE 3.1 Diagram showing the phases of the machine learning lifecycle

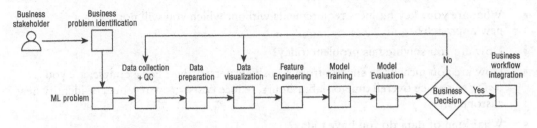

Every ML project should start with a business problem. Stakeholders from the business and ML teams should come together to first validate that the business problem is an ML problem and then the ML practitioners can frame the corresponding ML problem. Once this is done, you will need to source the data and perform quality control (QC) analysis on the data to assess the data quality. Then you may need to prepare the data for exploration and visualization. Following this exploratory analysis, you will have a sense of the features in your data and how they could be used to make predictions. You often will need to engineer new features or perform transformations on the existing features. We will cover this in depth in Chapter 7, "Feature Engineering."

Once the features are engineered, you can start training an ML model. You can then validate the model against the business goals you set at the outset. If the model meets your needs, you can proceed to put the model into production. If not, then you have to go back to gathering more data or exploring the data further to identify why the model was not predictive. You may also need to tune model parameters to improve model performance. In this chapter, we will start by identifying business problems that are suitable for ML. In subsequent chapters, you will learn how to convert the business problem into an ML problem-solving framework that will allow you to implement the solution.

Business Problem Identification

The first step in the ML lifecycle is to frame the business problem. This is also often the most important step as it requires buy-in from senior leaders and commitment that they should embark on an ML project. Since ML projects are resource intensive and hence require cost, your business stakeholders need to be willing to make that investment.

Once you have a top-down directive from senior leadership, the ML and business stakeholders should get together to identify the business problem and the goals and outcomes. It is important to remember that not all business problems are ML problems. As an ML leader, you will want to have a deep enough understanding not just of ML, but also of your core business to be able to determine which problems are ideally suited as ML problems and which are not.

Consider asking the following questions to your business stakeholders when attempting to identify an ML approach to solve a business problem:

- What are your key business requirements without which you will not adopt a new approach?

- How are you solving this problem today?

- How are you measuring success from a business perspective? For example, are you trying to reduce overall time or labor hours, reduce costs, grow revenue, or identify new customers?

- What kind of data do you have today?

- If you don't have sufficient data, then how much will it cost to source additional data and over what time frame?

- Who are the end users of this application and what is their desired experience?

- Does the business have the technical resources required to deliver the project or will they need to hire external resources to execute this? Have they factored in the resource cost?

If your organization is new to ML, it is helpful to work on problems where you can get a quick win to demonstrate success to the senior leadership in your company. Delivered results and earning trust with your leadership can then lead to more complex ML workloads.

Once these questions are satisfactorily answered, the ML team can then identify an ML approach to solving the problem and convert the business goals to an ML problem. We will cover this in detail in the next chapter, Chapter 4, "Framing a Machine Learning Problem."

 Real World Scenario

Optimizing Flight Path between Cities

Let's take a real-world example. Suppose you are in the airline business and your business stakeholder comes to you to ask you about using ML to find optimal flight paths between cities. This is not an ML problem but rather an optimization problem. If the problem asked you to forecast flight delays based on historical data, that is an ML problem.

Summary

In this chapter, we covered the first and most important step in the ML workflow—identifying a business problem. We described the CRISP-DM methodology for the stages of the ML lifecycle and outlined a set of questions to ask your business stakeholders when qualifying a use case as an ML problem.

Exam Essentials

Understand the steps in the ML lifecycle.   Know the CRISP-DM methodology. Although you don't need to read the entire referenced paper (https://www .the-modeling-agency.com/crisp-dm.pdf), it is useful to know the high-level steps.

Understand that not all business problems are ML problems.   It is important to not waste valuable business time attempting to solve a problem using ML when it can be more readily solved using other approaches.

Review Questions

1. The CEO of an organization recently attended a conference and would like to embark on an ML journey. While the CTO has a few data scientists working in her team, the CEO is unsure what the first step is to solve a problem using machine learning. As the chief architect under the CTO, what would you recommend to the CEO?

    A. Identify the data and check the data quality.

    B. Tell the CEO that ML projects rarely end up in production so it is not worth the time spent.

    C. Ask your data scientists to train a few models on public datasets and present the outcomes to the CEO.

    D. Ask the CEO to nominate a few lines of business (LoBs) that you can work with to identify a business problem that can be solved using ML.

2. Which of the following are the correct steps in the CRISP-DM methodology for the ML lifecycle? (Not all steps are included.)

    A. Business problem → ML problem framing → Data collection → Data exploration→ Model training

    B. Business problem → ML problem framing → Data collection → Model training → Data exploration

    C. Business problem → ML problem framing → Model training → Model evaluation

    D. Data collection → ML problem framing → Business problem → Model training

3. A business stakeholder comes to you with a business problem to extract a fixed set of known text from documents if they match exactly. He asks you if this problem can be solved using machine learning. As a data scientist, what advice would you give?

    A. Yes, you can solve this using image recognition.

    B. Yes, this is a classification problem in machine learning.

    C. This problem can be solved with simple regular expression (regex) matching, so it is not an ML problem.

    D. Yes, treat this as a natural language processing problem and solve it using named entity recognition (NER).

4. A business stakeholder comes to you with a business problem to predict anomalies in sales data. The business has a small set of rules to detect anomalies today but also has historical data of labeled sales anomalies going back a few years. However, the stakeholder is concerned that as the data size grows, the business rules will be insufficient and become cumbersome to maintain. How would you work with the business to implement the least complex solution? (Choose all that apply.)

   A. Develop a rule-based model initially that incorporates the business rules outlined by the stakeholders. As the data size grows, scale out the server to detect anomalies in parallel.

   B. Identify whether the historical sales data can be used to train a random cut forest anomaly detection model using Amazon SageMaker.

   C. Develop a rule-based model initially that incorporates the business rules outlined by the stakeholders. If the data size grows, simply scale up the server running the business rules.

   D. Since the rule-based approach is not scalable on its own, train a reinforcement learning model to learn the rules based on historical sales data.

5. Which of the following are the correct steps in the CRISP-DM methodology for the ML life-cycle? (Not all steps are included.)

   A. Business problem → ML problem framing → Data collection → Data exploration→ Model evaluation

   B. Business problem → Model hosting → Data collection → Model training → Data exploration

   C. Business problem → ML problem framing → Model training → Model evaluation

   D. Business problem → ML problem framing → Data collection → Data exploration→ Model training

6. Your CEO wants your organization to start investing in ML initiatives that are relevant to the business. The CEO is frustrated that most ML projects in the company are still using public datasets and not relying on first-party data and therefore are not insightful. You have worked with your AWS account teams and hosted a discovery workshop to identify a few strategic initiatives that are important for the business. What is a possible next step you can take?

   A. Of the use cases you have found, identify which ones can be solved with ML. Then quickly determine if you have the datasets available in order to train ML models. Then conduct a proof of concept on one of the use cases to quickly demonstrate value to your CEO.

   B. Pick any one use case of the ones you have identified, and train an ML model using public data relevant to that use case.

   C. Of the use cases you have found, identify which ones are ML problems. Then look for available public datasets from websites such as Kaggle.com that are closely relevant to your use case. Train an ML model and showcase the results to your CEO.

   D. Of the use cases you have found, identify which ones can be solved with ML. Then quickly determine if you have the datasets available in order to train ML models. For ones that do not have clean, labeled data available, start by labeling data.

7. A business stakeholder approaches their AWS Solutions Architecture team about predicting product defects in assembly lines using computer vision. What is the first question you should ask this stakeholder?

A. You should tell them that this is not an ML problem and will require humans to manually determine whether products are defective or not.

B. You should ask them if they have high-quality labeled images available that label defective and nondefective products.

C. While defect detection is an ML problem, it is not a computer vision problem and can be solved using a simple statistical algorithm like ARIMA.

D. Defect prediction does not require labeled data and can be accomplished using unsupervised learning algorithms such as principal component analysis.

8. Consider the same use case as in the previous question. The stakeholder goes back and reports that while they have some labeled data available, it is certainly not in the hundreds of thousands to millions of images. They have read that training deep learning algorithms requires a lot of data and are concerned that it will take a lot of time and money to source this data. What advice would you give the stakeholder? (Choose all that apply.)

A. They should consider using pretrained computer vision (CV) models available from open source and apply transfer learning on the small labeled dataset to begin with.

B. They should abandon the project because without millions of images, the ML model will not perform well.

C. They can consider a service like SageMaker Ground Truth Automated Labeling to automatically label images using ML as a way to scale the number of labeled images.

D. They should train a CV model from scratch on the small dataset they have.

Chapter

4

Framing a Machine Learning Problem

THE AWS CERTIFIED MACHINE LEARNING (ML) SPECIALTY EXAM OBJECTIVES COVERED IN THIS CHAPTER INCLUDE BUT ARE NOT LIMITED TO THE FOLLOWING:

✓ **Domain 3.0: Modeling**

- 3.1 Frame business problems as machine learning problems

Framing a Machine
Learning Pr

In this chapter you will learn about how to frame a business problem as a machine learning (ML) problem. Once you do so, you will be able to gather the data requirements, engineer features, and train and tune models.

ML Problem Framing

In the previous chapter, we covered the CRISP-DM framework, which provides a framework for understanding the stages in the ML lifecycle. Once you have identified a business problem and indeed verified that the business problem can be solved using a machine learning approach, the next step is to frame the ML problem.

> As always, remember that not all problems are machine learning problems or can be solved using machine learning.

The goal of machine learning is to predict the value or class of an unknown quantity using a mathematical model. To produce the model, you need some data that the model can use to "learn" from, which consists of independent variables and a dependent variable. This is often known as *training* data.

The model learns to predict the dependent variable based on the independent variables from the data provided. A good model should be able to then generalize what it has learned to unseen data, namely data where the dependent variable is unknown. A poor model that has simply memorized the training data will have poor generalization performance and therefore will not be usable in a business process.

In Chapter 8, "Model Training," we will dive deeper into the different kinds of machine learning and specific algorithms, but for now, this high-level understanding will suffice. We see that in order for any problem to be a machine learning problem, you need to have data that consists of independent variables and a dependent variable (also known as labels or a target variable). What if you don't have any dependent variable information? Can such a problem still be a machine learning problem?

The answer is yes—you can still use machine learning to *discover* patterns within the data in the absence of a dependent variable. This is a form of machine learning known as *unsupervised learning*, which we will discuss in Chapter 8.

Real World Scenario

Warehouse Inventory Demand Forecasting

Let's take a real-world example. Suppose you are a retail business and your business is interested in predicting demand for their products week over week to determine how to stock their warehouse with inventory. They have asked if this can be solved using machine learning.

First, this can be a machine learning problem since the business is likely to have daily or weekly data from points-of-sale on historical product sales. They are also likely to have related information about their warehouse inventory. In this case, you can build a machine learning model that uses independent variables such as the unit of time (day/week) to predict or forecast the dependent variable (total sales).

 Real World Scenario

Customer Segmentation for E-commerce

Let's take another real-world example. Suppose you run an e-commerce business and your business is interested in learning more about their customers. They have asked if this can be solved using machine learning.

First, this can be a machine learning problem since the business is likely to have data about their customers such as their age, gender, address, and purchase history from the e-commerce platform. However, in this case, there is no label attached to this data. You can use unsupervised machine learning methods such as clustering to discover patterns among the customer base and segment them into different groups based on their behavior.

Remember that machine learning is a tool, and whether or not you use machine learning should be driven by a concrete business outcome. Even if a problem is a machine learning problem, if you do not have the data or gathering the data is cost prohibitive, then ML may not be the right approach to solve the problem.

So let's take a look at some recommended practices you should apply when attempting to frame a business problem as an ML problem.

Recommended Practices

Consider the following questions and considerations when attempting to frame a business problem as an ML problem:

1. **How does the business identify success in the project?**

    Once you have a business metric, map this metric to a machine learning metric. Remember that a machine learning model has to optimize against some metric or quantity, which may be accuracy, precision, or recall. You will need to work with your business to convert a business metric, such as "maximizing profit" or "minimizing downtime," to a mathematical metric the ML model can understand.

2. **What are the inputs and what are the desired outputs?**

    Algorithms require concrete inputs, and for ML algorithms, that input is data. Remember the common ML adage, "garbage in, garbage out." ML models are only as good as the data they are trained on, and identifying the input data is key. Also focus on the outputs: What do you want the model to predict? Do you have existing data that relates the inputs to the outputs that the model can use to train? If not, can you label some data quickly and cost effectively? If not, can you scope this use case as a pattern identification use case where you want to learn patterns from the input data?

    Having concrete inputs and outputs and a quantifiable optimization metric will then help you determine the kind of machine learning algorithm to apply.

3. **What are the data sources and is labeled data available?**

    Dive deep into the kind of data your business has, the data sources, and the challenges in sourcing additional data. It is helpful to be broad at this stage and even consider data outside of your organization that may be relevant, such as the weather or public information or news (depending on the use case). Web scraping can often be a common way to source external data. Once you identify all the relevant data sources, then you can narrow them down to scope your project based on what is more readily available or most cost effective. It is important to beware of any data licensing restrictions that may apply to datasets that you use for machine learning or other applications.

    At this stage of the ML journey, it is also important to consider whether you want to use some kind of data annotation or labeling strategy to label data if you don't have sufficient labeled data to train a model. Some use cases such as fraud detection can be tricky in this regard as the number of total fraud cases can be extremely low. Absent sufficient fraudulent examples, you will not be able to develop a good ML model to predict fraud. Consider whether you first want to label some data using human experts prior to developing an ML model.

4. **Are there proxy metrics that may be useful to the business?**

    In the above fraud example, if you don't have sufficient labeled data and if labeling data as fraud is too expensive, you may want to ask your business if they look for other indicators of fraud. Banks, for example, often employ teams of individuals to identify fraud, and their domain expertise may come in handy to determine another label that could serve as a proxy to fraud.

5. Start simple and build complexity over time.

   Always start with a simple model and only employ more complex methods over time because more complex models take a long time to train, are more computationally expensive (hence costly), and can be harder to interpret. It is of no value to spend months training a deep learning model if your business requires interpretability, since deep learning models are notoriously hard to interpret. Simple models such as linear/logistic regression, decision trees, and random forests (which we will cover in Chapter 8) are popular for a reason.

6. Consider criteria such as model risk if they are relevant to your industry.

   As we alluded to earlier, sometimes regulatory considerations may require you to explain the outputs of your ML models. Although there are techniques for doing this such as Shapley values (SHAP) or local interpretable model-agnostic explanations (LIME), they generally work on linear or tree-based models, not deep learning algorithms. That may determine the kind of models you build and is an important consideration when framing an ML problem.

Summary

In this chapter we covered how you can frame a business problem as an ML problem and provided some recommended practices.

Exam Essentials

Understand the steps in the ML lifecycle.   Know the CRISP-DM methodology. While you don't need to read the entire paper (available at https://www.the-modeling-agency .com/crisp-dm.pdf), it is useful to know the high-level steps.

Understand at a high level some of the important considerations when converting a business problem to an ML problem.   Understand how your business defines success, what metrics they use, whether those are present in the data, what the inputs to the model should be, and whether there are any external risk factors you should consider.

Review Questions

1. A business stakeholder has approached you about creating a model to recommend items to users. However, although she has data about the users themselves, she does not have any labels. As a data scientist, which of the following options would you recommend to her to get started with most quickly?

   A. All machine learning problems require labels; since she does not have labels, this is not an ML use case.

   B. All ML problems require labels, so she should spend the next 6 months first getting labeled data users have purchased before building an ML model.

   C. Start simple by building a clustering algorithm that clusters the users into groups. Recommend items to new users based on the items purchased by users in their cluster.

   D. Train a classification model to predict the item for each user.

2. Which of the following are the correct steps in the CRISP-DM methodology for the ML life-cycle? (Not all steps are included.)

   A. Business problem → Data collection → Data exploration→ Model training → ML problem framing → Model evaluation

   B. Business problem → ML problem framing → Data collection → Data exploration→ Model training → Model evaluation

   C. Business problem → Data collection → Data exploration → Model training → Model evaluation → ML problem framing

   D. Data collection → ML problem framing → Business problem → Model training

3. A business stakeholder comes to you with a business problem to extract entities from documents. The documents are quite specific to your business and the entities have custom business verbiage that is not found in common parlance. Currently, the business stakeholder does not have much labeled data available. What advice would you give him to proceed with this use case?

   A. Entity recognition is an ML problem that doesn't require labeled data. You can use a clustering algorithm to discover entities.

   B. Entity recognition requires labels. Since the relevant entities correspond to verbiage that is not commonly found, you will need to train a custom model to detect them. For this, you will need to first develop a strategy to acquire labels. Advise the business stake-holder that you will need to factor in data labeling as part of this project.

   C. Entity recognition requires labels. Simply pick up an off-the-shelf entity recognition model that is trained on the Wikipedia text corpus for detecting the relevant entities.

   D. Entity recognition is not an ML problem. Advise him to write a set of rules to detect entities.

4. A business stakeholder comes to you with a business problem to extract entities from documents. The documents are quite specific to your business and the entities have custom business verbiage that is not found in common parlance. You have determined that the documents are currently in PDF format. What follow-up question would you ask the stakeholder?

    A. Nothing; simply tell them that Textract can process PDF documents and point them to the Amazon Textract documentation.

    B. Entity recognition requires labels. Since the relevant entities correspond to verbiage that is not commonly found, you will need to train a custom model to detect them. For this, you will have to first develop a strategy to acquire labels. Advise the business stakeholder that you will need to factor in data labeling as part of this project.

    C. Entity recognition requires labels. Remind the customer that there are several off-the-shelf entity recognition models that are trained on the Wikipedia text corpus for detecting the relevant entities.

    D. Ask the customer whether the PDF documents are in Amazon S3.

5. A business stakeholder comes to you with a problem to generate a know your customer (KYC) score for business-to-business (B2B) transactions. The stakeholder has public data about their customer, history of past transactions, dates, transaction amounts, and whether they were approved or denied. Today the KYC modeling is rules-based, but the stakeholder would like to augment this with machine learning to reduce false positives. What advice would you give the stakeholder? (Choose all that apply.)

    A. Tell the customer that a rules-based approach is likely to outperform ML since this is not an ML problem.

    B. Ask the customer whether they have considered stitching the transaction data with the Ground Truth data available about the quality of the customers to generate a labeled dataset.

    C. Consider a clustering approach to cluster customers based on the transaction data.

    D. Probe the customer on why they are considering augmenting the rules-based approach and what pain points they have with their current approach.

6. A business stakeholder comes to you with a problem to generate customer profiles and similarity scores to better understand their customers' purchasing behavior. The goal is to use this to upsell and cross-sell products to them based on items that related customers may have purchased. The stakeholder is not an expert in ML and is reaching out for advice on where to start. In particular, they are concerned about the cost of generating labeled data. However, they do have prior customer purchase data available. How would you help the stakeholder address this business problem?

    A. Tell them that customer segmentation is a supervised ML problem and therefore they will need to generate labeled data.

    B. Tell your customer that customer segmentation is a good place to start, and it can be addressed using unsupervised machine learning methods, so labeled data is not necessary to begin with.

   C. Tell your customer that Amazon Personalize is a service that lets you recommend items to customers based on prior purchase behavior and they should use that service.

   D. Tell your customer that Amazon Lookout for Metrics is a service that lets you recommend items to customers based on prior purchase behavior and requires no prior ML knowledge.

7. Consider the same use case as in the previous question. Having determined the kind of approach to take, the customer is satisfied that there is a path forward. However, it is unclear how the outputs of the model will impact the business. What questions might you ask to glean additional data in this regard?

   A. Ask them how the customer segments determined by the ML model are related to the key customer segments that are identified by the business.

   B. Ask them how the clusters produced by the ML model will be used to determine the cross-sell/upsell strategy.

   C. Ask them how they define success and how they plan to measure and monitor whether the customers are actually purchasing the products recommended by the strategy.

   D. All of the above options are correct.

Chapter

5

Data Collection

THE AWS CERTIFIED MACHINE LEARNING (ML) SPECIALTY EXAM OBJECTIVES COVERED IN THIS CHAPTER INCLUDE BUT ARE NOT LIMITED TO THE FOLLOWING:

✓ **Domain 1.0: Data Engineering**

- 1.1 Create data repositories for machine learning

- 1.2 Identify and implement a data ingestion solution

✓ **Domain 2.0: Exploratory Data Analysis**

- 2.1 Sanitize and prepare data for modeling

In this chapter, we continue along the CRISP-DM framework and discuss data collection. We first define some general data terminology and some machine learning (ML)–specific terminology that will become relevant to the next chapter on feature engineering. Then we will discuss ways to ingest data from different data sources and prepare it for machine learning. We will discuss tools for both batch ingestion and streaming ingestion of data.

Basic Data Concepts

To start collecting data for machine learning, you first need to understand some core concepts about data. Fundamentally, there are three kinds of data:

Structured Data   Structured data consists of data that has a well-defined schema and metadata needed to interpret the data such as the attributes and the data types. Tabular data is an example of structured data. A tabular dataset may have a number of different rows and columns. A given column may have a particular data type such as integers, floats, or strings. Depending on the column data type, you may have to perform different actions to prepare the data for machine learning. An attribute in a tabular dataset is a column, and a row corresponds to a data point or an observation.

Unstructured Data   Unstructured data is data that does not have a schema or any well-defined structural properties. In fact, unstructured data makes up the majority of the data most organizations have, and part of a data scientist's job is to either convert the unstructured data into some form of structured data for machine learning or train an ML model directly on the unstructured data itself. Examples include images, videos, audio files, text documents, or application log files.

Semi-structured Data   Semi-structured data is data that does not have any precise schema such as data that can be in JSON format or XML data that you may have from a NoSQL database. You may need to parse this semi-structured data into structured data to make it useful for machine learning.

With these basic concepts, we now introduce some machine learning–specific data concepts:

Labeled Data   Labeled data is data that has a single or multiple target columns (dependent variables) or attributes.

Unlabeled Data   Unlabeled data is data with no target attribute or label.

Feature   A feature is a column in a tabular dataset besides the label column.

Data Point   A data point is a row in a tabular dataset that consists of one or more features. For labeled data, a row also contains one or more labels.

Dataset   A dataset is a collection of data points that you will use for model training and validation.

Numerical Feature   A numerical feature is a feature that can be represented by a continuous number or an integer but is unbounded in nature.

Categorical Feature   A categorical feature is a feature that is discrete and qualitative, and can only take on a finite number of values. In most machine learning problems, you need to convert categorical features into numerical features using different techniques, which we will cover in the next chapter.

Image Data   Image data consists of images that are usually in different formats such as JPEG or PNG. An example of an image dataset is the popular handwritten digits dataset such as MNIST or ImageNet.

Audio Data   Audio data usually consists of audio files in MP3 or WAV formats. Audio data can arise from call transcriptions in call centers.

Text Data (Corpus)   In machine learning, text data is commonly referred to as a corpus and can consists of collections of documents. Text data can be stored in many formats, such as raw PDF or TXT files, JSON, or CSV. Popular text corpora include the newsgroups dataset, Amazon reviews data, the WikiQA corpus, WordNet, and IMDB reviews.

Time Series Data   Time series data is data that consists of a value varying over time such as the sale price of a product, the price of a stock, the daily temperature or humidity, measurements or readings from a sensor or Internet of things (IoT) device, or the number of passengers who ride the New York City Metro daily.

Training Data   This is the dataset that is used to train the model.

Validation Data   This is a portion of the dataset that is kept aside to validate your model performance during training.

Test Data   This should be kept aside from the outset so that your model never sees it until it is trained. Once your model is trained and you are satisfied with the model performance on the training and validation datasets, only then should you test the model performance on the test dataset. The test dataset should mimic as closely as possible the data you expect your model to serve during production.

It is helpful for the test to understand the different classifications of data for machine learning and the associated terminology.

Take a look at Table 5.1, which shows housing prices in different cities, and see if you can identify whether a column is a feature or a label. For the label, is it a continuous label or a discrete label? For the features, are there any categorical features in the data? How would you classify ZIP codes? Even though they are numerical, there are a finite number of ZIP codes. Does that make it a numerical or a categorical feature?

The label (price) is clearly a continuous label, and the other columns are features. City is a categorical feature because there is no inherent ordering (Brooklyn > Chicago, etc.). ZIP codes can also be considered as categorical for the same reason.

TABLE 5.1   Table of housing data

Item	City	Number of rooms	ZIP code	Square footage (sq. ft.)	Price (in USD)
1	Brooklyn, NY	5	11207	1350	1,500,000
2	Chicago, IL	3	60607	986	450,000
3	Washington, D.C.	4	20016	1200	650,000
4	San Francisco, CA	1	94133	700	600,000

Data Repositories

Having discussed the different kinds of data, we now need to cover the different data repositories where this data can be housed, read from, and queried.

Let's start with tabular data with a well-defined schema. Tabular data is often used for use cases such as online transaction processing (OLTP), analytics, and reporting, and analysts use a language like SQL to query this data.

OLTP applications typically run on relational databases, and AWS offers a service called AWS RDS to build and manage this kind of data. You can choose from a variety of underlying engines from AWS Aurora, MySQL, MariaDB, Oracle, Microsoft SQL Server, and PostgreSQL. Relational databases typically use row-wise storage and are suited for queries for specific rows, inserts, and updates.

For analytics and reporting workloads that are read heavy, consider a data warehouse solution like Amazon Redshift. Amazon Redshift uses columnar storage instead of row-level storage for fast retrieval of columns and is ideally suited for querying against very large datasets. Both Redshift and RDS store tabular data. It is worth noting that Amazon Redshift is now integrated with Amazon SageMaker via SageMaker Data Wrangler.

If your data is semi-structured, you should consider a NoSQL database like DynamoDB. DynamoDB stores data as key-value pairs and can be used to store data that does not have a specific schema. If your data currently lives in an open-source NoSQL store like MongoDB, you can use Amazon DocumentDB to migrate that data to AWS.

Most organizations have all the kinds of data just described, and AWS's recommendation is to use purpose-built databases for specific applications, whether it is OLTP or analytics, or reporting or bulk object storage like Amazon S3. This is opposed to a one-size-fits-all approach, which companies adopted in the past. When you have data in diverse data repositories, you may want to centrally manage and govern the access controls to these datasets and audit that access over time. AWS Lake Formation is a data lake solution that helps you centrally catalog your data and establish fine-grained controls on who can access the data. Users can query the central catalog in Lake Formation and then run analytics or extract-transform-load (ETL) workstreams on the data using tools like Amazon Redshift or Amazon EMR.

Finally, in order to actually train machine learning models, your data will need to land in Amazon S3 for Amazon SageMaker to consume it. Since S3 was already covered in Chapter 2, "Supporting Services from the AWS Stack," we will not cover it in detail here. In the next section, we will discuss how you can migrate data from these different data sources to S3.

This book will not cover different AWS data sources in great detail since those are covered in other Solution Architect exams such as the Solution Architect Associate Exam.

For the exam, you should have a basic familiarity with the different AWS data storage solutions.

Data Migration to AWS

To build machine learning models on AWS, you need to first migrate your data to AWS. Once your data lands in AWS, you need to move the data to Amazon S3 in order to train ML models. If your data is already on S3, then you're all set. In this section, we will cover different migration tools available on AWS to move your data to S3.

At a high level, there are two use cases for migrating data onto AWS: batch and streaming. In the batch case, you want to bulk transfer some data, whereas in the streaming use case, you have a streaming data source such as a sensor or an IoT device and you want to stream that data into S3. You can use different solutions for each use case.

Batch Data Collection

If your data is already on AWS, you can use AWS Data Pipeline to move the data from other data sources such as Redshift, DynamoDB, or RDS to S3. Data Pipeline uses a concept called activity types to perform certain actions (see `https://docs.aws.amazon.com/datapipeline/latest/DeveloperGuide/dp-concepts-activities.html`).

An activity type is a pipeline component that tells Data Pipeline what job to perform. Data Pipeline has some prebuilt activity types that you can use, such as CopyActivity to copy data from one Amazon S3 location to another, RedshiftCopyActivity to copy data to and from Redshift tables, and SqlActivity to run a SQL query on a database and copy the output to S3.

Once your data is in S3, you can run ETL jobs on the data using Amazon EMR. Data Pipeline can be used to migrate the data to EMR for processing, Hive for running Hive queries, Pig to run Pig scripts, and so forth. Data Pipeline also allows you to copy data out from S3 or DynamoDB to Redshift. Data Pipeline uses EC2 instances under the hood to migrate your data and can be run in an event-driven manner or on a schedule. See Figure 5.1.

FIGURE 5.1   Various data sources you can use with AWS Data Pipeline to land data in S3

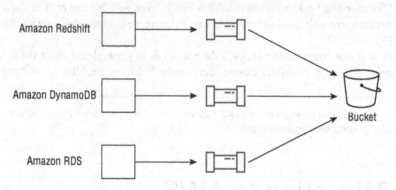

If your data is in a relational format and you want to migrate data from one database to another, you can use AWS Database Migration Service (DMS). For example, your data may be in an Oracle on premises or on EC2, and you want to land that in an Oracle database in Amazon RDS. This is an example of a homogenous migration. An example of a heterogenous migration would be when you have data in a MySQL database either on premises or on AWS and you want to land that in Amazon Aurora. In the latter case, you may need to convert the schema of the dataset along the way. You can do this using the Schema Conversion Tool. You can also use DMS to land the data from one relational database to Amazon S3. See Figure 5.2.

FIGURE 5.2 Various data sources you can use with AWS DMS to land data in S3

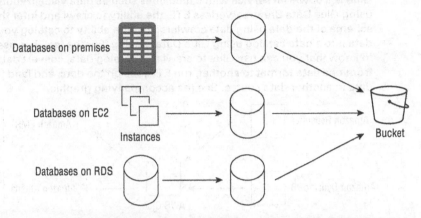

Databases on premises

Databases on EC2

Instances

Databases on RDS

Bucket

Understand the differences at a high level between DMS and Data Pipeline. Remember that Data Pipeline can be used with data warehouses such as Redshift and NoSQL databases such as DynamoDB, whereas DMS can only be used to migrate relational databases such as databases on EC2, AzureSQL, and Oracle. If your data is already in a relational database on AWS such as RDS and you want to migrate it to S3, choose AWS Data Pipeline instead of DMS.

Remember that for heterogenous migrations, you will also need to use the Schema Conversion Tool to facilitate the migration.

The third tool we will discuss in the context of data migration is AWS Glue. AWS Glue is a managed ETL service that allows you to run serverless extract-transform-load workloads without worrying about provisioning compute. You can take data from different data sources, and use the Glue catalog to crawl the data to determine the underlying schema. Glue crawlers will try to infer the data schema and work with a number of data formats such as CSV, JSON, and Apache Avro.

Then you can create a data catalog using Glue Data Catalog to serve as a metadata repository for your data. In fact, Lake Formation uses Glue Data Catalog to provide a centralized data catalog.

Once the schema is determined, you can run your own ETL scripts to change the data format, such as changing Apache Parquet data to CSV, or to run custom preprocessing scripts on the data. Recently, Glue released Glue Data Brew, which is a service that allows you to visually prepare and clean your data, normalize your data, and run a number of different feature transforms on the dataset. We will cover these different feature transformations in the next chapter.

TIP

Glue is a powerful service with capabilities such as data visualization using Glue Data Brew, serverless ETL, the ability to crawl and infer the schema of the data using data crawlers, and the ability to catalog your data into a data catalog using Glue Data Catalog. For the test, it is useful to know that you can use Glue to crawl and catalog data, convert data from one data format to another, run ETL jobs on the data, and land the data in another data source. See the accompanying graphic.

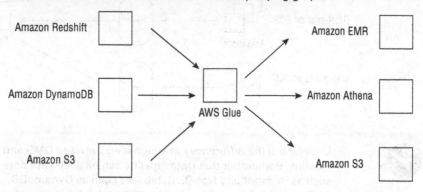

NOTE

We recommend that you go over the FAQs for AWS Data Pipeline, AWS Glue, and AWS DMS prior to taking the test.

Streaming Data Collection

For many applications such as sensors and IoT devices, video or news feeds, and live social media streams, you may want to upload the data to AWS in a streaming manner rather than in batch. For streaming use cases, think of the Kinesis family of services. We will describe each of the Kinesis services at a high level in this section.

NOTE

If the exam question has key words such as streaming, sensors, and IoT and concerns data collection, immediately think of the Kinesis family of services, which we will cover now.

There are four key Kinesis services that we will describe here:

- Kinesis Data Streams
- Kinesis Data Firehose
- Kinesis Data Analytics
- Kinesis Video Streams

Kinesis Data Streams

Kinesis Data Streams is a service you can use to collect and process large streams of data records in real time (Figure 5.3). Once the data streams are in AWS, you can run a number of downstream applications such as real-time data analytics by sending the data to a dashboard. Similarly, you can intake logs from different applications and sensors and process them and generate real-time metrics and reports.

FIGURE 5.3   Conceptual diagram of Kinesis Data Streams

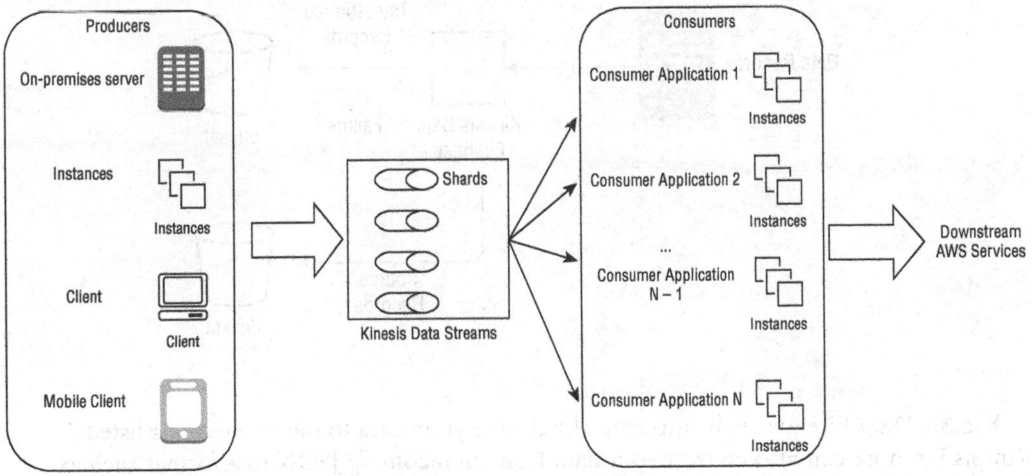

The basic concepts are as follows:

- A data stream represents a group of data records, where a data record is a unit of data. Data records are distributed into shards. A shard represents a sequence of data records. Each shard supports 5 transactions/second for reads or up to 2 MB per second and 1,000 records/second up to 1 MB per second for writes. When you create a Kinesis Data Stream, you specify the number of shards.

- The retention period corresponds to the length of time the data is available in the stream. The default is 24 hours, but you can increase it to 365 days (8,760 hours).

- A producer puts records into the streams such as a web log server. You can use the Kinesis Producer Library (KPL) to build your producer application.

- A consumer gets records from the stream and processes them. Consumer applications often run on a fleet of EC2 instances. Kinesis Client Library abstracts a lot of the lower-level Kinesis data streams APIs to allow you to manage your consumer applications, distribute load across consumers, respond to instance failures, and checkpoint records.

- Downstream AWS Services include services such as S3, EMR, and Redshift that consumers send the outputs of the processed stream to for various end applications.

Kinesis Data Firehose

Often you may need to send streaming data directly to an end service such as Amazon S3 for storage, Redshift for querying, or Elastic Search/Splunk or some custom third-party endpoint such as Datadog. In this case, instead of writing complex producer-consumer applications like Kinesis Data Streams, you can simply use Kinesis Data Firehose (Figure 5.4).

FIGURE 5.4   Conceptual diagram of Kinesis Data Firehose showing how data can be directly streamed to S3. Note that the lower bucket is optional.

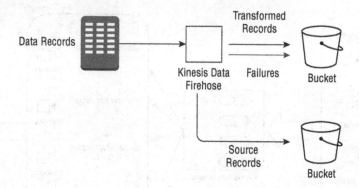

Kinesis Data Firehose will automatically deliver your data to the services just listed. Kinesis Firehose can also convert your data from an incoming JSON to a format such as Parquet ORC prior to storing the data in S3. Kinesis Data Firehose also allows you to use AWS Lambda functions to process the incoming data stream before it is delivered to the final destination service.

To deliver data to Redshift as the final destination, note that Firehose will create an intermediate S3 bucket to store the transformed records. A Redshift Copy command is then issued to move the data from S3 to Redshift.

Kinesis Data Analytics

Kinesis Data Analytics lets you run SQL queries directly on streaming data. The output of Kinesis Data Analytics can be sent to Kinesis Firehose (to then send to S3, Redshift, ElasticSearch Service, or Splunk) or Kinesis Data Streams as destinations.

Kinesis Data Analytics can be used to generate metrics and aggregated analysis over windows for time series data and then stream those outputs to S3 or to a data warehouse.

Kinesis Data Analytics can be used to feed real-time dashboards or create real-time metrics and triggers for monitoring, notifications, and alarms.

Kinesis Data Analytics does not source data from streaming sources directly, unlike Firehose or Data Streams. It requires either Data Firehose or Data Streams or S3 as an input, and sends the output of the SQL query back to either Kinesis Data Streams or Firehose for downstream processing to other consumers or AWS services. See Figure 5.5.

FIGURE 5.5   Diagram showing streaming data flow pattern for Kinesis Data Analytics

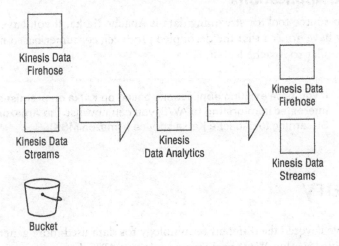

Streaming SQL is different from standard SQL queries on batch data since the query must occur over a particular time window. Although this is not an important topic for the ML Specialty, if you wish to take the Data Analytics Specialty, then having a good understanding of the windowed queries is important. This is covered in more detail in the following section of the documentation: https://docs.aws.amazon.com/kinesisanalytics/latest/dev/streaming-sql-concepts.html.

Kinesis Video Streams

The fourth service in the Kinesis family is Kinesis Video Streams. As you may have guessed, you use this service when you want to stream live video feeds into the AWS cloud. Kinesis Video Streams allows you to stream massive amounts of live video from sources like webcams, embedded cameras in cars, drone footage, security cameras, and smartphones. You can also use this service for non-video data such as audio data and RADAR data.

Kinesis Video Streams works similar to data streams in that it has the concept of a producer, which is any video-generating device, and a consumer, which is an EC2-based application that processes the streaming video and analyzes it. Recall in Chapter 1, "AWS AI ML Stack," where we covered Amazon Rekognition Video. Rekognition video can be used as a downstream "consumer" of a Kinesis Video stream.

Covering the Kinesis services in greater depth is beyond the scope of this book and the exam. We highly recommend that prior to taking the ML Specialty exam, you should at least read the FAQs for the different Kinesis services covered in this section.

Kafka-Based Applications

A common open-source tool for streaming data is Apache Kafka. If you have used Kafka before, you may have noticed that the decoupled producer, consumer-based model for Kinesis is very similar to Apache Kafka.

If you have existing applications based on Kafka on premises that you are interested in migrating to AWS, you can now use the Amazon Managed Streaming for Apache Kafka service (Amazon MSK).

Summary

In this chapter we covered the different terminology for data used more generally as well as specific to machine learning. We then discussed relevant AWS data repositories and their end uses. We also explored various AWS tools for bringing data into AWS and then into S3 for machine learning. We separately discussed two data collection patterns: batch and streaming.

Exam Essentials

Understand where data collection fits in the CRISP-DM model for the ML lifecycle.   Recall the CRISP-DM model from Chapter 3, "Business Understanding." At a high level, it is useful to remember the stages in the ML lifecycle.

Know the different kinds of data (structured, semi-structured, unstructured) and some examples for each.   The exam often asks questions that require you to know whether a dataset is tabular (structure), image or textual (unstructured), or in JSON format (semi-structured). Your approach to data ingestion and the ML algorithms used will vary based on the data type.

Understand clearly the difference between training, validation, and test data.   Remember that test data should be kept aside and only used when you are ready to fit the model after training. To test your model during training, use a validation dataset. By comparing the performance of your model against the training and validation datasets, you can identify whether the model is overfitting/underfitting your data.

Know the difference between continuous and categorical variables.   Remember that categorical variables are discrete and finite and don't have an ordinal relationship (Monday is not "greater" than Tuesday, etc.)

Understand the different data collection use cases and the relevant services for each.   The most common data collection use cases are streaming and batch. For batch use cases, think databases, data lakes, and data warehouses; for streaming use cases, think Kinesis, Kafka, message queues, IoT services, and so on.

Know the difference between Data Pipeline and Database Migration Service.   If your data is already on a database on AWS, and you want to move it to S3, consider Data Pipeline. If you want to migrate from one database to another, either homogeneous or heterogeneous, consider Database Migration Service. Know that you will need the Schema Conversion Tool to change the data schemas.

Know the difference between Kinesis Data Streams and Kinesis Data Firehose.   Kinesis Data Firehose can be used to directly stream data into a data source such as S3, without the need for producers/consumers.

Review Questions

1. You are building an ML solution to identify anomalies in sensor readings from a factory. The sensor publishes numerical data every second. What kind of data is sensor data?

    A. Structured, time series

    B. Unstructured, time series

    C. Image data

    D. Text data

2. You are building an ML solution to identify the sentiment of news and social media feeds about a company. What kind of data is the incoming news data and what kind of ingestion use case is it?

    A. Structured, CSV data, streaming data collection

    B. Semi-structured, JSON, streaming data collection

    C. Unstructured, text corpus, batch data collection

    D. Unstructured, text corpus, streaming data collection

3. Refer to Table 5.1 for this question. If you are trying to predict the housing price, the column "Price (in USD)" represents what ML data concept?

    A. Label

    B. Categorical feature

    C. Data point

    D. Continuous feature

4. Refer to Table 5.1 for this question. If you are trying to predict the housing price, the column "ZIP code" represents what ML data concept?

    A. Label

    B. Categorical feature

    C. Data point

    D. Continuous feature

5. As the head of AI/ML for a large enterprise, you are building an ML platform. Since the platform will be used by different lines of business (LoBs), you are creating separate S3 buckets for data scientists in those LoBs in different AWS accounts. Your IT security team has asked you to ensure that the data stored in those LoB buckets has fine-grained access controls and entitlements established at the column level and is cataloged in a central repository. What AWS service would you use to achieve this?

    A. AWS IAM to establish access controls and AWS Glue Catalog to catalog data

    B. Store the data catalog as a table in Amazon Redshift

    C. Hive Catalog

    D. AWS Lake Formation

6. You have a large amount of data stored in Redshift in Parquet format that you need to convert to CSV before storing in S3. What is the simplest data ingestion solution to sanitize this data into the proper format for machine learning?

   A. Use AWS Data Pipeline using a CopyActivity to copy data directly from Redshift to S3.

   B. Use AWS Glue to move the data from Redshift to S3 and run an ETL job to convert the data type to CSV from Parquet.

   C. Use AWS Database Migration Service with the Schema Conversion Tool to convert the data schema.

   D. Use AWS Lake Formation.

7. You have a large amount of data stored in a PostgreSQL database on EC2 that you want to migrate to Amazon Aurora. What AWS service would you use for this?

   A. AWS Lambda

   B. AWS Database Migration Service

   C. AWS Data Pipeline

   D. AWS Glue

8. You have data incoming from a number of IoT devices that are deployed on your factory floor. You want to take the inputs from these devices and run some interactive SQL queries on the data to power a real-time dashboard as well as set up alarms to alert admins when there is an issue. What AWS streaming services can you use to build this solution?

   A. Use Kinesis Firehose to ingest the data and output to ElasticSearch. Run a real-time dashboard using Kibana on top.

   B. Use Kinesis Data Streams to ingest the data and use EC2 as a consumer to run SQL queries. Send the outputs to these queries to a custom dashboard application.

   C. Ingest streaming data with Kinesis Data Streams but use Kinesis Data Analytics to run SQL queries over windowed streaming data. Create alerts on the incoming data stream as well. Send the outputs to Kinesis Data Streams to output to a DynamoDB table. Build your dashboard on the DynamoDB table.

   D. Ingest the data into S3 using S3 copy APIs. Use Amazon Athena to run SQL queries on the S3 data and send the outputs to a custom dashboard built using QuickSight.

9. You have performed OCR on textual data and extracted the outputs in JSON format. The outputs consist of key/value pairs as well as some raw text fields. What kind of data is this?

   A. Structured data

   B. Semi-structured data

   C. Unstructured text data

   D. Unstructured image data

10. You have split video frames into images and stored the images in S3 for further processing. Your ML scientists want to build image classification models on top of this image data directly in JPEG format. What kind of data is this?

   A. Structured image data

   B. Semi-structured image data

   C. Unstructured text data

   D. Unstructured image data

11. You are given a dataset that consists of a day_of_week field. What kind of feature is this?

   A. Label

   B. Continuous feature

   C. Categorical feature

   D. Data point

12. You have a large amount of streaming video data incoming from various video feeds you have in place. You need to quickly ingest this video data and perform some image analysis and object detection on the video. What architecture might you propose that the customer use in this use case that will minimize the amount of code the customer needs to manage?

   A. Ingest the video using Kinesis Data Streams. Build an ML model to do object and scene detection using Amazon SageMaker, and host the model using EC2. Set up an EC2 consumer to process the video.

   B. Ingest the video using Kinesis Data Streams. Build an ML model to do object and scene detection using Amazon SageMaker, and host the model using Lambda. Set up a Lambda consumer to process the video.

   C. Ingest the video using Kinesis Video Streams. Build an ML model to do object and scene detection using Amazon SageMaker, and host the model using SageMaker Endpoint. Set up a SageMaker consumer to process the video.

   D. Ingest the video using Kinesis Video Streams. Use Amazon Rekognition Video as a consumer to use prebuilt ML models to process the video.

Chapter

6

Data Preparation

THE AWS CERTIFIED MACHINE LEARNING (ML) SPECIALTY EXAM OBJECTIVES COVERED IN THIS CHAPTER INCLUDE BUT ARE NOT LIMITED TO THE FOLLOWING:

✓ **Domain 2.0: Exploratory data analysis**

- ■ Sanitize and prepare data for modeling

In this chapter, we continue along the CRISP-DM framework and discuss data preparation. We will describe a few AWS services that you can use to extract, transform, and load (ETL) your data and sanitize and prepare your data for machine learning.

Data Preparation Tools

In the previous chapter, we discussed the various kinds of data and the terminology about data more broadly and for machine learning (ML). Then we covered a number of AWS services for data collection, whether it is streaming data or batch data.

Simply having your data in an S3 bucket or in Redshift does not mean it is ready for ML. You need to prepare the data for machine learning, which may involve running Structured Query Language (SQL) queries to join data across different tables, such as matching customer data to order data to sales data in order to build a single view of customer purchases. It may involve sanitizing the data, such as converting the data type from Parquet to CSV; removing missing values; or converting integers to floats. Finally, you may need to generate some labels using a data-labeling tool.

In this chapter and the next, we will discuss how to take raw data and convert it to features for machine learning. This chapter will focus on some relevant AWS tools for data preparation, and the next chapter will cover the key concepts for feature engineering.

SageMaker Ground Truth

 Real World Scenario

Labeling Street Data for Autonomous Vehicles

Let's start with a real-world example of an autonomous vehicle business that wants to label objects on the street as cars, persons, stop signs, pets, buses, stores, and so forth. Your cloud engineering team has just uploaded a massive amount of sensor data from cameras mounted on top of cars to the AWS cloud and the data is stored in S3. Now that the data is in S3, you as the lead data scientist have identified that this is indeed unstructured image data and you need to build an object detection model to detect the various objects in the image. However, there's a problem; the camera images are unlabeled. Without labels you cannot train a model to detect objects in an image.

Amazon SageMaker Ground Truth is a service that you can use to label your image, text, audio, or even tabular data. SageMaker Ground Truth lets you outsource the labeling task to a public workforce (via Amazon Mechanical Turk) or a private workforce (either a third-party labeling company or your own private workforce within your organization) to label data. Ground Truth has built-in workflows for image and text labeling use cases such as image classification, object detection via bounding boxes, segmentation, text classification, entity recognition, video and audio labeling, or even 3D point cloud labeling. Furthermore, you can create custom workflows using Ground Truth if your use case doesn't fit into these built-in types.

To use SageMaker Ground Truth, you can reference the architecture pattern shown in Figure 6.1.

FIGURE 6.1   Diagram showing SageMaker Ground Truth data labeling tool

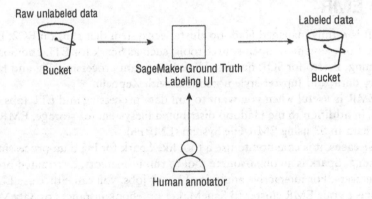

Once you create a team of workers on AWS, who are authenticated using either AWS Cognito or your own custom identity provider, SageMaker Ground Truth handles the routing of tasks to individual labelers and publishes the outputs to an S3 bucket. Ground Truth can also aggregate outputs if the same labeling task goes to multiple workers to label.

Real World Scenario

Labeling Street Data for Autonomous Vehicles

Now let's return to our case study. Ground Truth is the right solution for you to get started with for labeling your data. You can use the semantic segmentation or the object labeling task in Ground Truth to identify if a particular pixel belongs to a specific object or draw bounding boxes around the objects.

Generally, in this kind of use case, you may need to labels hundreds of thousands of images, which can start to get quite expensive if using only manual labor.

Ground Truth also has an active learning capability where a machine learning model learns the labels provided by the human annotators. This is known as automated data labeling. The model then automatically labels images it has a high confidence in and only sends the low-confidence images to the human annotators for labeling. This can allow you to scale your labeling to a large number of images.

Amazon EMR

Amazon EMR is a fully managed Hadoop cluster ecosystem that runs on EC2. EMR allows you to choose from a menu of open-source tools, such as Spark for ETL and SparkML for machine learning, Presto for SQL queries, Flink for stream processing, Pig and Hive to analyze and query data, and Jupyter-style notebooks with Zeppelin.

Amazon EMR is useful when you want to run data processing and ETL jobs over petabytes of data. In addition to the Hadoop distributed filesystem for storage, EMR integrates directly with data in S3 using EMR File System (EMRFS).

For ML use cases, it is common to use a tool like Spark for big data processing prior to machine learning. Spark is an open-source tool to run in-memory, distributed processing jobs on massive datasets. For interactive analysis of Spark jobs, you can either use EMR notebooks or connect your EMR cluster to SageMaker notebook instances or SageMaker Studio.

EMR is a big topic and a big part of the AWS Data Analytics Specialty. For the ML Specialty, you simply need to know what EMR is and that it allows you to run Spark-based workloads on EC2 instances. It is helpful to review the EMR FAQs prior to the exam. Also, if you plan to use EMR in your workloads, refer to the EMR best practices whitepaper here: https://d0.awsstatic.com/whitepapers/aws-amazon-emr-best-practices.pdf.

Amazon SageMaker Processing

EMR gives you the scale to process petabyte-scale data on AWS, but sometimes your data-sets are not as large or your data science team may not have the relevant Hadoop/big data experience that is required to run EMR jobs.

For such use cases, you also have the option of using a tool like SageMaker Processing directly within SageMaker itself. SageMaker Processing lets you implement your processing logic using scikit-learn or PySpark, or via a custom container. Since SageMaker Processing has been covered briefly in Chapter 1, "AWS AI ML Stack," we will not describe it in more detail here.

 A common design question is when to use SageMaker Processing versus EMR or Glue. SageMaker Processing is ideally suited for data scientists, and though it can process large amounts of data using, for example, PySpark, it is fully managed and the underlying compute runs in an AWS managed account. As of this writing, SageMaker Processing does not support spot instances or persistent clusters. EMR is ideally suited for the extremely large-scale (petabyte-scale) data requirements, but it does require familiarity with the Hadoop ecosystem. It runs on EC2 instances in your AWS account, and you can set up transient or persistent clusters depending on your workload. It is ideally suited for big data engineers.

AWS Glue

We covered AWS Glue in Chapter 5, "Data Collection," in the context of cataloging data with Glue Crawlers and Glue Data Catalog, converting the schema of your data, such as from Parquet to CSV, and using Glue to automatically detect the data type of your data.

Here, we discuss Glue as an ETL tool. Glue has the benefit over EMR in that it is serverless—users have no need to manage the underlying compute or clusters to run their processing jobs. You can run your ETL scripts using Python, PySpark, or Scala. Glue offers several built-in data transforms and can even build the processing script for you, or you can bring your custom scripts.

Figure 6.2 shows the high-level Glue workflow. First, point your data sources to Glue and define a data crawler to crawl your data, and populate the Glue Data Catalog with your table metadata. Now you can run a custom processing script on your data. Simply point Glue to your data source and a custom or prebuilt script, and schedule a job or use an event trigger to trigger the Glue workflow. The processed outputs will be stored in the specified destination, such as an S3 bucket or Redshift. Glue works with data sources and destinations that support JDBC connectivity such as Amazon Redshift or Amazon RDS, in addition to Amazon S3.

FIGURE 6.2   Diagram showing AWS Glue as an ETL tool

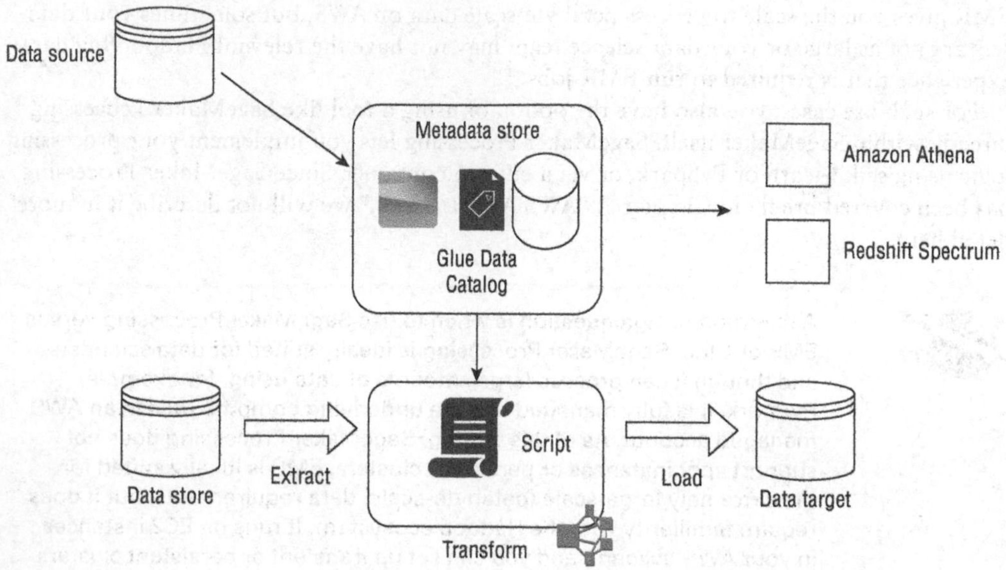

Note that the Glue Data Catalog is also used by AWS Lake Formation to catalog your data. You can also run Athena or Redshift Spectrum queries on data in S3 using the Glue Data Catalog as the underlying metadata store. If you prefer to use Amazon EMR, you can also use EMR in the Transform step of the diagram in Figure 6.2 instead of Glue by referencing the Glue Data Catalog.

> It is helpful to read the Glue FAQs prior to taking the exam. Glue supports a wide variety of AWS services for data ingestion and ETL such as S3, Redshift, RDS, DynamoDB, and even Kinesis Data Streams, Amazon MSK, and Apache Kafka.

In 2020, AWS released Glue Data Brew, which is a service to help data scientists visually inspect their data, explore the data, define transformations, and engineer features. They can then run these transformations as a Glue job to prepare their data for ML.

In Chapter 1, we covered SageMaker Data Wrangler, which is another data preparation tool for ML within SageMaker. Although the exam is unlikely to test you on SageMaker Data Wrangler versus Glue Data Brew, it is helpful to watch the following video blog in case you are deciding between the two services: https://julsimon.medium.com/ data-preparation-aws-glue-data-brew-or-amazon-sagemaker-data-wrangler-d8e76d1510cb.

Amazon Athena

Amazon Athena is a service that allows users to use SQL to access data directly on S3 without moving the data out of S3. You can use Athena to run ad hoc queries to explore data, extract specific relevant rows and columns, or even perform SQL-based transformations and aggregations and joins on the data.

First you need to register a table using the AWS Glue catalog we discussed earlier. Refer to Figure 6.2 for more details on this. You can either automatically create a Glue Data Catalog table or create one manually using the HiveQL data definition language.

Once the table is created, you can run Athena queries against that table. Athena uses Presto, which is a distributed SQL query engine under the hood to run the queries.

Redshift Spectrum

Redshift Spectrum is another analytics service similar to Athena that allows you to interactively query data on S3 without moving the data. The difference is that Redshift Spectrum requires a running Redshift cluster and a connected SQL client, unlike Athena.

Since Spectrum runs on Redshift, it has the advantage of Redshift-level scale and can run on exabytes of data using massive parallelism.

If you are architecting for an analytics solution to interactively query data in S3 and already have a Redshift cluster up and running, consider Redshift Spectrum. Otherwise, consider using Athena instead.

Summary

In this chapter, we discussed the different AWS tools for preparing your data for machine learning. Remember that the data preparation stage follows the data ingestion stage where data is first ingested into a data repository like S3 or Redshift. Once data is in these data sources, you can use interactive query tools like Athena or Redshift, perform ETL jobs using AWS Glue, catalog your data with AWS Glue data catalog, or run big data processing using Hadoop framework with EMR. In order to source labeled data for training ML models, you may first need to use SageMaker Ground Truth.

Exam Essentials

Understand where data preparation fits in the CRISP-DM model for the ML lifecycle. Data preparation follows data collection, which is the ingestion of data. Preparing data may involve cataloging data into a metadata registry, running ad hoc SQL queries, or running large-scale ETL jobs on massive amounts of data to transform it from one form to another.

Know the difference between EMR and Glue.   Glue is serverless, whereas EMR requires provisioning of compute. EMR runs Hadoop in the background and allows you to choose from various Apache big data tools such as Hive, Presto, Pig, Spark, Flink, and others. With Glue, you can run ETL jobs using PySpark, Python, or Scala.

Remember that you can use the Glue Data Catalog to catalog data but you don't have to run ETL jobs on Glue itself.   You can use the data catalog to run ETL using EMR or SQL queries and analytics using Athena or Redshift Spectrum.

Remember that the Glue Data Catalog is also used to catalog data for Lake Formation or even SageMaker Feature Store.   SageMaker Feature Store is a service you can use to reuse, catalog, search, and store features for ML, which was covered in Chapter 1, "AWS AI/ML Stack."

Be familiar with best practices on data preparation.   Refer to the following white-paper: https://docs.aws.amazon.com/wellarchitected/latest/machine-learning-lens/data-preparation.html.

Be familiar with the EMR documentation for a high-level understanding of the different tools in the Hadoop ecosystem.   Although the ML Specialty doesn't test knowledge of all the Hadoop ecosystem in great detail, knowing the different tools is helpful when architecting solutions with EMR.

Review Questions

1. You are building an ML solution to extract entities from financial documents submitted to the Securities and Exchange Commission (SEC). These entities will be fed into an entity recognition model. You have collected the relevant SEC filings and stored them on S3. To prepare the data for your ML model, you need to first label the entities. You have experts in your company but do not want to build a labeling tool. You have asked your AWS Solutions Architect to give you some guidance. What guidance should the Solutions Architect give you?

    A. Use Redshift ML.

    B. Use SageMaker Ground Truth.

    C. Use Glue Data Labeler.

    D. AWS does not offer any data labeling tools. You have to build your own on premises.

2. You have a large amount of data on S3 and want to run queries on exabyte-scale data. You are using Redshift as your data warehousing solution already, but you are concerned with the added cost of moving this data to Redshift. What tool should you use to run SQL queries on the S3 data without moving the data?

    A. Nothing; you always have to move the data out of S3 to run queries.

    B. Use Amazon Athena so you don't have to move the data out of S3.

    C. Use Redshift Spectrum. The data does not leave S3, so no additional storage costs are incurred.

    D. Move the data to HDFS on an EMR cluster. Then use Presto on EMR.

3. You need to train a deep learning image model to recognize images of products in your warehouse and identify any malformed or faulty packages. However, you don't have any labeled data. You can start labeling data using a public workforce but are concerned about the cost for labeling hundreds of thousands of images for training an ML model. What advice should your AWS Solutions Architect give you to circumvent this issue?

    A. Use SageMaker Ground Truth with Amazon Mechanical Turk. Wait a few months for all images to be hand labeled.

    B. Train an ML model on SageMaker using a handful of labels. Turn this model on to label the rest of the images. Retrain the model periodically to ensure that it is seeing more data.

    C. Use SageMaker Ground Truth with Amazon Mechanical Turk. Turn on automated labeling to speed up labeling of high-confidence images, sending only low-confidence images to human reviewers.

    D. Train an ML model using Spark ML on EMR using a handful of labels. Turn this model on to label the rest of the images. Retrain the model periodically to ensure that it is seeing more data.

4. You need to run some large-scale distributed ETL jobs on EMR and run some machine learning models on top of that processed data. Which EMR tool is ideally suited for running in memory-distributed computing and for ML workloads on that data?

    A. SageMaker Processing and SageMaker

    B. Pig for distributed processing and Spark ML for ML

    C. HBase for distributed processing and HiveML for ML

    D. Spark for distributed processing and Spark ML for ML

5. Which of the following EMR tools is an interactive web application that allows users to author code, equations, text, and visualizations?

    A. Jupyter Notebook

    B. Hue

    C. Ganglia

    D. Presto

6. You have trained an ML model for fraud detection and have hosted that model on Sage-Maker. However, your customer data is stored in Redshift. The users who need to perform downstream analytics on the fraudulent cases are not proficient in ML, but they are familiar with Standard SQL, and you are concerned about the cost of engineering a custom UI and inference service for these users. What solution might you employ to make the predictions of the ML model usable by the end customers?

    A. Have your customers call a Lambda function that runs the inference on the SageMaker model. Import the inferences into Redshift.

    B. Replace the SageMaker endpoint with SageMaker batch transform. Store the outputs of the model in S3 and use the COPY command to load the data into Redshift from S3.

    C. Replace the SageMaker endpoint with SageMaker batch transform. Store the outputs of the model in S3 and use the UNLOAD command to load the data into Redshift from S3.

    D. Use Redshift ML. Analysts can write SQL queries that call the SageMaker model using SQL and generate inferences on the fly directly within Redshift itself.

7. Your data engineers have authored some extract-transform-load (ETL) code using PySpark. Given that you are a small startup with a lean engineering team, you don't want to worry about managing a persistent Hadoop environment, so you are interested in implementing a serverless ETL solution. However, you also want the solution to be event driven and triggered whenever new data lands in your raw data bucket. What AWS tools might you use to build such an architecture? (Choose all that apply.)

    A. Write a Lambda function that calls AWS Glue APIs to kick off a Glue job using the code authored by your engineers. Set the Lambda to be triggered by an S3 prefix.

    B. Write a Lambda function that sets up an EC2 instance from a snapshot containing the code and associated dependencies authored by your engineers. Set the Lambda to be triggered by an S3 prefix.

    C. Set up an ephemeral EMR cluster to run the job. The cluster will automatically spin down once the processing is completed.

    D. Use a SageMaker Processing job to run your ETL scripts in a serverless manner. Trigger the SM Processing job using AWS Lambda.

8. Consider the same use case as in the previous question. You have chosen to go with AWS Glue for ETL, and the processed data is staged in S3. Data scientists would like to have a UI that can import the data from S3 in tabular format, visually inspect the data, run simple transformations, and feature engineering steps to produce prepared data for ML. What tool would you recommend?

    A. Build a custom data viewer on Amazon EC2 and use Amazon Athena to write SQL queries to transform the data.

    B. Use Glue Data Brew.

    C. Import the data into SageMaker Data Wrangler.

    D. Build a custom UI on Amazon EKS to inspect the data and use SageMaker Processing to run your data transformation logic.

9. Which Apache tool would you use to perform event-driven computations on incoming data streams from clickstream data, log data, or IOT data?

    A. Apache Spark

    B. Apache Flink

    C. Hue

    D. Hive

10. You have built fraud models on premises using data stored in the Hadoop Distributed File System (HDFS) that you are now migrating to S3. However, you are under a deadline to deliver the models in production in the cloud and would like to minimize as much code refactoring as possible. The models are trained using PySpark using the pyspark.ml and mllib libraries. What suggestion would you provide to the customer as their AWS Solutions Architect?

    A. Move their code and dependencies into a custom docker container and use Amazon SageMaker for training ML models since SageMaker is the leading ML platform on AWS.

    B. Given the tight timelines, set up an EC2 cluster with the PySpark code and dependencies to run your training job.

    C. Transform their code to PyTorch instead and run the model training on SageMaker since PyTorch is a growing open-source framework for ML.

    D. For the time being, given that the customer is under a deadline, spin up an EMR cluster leveraging existing code to train the models.

Chapter

7

Feature Engineering

THE AWS CERTIFIED MACHINE LEARNING (ML) SPECIALTY EXAM OBJECTIVES COVERED IN THIS CHAPTER INCLUDE BUT ARE NOT LIMITED TO THE FOLLOWING:

✓ **Domain 2.0: Exploratory Data Analysis**

  ▪ 2.2 Perform feature engineering

One of the most important stages of machine learning is feature engineering. We will cover some key concepts of engineering features for different kinds of datasets as well as describe a few AWS tools that are designed to help with feature generation and reusability.

Feature Engineering Concepts

In the previous chapter, we discussed how you can collect and prepare your data for machine learning. This often involves basic data transformations such as converting data types or data formats (say from Apache Parquet to CSV) or data aggregation using SQL queries such as merging or joining datasets or grouping data by relevant columns. Once these steps are complete, you have a dataset that contains all the relevant rows and columns that you can use for your machine learning (ML) models.

However, the data may still not be ready to be fed into an ML algorithm. The inputs to machine learning algorithms are numbers or vectors of numbers, and your prepared dataset may still contain categorical values or missing values such as missing rows. It may contain outliers, which can potentially skew your model, especially if you don't have many outlier examples. In this chapter, we will discuss how you can transform your data, or combine multiple columns in your data into "features" that can be directly fed into an ML algorithm.

There is an art to feature engineering, and a number of the common feature engineering strategies employed by data scientists are often drawn from experience, rather than precise mathematical methods. We will discuss the most common strategies for feature engineering with different datasets in this chapter.

The kind of data determines how you will engineer features. Most of the feature engineering tools and techniques apply to tabular data. We will also briefly cover strategies you can use for textual and image data as well as for time series data.

Feature Engineering for Tabular Data

Let's start with the most common types of feature engineering required for tabular datasets:

Duplicate Data   As a best practice, remove any duplicate data/rows you may have in your dataset. Later on, we will discuss data leakage between training and test datasets and how having duplicates can increase the risk of data leakage in your dataset.

Normalization   Normalization applies to columns in your dataset, which are numerical. Imagine you have a dataset where you are trying to predict housing prices and you have one column for the total number of bedrooms and another column for the average square footage. While the total number of bedrooms will mostly range between, say, 1 and 10, the square footage can range in the hundreds to thousands. However, to an ML algorithm, these are all simply numbers, and the size of the numbers can have an influence on the step size of the gradients for algorithms that use gradient descent. This can lead to convergence issues, ultimately generating models with low accuracy. Normalization simply scales all the features to lie between [0, 1].

Standardization   A related technique to normalization is standardization, where instead of restricting all features between [0, 1], you center all the values around the mean value for that column with unit standard deviation. Standardization is useful when your data has a normal distribution or a close to normal distribution.

TIP   Not all ML algorithms are sensitive to standardization/normalization. The accuracy and convergence of linear and logistic regression algorithms can be improved by these methods, whereas tree-based algorithms are relatively insensitive. This is because tree-based algorithms split a node based on a single feature. Therefore, that particular node split decision is unaffected by other feature values.

Outlier Detection   Outliers are data points that lie beyond a certain number of standard deviations (2σ, 3σ) from your mean. The challenge with outliers is that you often don't have enough outlier examples for an ML model to meaningfully learn, which in turn means that ML models will not generalize well to an outlier example. Alternatively, retaining outliers in your dataset can also skew your model because the model may adjust its weights to better predict the outlier, which in turn reduces the model performance overall on the majority of data points.

The most common strategies for dealing with outliers are as follows:

Outlier Removal   Simply truncate any data points that lie beyond a certain standard deviation from your dataset.

Log Transformation   If your data distribution is heavily skewed and you have a large number of outliers, consider using a log transformation to first transform your data to a distribution that looks similar to a normal distribution and then use standardization. In the popular Python Library NumPy, you can use the $log1p$ function for this. See Figure 7.1.

FIGURE 7.1   Diagram showing how you can deal with skewed distributions using log transforms

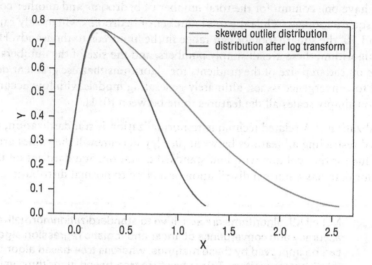

Note that there is a separate class of machine learning problems that focus specifically on detection of outliers or anomalies. Here we are referring to outlier removal as a feature engineering technique and simply use standard deviation as a way to measure whether a data point is an outlier. We cover one of these algorithms in Chapter 8, "Model Training," and they apply to use cases such as detecting network intrusion events from security log data.

Label Encoding   When dealing with categorical variables, there are two strategies you can consider. Label encoding refers to simply labeling the unique values in a categorical column with integers. For example, if you have a categorical feature such as Day_of_ Week, you can do {"Monday": 1, "Tuesday": 2, "Wednesday":3 and so on}. The key benefit of label encoding is its simplicity, particularly when you have large numbers of unique categorical values. The main downside is that an algorithm can misinterpret the label encoding to mean that one value is somehow greater or less than the other. For example, 3 is greater than 2, but Wednesday is not "greater" than Tuesday.

One-Hot Encoding   To avoid this issue, a better approach is to one-hot encode categorical values. In this case, you can convert each value to its own column and assign a 1 or 0 depending on whether that row has that value. A benefit of one-hot encoding is that by converting each value to its own column, it avoids any misinterpretation that could occur with label encoding. However, if you have a large number of categorical values (e.g., ZIP codes in the United States or types of colors) in your dataset, then one-hot encoding can produce a very large feature matrix. You then need to scale up your compute accordingly to train the model on large numbers of columns.

Binary Encoding   Another common encoding strategy, particularly if you have a categorical column with just two values such as "yes" or "no," is to use binary encoding. Binary encoding is similar to label encoding where you set `{"value_1":0,` `"value_2":1}`.

Handling Missing Values   A common issue you find in datasets is that some rows may have missing values for one or more columns. Depending on the number of missing values, there are a few strategies you should consider:

Collect More Data   The best approach is to try to collect the missing data. However, data collection can be expensive or time consuming. In that case, the following strategies can be used as suitable alternatives.

Drop Column   If you have a column for which the majority of the values are missing across all data points, then simply drop that column.

Constant Imputation   For small numbers of missing values, a good strategy is to perform imputation where you "impute" or replace the missing value with either the mean or the median of the values in the column or even the most frequent value. For columns with a normal-like distribution, you may consider mean imputation. Median imputation is better for skewed column distributions. Remember that this strategy is not suitable when you have a large number of missing values because you could be adding bias to the data.

Supervised Learning   You can also train an ML model to predict the value of a column based on the other rows in the dataset. This strategy is useful since it reduces the potential bias introduced by constant imputation and still allows you to keep the column. However, it can be computationally expensive because you are now training another ML model.

Label Sampling   In certain problem types, there may be a large imbalance in the label values themselves. A common example is fraud detection, where the number of fraudulent examples is often much lower than the number of nonfraudulent cases. In these situations, there are typically five approaches you can take:

Collect More Data   The best approach is to try to collect more minority label data. However, data collection can be expensive or time consuming. In that case, the following strategies can be used as suitable alternatives.

Downsampling   In this case, you can downsample the majority class to try to produce a more balanced dataset by simply removing a fraction of the rows that have the majority label. Here majority class means the label with the most values. Downsampling is a good strategy when you have a large amount of data, so you can afford to reduce the number of majority examples.

Upsampling   The opposite of downsampling, here you upsample the minority class (the fraud label in the previous example) by simply replicating the rows that have the minority label. Upsampling is good when your data size isn't large enough to downsample, but it generally introduces other issues since you are simply making copies of the data points.

SMOTE, or Synthetic Minority Oversampling Technique   This is a method to use unsupervised learning to generate minority class examples. SMOTE is suitable when the number of features greatly exceeds the number of samples. SMOTE takes a data point in the minority label class and first extracts the k - *nearest* neighbors. Then it constructs a new data point by taking a vector between one of the neighbors and the data point and multiplying it by a random number.

Weighting   Another strategy for dealing with imbalanced data is to penalize the algorithm more for misclassifying a minority label by using a weighting technique to modify the loss function. This strategy avoids having to down- or upsample data.

Data Splitting   Finally, to train an ML model, you need to split your data into training, validation, and testing data or training and testing data. Generally, data scientists use an 80-10-10 or 80-20 split for train-val-test or train-test respectively. It is also a common practice to use a technique like k-fold cross-validation during training, where you train k models by splitting the data into k even splits, known as folds. Then you train model 1 on folds $1 \ldots k - 1$, and validate the model on fold k; model 2 on folders $2 \ldots k$ and validate on fold 1, model 3 on folds $1, 3 \ldots k$ and test on fold 2, and so forth. The k-fold cross-validation method is popular for small datasets but can be quite expensive for large datasets since you are training k times, hence incurring k times the cost.

Regardless, you should always split your data into train and test sets. As a best practice, make sure that the test set retains the original label distribution (before upsampling, downsampling, etc.) so that it mimics your real production data. Often it is common to use a third validation dataset that is provided to your algorithm at training time to evaluate your model's performance during training. As a general rule, do not use your test set on your model unless you have completed training.

A common mistake is to introduce *data leakage*, where some of the test data "leaks" into the training dataset. As a best practice, you want to avoid this at all costs because, to evaluate your model, you need to ensure it has never seen the test data. Only then can you truly determine the model performance.

One of the most common ways data leakage gets introduced in ML is during the normalization/standardization process. Always normalize/standardize after you have already split your data into train/test sets. Then you can normalize the training data and use those normalization scores (such as mean and standard deviation) to normalize the test set. If you normalize the entire dataset, and then split into train-test, leakage will often get introduced.

Feature Engineering for Unstructured and Time Series Data

We will also briefly cover feature engineering methods for unstructured or time series data:

Data Augmentation   Often, when dealing in particular with image data, you may want to augment the data to provide your model with more examples. There are many different strategies for augmenting image data, such as rotating an image, flipping an image, adding some random noise to an image, changing the brightness, shifting the image vertically or horizontally, or zooming in or out and others. The popular machine learning library Keras provides a handy data preprocessing class that you can use to preprocess your images (see https://keras.io/api/preprocessing/image). For image labeling problems, since none of these transforms change the label of the data, you can cheaply augment your data while providing your model with more examples of a given label.

Windowed Splitting of Time Series Data   For time series problems, you often need to test your model on historical data where you have ground truth labels. For example, imagine you are building a model to predict stock prices. Once your model is trained, you can test it on historical stock prices where you know whether a stock went up or down. This is often called *backtesting*.

To properly backtest data for time series, you cannot use the simple k-fold cross-validation strategy, and the reason is that you cannot randomly split a single time series because the different time intervals are related to one another. In this case, you should use a strategy where you first pick a prediction window (striped pattern bar in Figure 7.2). Then you take a window of your time series (solid bar) and predict over the prediction window. Then you expand your training window to include the previous prediction window, train the model again, and predict for the next prediction window. This is illustrated in Figure 7.2.

Preprocessing for Natural Language Processing (NLP)   NLP models often require considerable preprocessing before they can be fed into a model. Models such as Word2Vec or BERT rely on tokens, and so the data first needs to be tokenized. Tokenization refers to splitting a dataset into individual words or tokens that form part of the vocabulary. Each word is then assigned a numerical value in the vocabulary, which is often stored as a dictionary of key value pairs. A sentence is converted into a numerical sequence based on the values of each token.

Other common text preprocessing techniques include removal of stop words such as "is," "and," and "the"; removal of frequent or extremely rare words; changing all the text to lowercase; stemming; and lemmatization. Stemming refers to converting derived words into their root form or word stem. For example, the words "organize," "organizes," and "organizing" may all be converted to "organize." Lemmatization is a related technique that converts words to their lemmas. Lemmatization has the benefit that it relies on the context; for example, the word "better" has "good" as its lemma. You should be careful when applying stemming or lemmatization because they tend to affect the model's performance. According to the Stanford NLP group, stemming can increase model recall but harm the precision (see `https://nlp.stanford.edu/IR-book/html/htmledition/stemming-and-lemmatization-1.html`). A popular open-source tool for text preprocessing and NLP is the Spacy library (available at `https://spacy.io`).

FIGURE 7.2   Diagram showing how you backtest on time series data

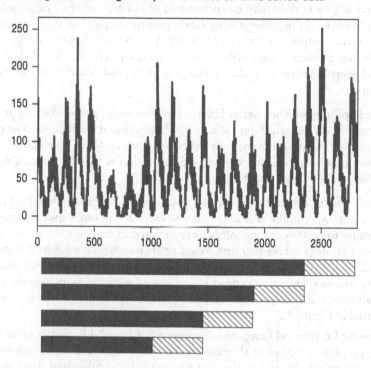

Feature Engineering Tools on AWS

In the previous chapter, we covered two big data tools that can be used for feature engineering: Amazon EMR and AWS Glue. Glue can be used for serverless Extract, Transform, and Load (ETL)—that is, where you don't have to worry about provisioning compute. You simply author your data transformation and feature engineering code in Python, Scala, or PySpark and let Glue run the job and send the outputs to your S3 bucket. With EMR, you can spin up a cluster and submit Spark jobs to the cluster for large-scale processing using Spark.

In 2020, AWS launched two new services that offer developers a *low-code* way to perform feature engineering. Glue announced Glue Data Brew, which is a visual data preparation tool. With Data Brew, you can visualize your data, clean your data, normalize your data, and use over 250 transformations to run common feature engineering transforms without authoring any code. You can combine these transformations into a recipe and then submit the recipe as a single job that you can run on a schedule or on demand. Since Glue Data Brew integrates with the Glue Data Catalog, it supports a number of data sources such as S3, Redshift, RDS, and Aurora and provides connectors for third-party data warehouses such as Snowflake.

Also in 2020, SageMaker announced a service called Data Wrangler on SageMaker Studio, which pulls in data from S3 or Redshift, or by using Athena into SageMaker. Data Wrangler offers similar user interface (UI) capabilities and 300+ transforms, as well as the ability to author custom transforms with your own code. Data Wrangler also allows you to quickly build an ML model on a subset of the data with no code to get a baseline model. Similar to Data Brew, once you are satisfied with your feature engineering, you can build a pipeline and run the engineering steps as a processing job on the entire dataset.

It is unlikely that the test will ask you to compare between Data Brew and Data Wrangler, but just know that they are both low-code, UI-based feature engineering tools on AWS. In contrast, Glue and EMR both require you to write your own processing and feature engineering code.

Summary

In this chapter, we discussed the different feature engineering techniques commonly used in data science. We explored how you can impute data, deal with missing values, and handle categorical features and imbalanced data, and the importance of splitting your data into training, validation, and test sets. We also covered some tools on AWS that can help you with feature engineering.

Exam Essentials

Understand where feature engineering fits in the CRISP-DM model for the ML lifecycle. Feature engineering follows data preparation. Most data scientists spend 80 percent of their time in an ML project collecting and preparing data and engineering features. Without properly engineered features, your ML model will generally not perform well, so this is an extremely important step in the process.

Remember that not all ML models are sensitive to standardization/normalization. Linear/logistic regression or distance-based algorithms (Principal Component Analysis, k-means) are sensitive to this, whereas tree-based models are not.

Understand the difference between label encoding and one-hot encoding and which one to use when.   This can be a popular exam topic; unless there is a meaningful mathematical relationship between each value in your categorical feature or you just have too many possible values for that feature, you should one-hot encode.

Know the different data imputation strategies.   Another common exam question relates to different data imputation strategies. Know that removing a column is only suitable if most of the values are missing. If only few values need to be imputed, mean/median imputation is good, but it can introduce data bias. To avoid this, you can use supervised learning to train a model to predict the missing values.

Understand how to avoid data leakage.   Data leakage can be a serious problem and lead to models that seem highly performant during training but perform poorly in production. Be careful when splitting data into train and test sets to make sure that no leakage is introduced. Remember that the test data should only be used to verify model performance once all training is complete.

Understand different strategies for outlier detection.   The most common approach is simply to remove outliers. Taking a log transform is also often used.

Understand the different strategies for data normalization.   Know the difference between normalization (min/max scaling) and standardization.

Know the difference between Glue Data Brew and Glue.   Glue Data Brew is a low-code visual data preparation or feature engineering tool, whereas Glue requires you to submit code scripts.

Review Questions

1. You are a company that is just starting out in machine learning and need to engineer features on a large dataset. However, your team currently is composed of analysts who lack data engineering skill sets such as PySpark and Scala. What tools would you recommend they start with to prepare data and engineer features? (Choose all that apply.)

    A. SageMaker notebooks

    B. Amazon EMR

    C. AWS Glue Data Brew

    D. SageMaker Data Wrangler

2. You are a company that is just starting out in machine learning and need to engineer features on a large dataset stored in an Amazon Aurora database. Which AWS tool could you use to visualize the data and engineer features with little to no code?

    A. Jupyter Notebooks on EMR

    B. AWS Glue Data Brew

    C. Spark Cluster on EMR

    D. SageMaker Data Wrangler

3. You are a data scientist and your engineering team has provided you with a dataset to build ML models on, but one of the columns has 30 percent of the values missing. What strategy would you use to fill in the missing dataset to avoid introducing bias in the data?

    A. Nothing; just remove the column.

    B. Replace with the most frequent value to reduce the bias.

    C. Replace with the mean.

    D. Train an ML model to predict the missing values.

4. Which of the following is a valid data engineering strategy?

    A. Split raw dataset into train/test ➢ standardize training dataset ➢ use the mean/standard deviation values to standardize the test set ➢ train the model on the training data and make predictions on the test set.

    B. Standardize entire dataset ➢ split standardized dataset into train/test ➢ train the model on the training data and make predictions on the test set.

    C. Split raw dataset into train/test ➢ convert categorical values in the training dataset alone to one-hot encoded values ➢ train the model on the training data and make predictions on the test set.

    D. Split raw dataset into train/test ➢ use a mean imputer to impute missing values with the mean in the training dataset ➢ train the model on the training data and make predictions on the test set with some missing values.

5. You are a data scientist at a bank working on a fraud detection problem. You notice that the number of fraudulent examples in your dataset is extremely small. You are concerned that your model will not be able to detect fraudulent examples well due to the lack of examples in the training data. What are some techniques you can apply to mitigate this? (Choose all that apply.)

   A. Write a custom loss function that penalizes the model more for incorrectly predicting fraudulent examples.

   B. Perform SMOTE upsampling on the fraudulent class.

   C. Upsample the fraudulent class.

   D. Simply drop the minority class since you have too few examples and the model will not be able to learn from them.

6. Which of the following are valid data augmentation strategies for image labeling use cases? (Choose all that apply.)

   A. Use SageMaker Ground Truth to label more images for use in your ML model.

   B. Duplicate each image by converting the format from PNG to JPEG.

   C. Rotate each image by a random angle.

   D. Stem the images.

7. You would like to build an image classification algorithm but you are concerned with the lack of labeled data and the expense and time in labeling data. In order to convince leadership of the need for new data, you need to create a baseline model with good performance. What simple strategy can you use to generate more labeled data?

   A. Use a log transform data augmentation strategy.

   B. Use SMOTE to upsample the images.

   C. Augment the images by rotating, cropping, and changing the RGB contrasts to generate more labeled images to train a more robust model.

   D. Use an external third-party vendor to generate more labeled data. There is no other way.

8. A data scientist has noticed that one of the columns in her tabular dataset has over 20 percent missing values. Upon plotting the data distribution, she finds that the distribution is skewed and non-normal, with several outliers. What strategy should she consider to treat the missing values to quickly start building an ML model?

   A. Use a mean imputation strategy.

   B. Use SMOTE to impute missing values.

   C. Drop the rows containing missing values; it won't affect the model performance much.

   D. Use median imputation.

9. A data scientist has engineered features, normalized the data using a standard scaler, and then split the data into train, test, and validation. The modeler is getting near 100 percent accuracy on training, test, and validation datasets and is very satisfied. As the lead data scientist, you are asked to approve the model, but what may the data scientist have missed to get such good performance?

   A. The data scientist should have used a MinMaxScaler normalizer.

   B. A standard scaler is only useful if the feature is normally distributed.

   C. Nothing; you should approve this model for production.

   D. The scientist should have split the data into train, test, and validation before normalizing the data, not after.

10. A data scientist is attempting to improve his model performance. He has observed that the performance appears to be insensitive to normalizing the features; however, he believes that normalization is important as the features have very different scales. What might be true of the model?

   A. The model is likely unsupervised; unsupervised ML is insensitive to feature normalization.

   B. The model is likely a linear model; linear models are insensitive to feature normalization.

   C. The model is likely a tree-based model, which are typically insensitive to feature normalization.

   D. All ML models are insensitive to normalization, and as such, it is not a particularly useful feature engineering technique.

Chapter

8

Model Training

THE AWS CERTIFIED MACHINE LEARNING (ML) SPECIALTY EXAM OBJECTIVES COVERED IN THIS CHAPTER INCLUDE BUT ARE NOT LIMITED TO THE FOLLOWING:

✓ **Domain 3.0: Modeling**

- 3.3 Train machine learning models

- 3.4 Perform hyperparameter optimization

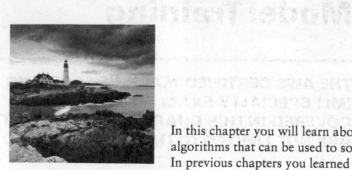

Model Training

In this chapter you will learn about common machine learning algorithms that can be used to solve various business use cases. In previous chapters you learned how to source, label, wrangle, and clean data, as well as engineer the necessary features required to train machine learning models. Now we will cover the actual models themselves that you train on your data. We will discuss training models locally for experimentation versus using distributed training for large datasets. As you have no doubt figured out, the machine learning process is highly iterative and you will almost never put the first model you train into production. For this reason, we will explore strategies for tuning model parameters to obtain the best model.

Common ML Algorithms

The goal of machine learning is to allow you to make inferences on data using induction. For this reason, a machine learning model needs to be able to generalize—that is, perform accurate inferences on data it has not previously "seen" or trained on. Otherwise, the model would be doing little more than simply memorizing the data, which is not a desired outcome. Depending on the kind of data, machine learning use cases fall primarily into three categories:

Supervised Learning   Supervised learning refers to when a model is shown labeled examples of ground truth values and learns to predict the label based on the input data or features.

Unsupervised Learning   Unsupervised learning refers to when you do not have labeled data available and you want the model to discover patterns in the unlabeled data.

Reinforcement Learning   Reinforcement learning is when a model or agent learns by interacting with its environment. Reinforcement learning is similar to trial-and-error learning, where an agent is given rewards and penalties for actions taken and its aim is to maximize the long-term rewards.

These are the primary classes that most of the machine learning use cases fall into and that are likely to appear on the exam, but it is worth noting that semi-supervised learning is another branch of machine learning where you have some labeled data and a lot of unlabeled data. Semi-supervised learning is an growing and active area of research partially due to the high costs of data labeling and the availability of unstructured data.

Supervised Machine Learning

Perhaps the most common form of machine learning problem you will encounter is supervised machine learning, where you have data and accompanying labels. Example real-world problems might include credit card fraud, where you have transaction data and fraud/not fraud labels; housing or commodity price precision, where you have data on the square footage of a home, number of rooms, and so forth, and the label is the house price; data about taxi rides or bike share rides in New York City, and the label is the cost of the ride; or a number of documents or news articles, with labels being the news topics and many more.

 The data type (whether it is structured or unstructured) does not dictate whether learning is supervised. As in our examples, the data could be numerical data (transactions, ride share data, etc.) or images (such as images of pets) or even raw text (such as documents). It is the presence or absence of *labels* that dictates whether learning is supervised or unsupervised.

Supervised learning itself comes in a few flavors:

- Binary classification, where the label is binary, such as fraud/not fraud, cat/dog, spam/not spam
- Multiclass classification, where the label can have more than two classes
- Regression, where the label is a continuous number such as a house price

We start by discussing common supervised learning algorithms using structured data.

Linear and Logistic Regression

Linear models are a form of supervised machine learning where a model predicts a linear relationship between the data and the labels. Linear regression is used when you have a continuous label (regression task), where the assumption is made that the label is linearly related to the data.

If you have labels y_i and features $x_{1i}, \ldots x_{ni}$, linear regression assumes

$$y = \beta_1 x_1 + \ldots + \beta_n x_n + \varepsilon$$

where bold values denote the vector over the entire dataset of size $i \in N$. Here β_i are the coefficients or weights the model will learn and the ε corresponds to a noise term, which should be a random variable. Viewed mathematically in this manner, your goal is to predict the coefficients β_i which will minimize the error ε across the dataset.

Generally, it is common to use the sum of squares of the errors as the quantity to minimize, also known as the loss. When the sum of squares is used, the loss is often also known as mean-squared loss. Figure 8.1 shows a one-dimensional example of linear regression.

FIGURE 8.1   Linear regression example. The error terms shown by the vertical arrows are what you want to minimize.

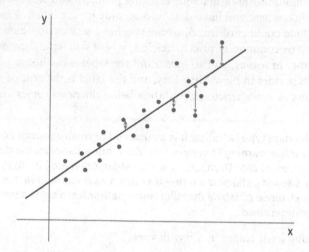

Linear regression models are powerful because they are easy to interpret. However, this ease comes at a price: the model makes multiple assumptions that need to be tested before a linear model can be accurately fit to the data. The first one is linearity—that the label is a linear combination of the input data or feature vectors. Second, these models assume a constant variance (see Figure 8.2)—that the statistical variance in the label is identical, regardless of the value of the input data. For example, if you are predicting a house price, the variance in the house price is identical whether you have homes with one bedroom or

FIGURE 8.2   Example showing lack of constant variance. The error terms shown as vertical arrows are growing as x increases.

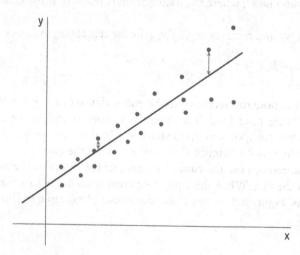

five bedrooms. This assumption is often challenged by real data, limiting the utility of these models. A third key assumption is that features cannot be strongly correlated with one another; in the extreme case, if two features are multicollinear (where one feature can be linearly derived from the other, in the most trivial example; they are related by a constant), then the previous equations of linear regression become unstable.

If you have highly correlated features in your data, are linear regression models unusable? You can mitigate this by using a technique known as *regularization*. Regularization is often used in machine learning as a way to penalize the model from learning weights that do not generalize well to unseen data. This reduces the overall model complexity and prevents overfitting.

The most common forms of regularization are *ridge* (where you add an L2 penalty or quadratic penalty to the weights), *lasso* (where you add an L1 penalty or absolute value penalty to the weights), and *elastic net* (which combines the two). It is helpful to note that ridge regression tends to reduce the values of weights that are unimportant in predicting the labels, whereas lasso tends to shrink the weights to zero.

If you have a linear regression problem with a lot of features, using lasso penalty as a start is a good solution to eliminate features that are unimportant. For this reason, lasso regression is also known as shrinkage. Note that ridge, lasso, and elastic net are all different forms of regression; they differ only in the `loss` function.

Consider Figure 8.3. In this case, can you still use linear regression? Yes, you simply define a new variable $x_2 = x^2$, and now you see that the label y is linear in x_2. This is often known as polynomial regression and is a generalization of linear regression. Creating a new feature by constructing a polynomial from the original feature is a simple example of feature engineering. Notice how we used feature engineering to still enable us to use a simple model such as linear regression. Often in machine learning, it is not the model but how you engineer features that determines model performance and ultimately business value.

Logistic regression is the application of linear regression to binary or multiclass classification problems. To do so, logistic regression uses what is known as a *logit function*, where the label y is modeled in the following way:

$$log\frac{p}{1-p} = y = \beta_1 x_1 + \ldots + \beta_n x_n + \varepsilon$$

The implication of this is that you can now interpret p as a probability given by

$$p = \frac{1}{1 + e^{-y}}$$

FIGURE 8.3   Example showing violation of linearity assumption

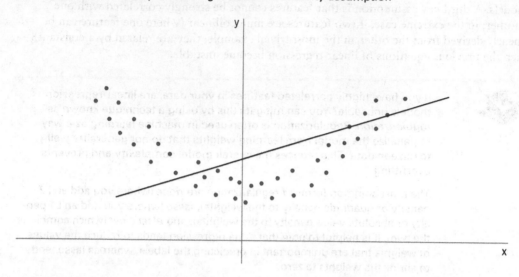

Note that when y is large and negative, this approaches 0, whereas when y is large and positive, it approaches 1 and is therefore bounded between [0, 1].

Logistic regression solves binary classification problems by simply thresholding this probability: if the probability exceeds 0.5, then the model predicts one class; if it is less than 0.5, it predicts the other. To do so, it uses a loss function known as the *cross-entropy loss* defined next:

$$L = -\frac{1}{N}\sum_{i \in N} p_i \log \hat{p}_i + (1-p_i)\log\left(1-\hat{p}_i\right)$$

where p_i is the true probability and $\hat{p}_i$ is the predicted probability by the model during training. The sum is over all data points in your dataset.

You can generalize this to multiclass classification problems, but we will not cover that mathematically here. But know that logistic regression can apply to both binary and multiclass classification problems. The cross-entropy loss is one of the most common loss functions for classification problems in machine learning irrespective of the underlying algorithm.

Finally, from a production perspective, unlike deep learning models, which can be quite large (sometimes several gigabytes), logistic regression models only store coefficients and can thus be quite small. It is often recommended to start with simple models like logistic regression before moving to more complex deep learning or tree-based algorithms, because the logistic regression often serves as a benchmark for model performance.

Don't get confused by the term *regression* in logistic regression. Logistic regression is used to solve classification problems; linear regression is used for regression problems.

Amazon SageMaker has a built-in algorithm that covers both linear and logistic regression use cases called *linear learner*. The test may ask you what data formats this model assumes. This algorithm is built using the MXNet framework, which recognizes a data format known as RecordIO-wrapped protobuf, or RecordIO for short. Also, since the majority of data is in CSV format, this algorithm also recognizes CSV data.

We recommend that you read the documentation on this algorithm prior to taking the test: https://docs.aws.amazon.com/sagemaker/latest/dg/linear-learner.html.

Factorization Machine

Sometimes in addition to a linear relationship between the data and the label, the label may also be proportional to interaction terms between different independent variables, such as the product of two features $x_i x_j$. SageMaker's Factorization Machines algorithm takes this into account in building the model. Factorization Machines can be used for supervised learning for both classification and regression tasks.

Consider using the Factorization Machines algorithm when dealing with large sparse data. This usually occurs in use cases in advertising such as clickstream prediction or in item recommendation. Factorization Machines, as the name suggests, works by a method known as matrix factorization, which is a popular method in recommendation systems.

Similar to the linear learner, this is also built on top of the MXNet framework and accepts RecordIO format. Note that this algorithm does not accept CSV, since CSV is generally not a good format for storing large, sparse matrices.

You might see a question on which built-in algorithm to use when dealing with recommender systems or item recommendation use cases. Although you can use algorithms like linear learner or the XGBoost algorithm we cover later, generally AWS recommends using Factorization Machines for such large sparse matrix use cases.

k-Nearest Neighbors

Another supervised learning algorithm on structured data is called *k*-nearest neighbors (KNN). This algorithm works by first building an index consisting of the distance between any two data points in your dataset. When a new point whose label is unknown is provided, the KNN algorithm calculates the *k*-nearest neighbors to that point based on a specified distance metric and either averages the label values for those *k*-points in the case of regression or uses the most frequently returned label as the label for classification.

Training for this algorithm mainly corresponds to building an index. Inference corresponds to performing fast lookups against that index. The index here refers to a vector representation of every data point in the input dataset that can be quickly loaded into memory for performing the lookup analysis later. Note that larger the dataset, larger the model.

To do this efficiently, you first need to sample your dataset so that it can fit into memory. Next, you need to reduce the dimensionality of the dataset to avoid the so-called *curse of dimensionality*, which affects distance measurements in high dimensional space. By reducing the dimensionality, you can also efficiently measure distances using Euclidean distance, cosine distance, Manhattan distance, or other distance metrics.

The process of taking a high dimensional vector and effectively representing it in a lower dimensional space is often called dimensionality reduction or compression. Following this, each vector is assigned to a cluster based on some similarity metric. A separate algorithm called *k-means clustering* is often used for this, which we will cover later.

Now the index stores the vector representation, along with the cluster that vector belongs to. Each cluster has a centroid, represented by the centroid vector. This method of storing data is known as an inverted list.

During the inference or lookup phase, first the algorithm identifies the cluster a point belongs to by comparing distances against the centroid. Then, a second similarity search is conducted within that cluster to find the k closest points to use to determine the final label.

If you are interested in more details, in particular on a highly efficient library for k-NN developed by Facebook known as Faiss, we refer you to this paper: `https://arxiv.org/abs/1702.08734`.

Support Vector Machines

Yet another popular machine learning model to know about is the support vector machine (SVM). This algorithm is particularly popular in biological fields such as neuroscience and continues to be popular today.

The concept behind the support vector machine is simple: it aims to find the separating hyper-plane that separates two classes by the widest so-called margin. The wider the margin, the better the quality of the algorithm and its ability to generalize.

Figure 8.4 intuitively demonstrates the idea behind the SVM, where the model aims to find the solid line that best separates the two clusters of points.

SVMs also generalize to nonlinear situations where the separating boundary may not be linear. This can be done by introducing a so-called kernel trick, which goes beyond the scope of this book. The basic idea, however, is to represent the points in a higher dimensional space where separating them becomes easier. However, for the test it is essential to note that a non-linear SVM can be used to distinguish between points that cannot be separated by a line, as shown in Figure 8.5. In this case, the kernel function you choose must be able to represent a circle given by the form $r^2 = a^2 + b^2$, where r is the radius, and a and b correspond to the x- and y-axes.

FIGURE 8.4   SVM conceptual example showing the separatrix by the solid line and the margin indicated by the dashed black lines. The SVM aims to maximize the margin.

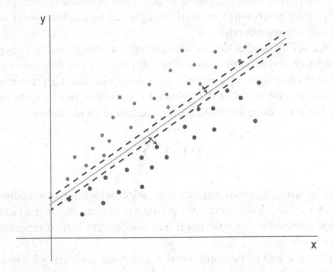

FIGURE 8.5   You can use a kernel SVM to separate the points. Although they clearly cannot be separated by a linear line, by lifting the points into a higher dimensional kernel representation, you can separate them.

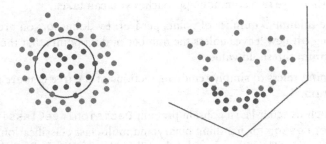

Tree-Based Models

No discussion of supervised learning on tabular data is complete without discussing the tree family of models, namely decision trees, random forests, and XGBoost.

Let's start with a single decision tree: a decision tree consists of a root node or parent node and spawns off child or leaf nodes based on certain criteria. Most businesses use decision trees today as part of rule-based systems, where a rule dictates whether or not to split a node. Although rule-based systems are highly popular and will continue to be, in order to encode business insights, decision tree learning lets the tree learn when to spawn off new nodes based on the input data.

There are a few popular algorithms for decision tree learning, the most popular being Classification and Regression Trees (CART). CART first uses a metric to decide when it is appropriate to split a parent node into child nodes. Then this rule is recursively applied to the child nodes. Splitting stops when no further gains can be made or some other condition is met, which we will discuss shortly.

How does the CART algorithm decide when to split a parent node? Two popular metrics are the Gini impurity or the entropy metric. The Gini impurity is a measure of the probability of incorrectly classifying a data point with a particular label. In this manner, it represents some information gained about the system. In particular, the formula below represents the Gini impurity for a multiclass classification problem with K classes:

$$I_G(p) = 1 - \sum_{i=1}^{K} p_k^2$$

CART operates by using a greedy algorithm to select which input variables to split on and for that input variable, all different split points are evaluated for the Gini impurity. The lowest value is then selected as the split point and the process is then repeated for each child node of the parent node.

What are some limitations of decision trees? A common problem with decision trees is their tendency to overfit the data; this means, in the extreme case, that every data point gets its own leaf node and the tree can become extremely deep. This is a limitation because in this example, your decision tree has simply learned the data, so it lacks the ability to generalize to unseen data.

To avoid this, there are two common approaches you can take:

- Increasing the minimum number of points per leaf: By doing so, you prevent the tree from spawning off new leaves unless the number of data points that the leaf represents meets a minimum threshold value.

- Pruning: Pruning refers to simply removing sections of the tree that are not relevant to the classification.

Frameworks such as scikit-learn contain prebuilt `DecisionTreeClassifier` and `DecisionTreeRegressor` for handling binary and multiclass classification and regression tasks with decision trees. These frameworks also allow you to simply limit the `max_depth` of the trees as a parameter. This also prevents overfitting by making sure that the algorithm does not create very deep trees. Note that the discrete nature of decision trees naturally implies that they cannot output labels not present in the original data. For regression problems, for example, the tree outputs the closest point in the training dataset (which belongs to a leaf node on the tree).

Another viewpoint on decision trees can be in terms of what is known as *bias-variance trade-off*. But before we discuss that, we will cover random forests and XGBoost.

As you saw earlier, a key limitation of decision trees is that they can overfit. Random forests are designed to reduce this problem by creating a collection of decision trees, or a "forest." A random forest works by building many trees, but each tree is trained on only a subset of the input features using a method known as bootstrap aggregation or *bagging*. Bagging essentially refers to sampling but with replacement.

To understand sampling with replacement, suppose you are asked to randomly pick samples of 10 individuals from a population. If you are sampling without replacement, once you pick the first 10 individuals, this affects the next batch of 10 you will pick since the first 10 cannot be picked again. Sampling with replacement simply allows different samples to be independent of one another, by allowing the original 10 to be part of the sampling pool in subsequent iterations.

In this manner, random forests try to ensure that different trees are constructed independently of one another by sampling with replacement, from a subset of features. Random forests then use the same techniques, such as specifying a maximum tree depth and/or a minimum number of data points per leaf node, to build the tree. However, the final prediction or regression task is done by averaging the results of all the trees.

Once again, frameworks like scikit-learn offer easy-to-use packages to train random forest regressors and classifiers.

For the test, it is worthwhile to take a look at the scikit-learn implementations of decision trees/random forests to understand how you can prevent them from overfitting. Remember, to avoid overfitting, you want to increase the minimum samples per leaf but decrease the maximum depth of the trees.

Random forests have the benefit of training multiple trees in parallel. However, one disadvantage of random forests is that different trees do not work together to reduce the overall errors. This is where sequential learning or XGBoost comes in.

XGBoost (depicted in Figure 8.6) takes the same ideas behind decision trees, namely the CART algorithm, but instead of bagging, uses a technique called *boosting*. Boosting refers to sequential learning where each subsequent tree aims to correctly classify the errors that were misclassified by its predecessor. This can also prevent overfitting, as each individual tree can be a so-called weak learner or a shallow tree, but collectively, they can become a strong learner.

There are many popular boosting algorithms, such as AdaBoost and Logit Boosting, which are examples of *gradient boosting*. Gradient boosting refers to the ability to treat the error terms as continuous variables and to use Taylor's expansion to expand them in terms of their gradients or derivatives. Coupled with the regularization techniques we discussed earlier (L1 and L2 norm), this can become a highly powerful algorithm. You can also leverage infrastructure like GPUs to rapidly calculate gradients, which has allowed XGBoost to become one of the most popular algorithms in machine learning today.

Given its popularity and success in generating highly accurate models, SageMaker offers a built-in XGBoost algorithm that works both on single CPUs and on multiple CPUs or on single GPUs as of this writing. It can be used on CSV and LIBSVM data formats, although there are libraries that convert your data from Parquet to CSV for subsequent use with XGBoost. A key benefit of XGBoost is its ability to scale to very large datasets, which can occur for common machine learning problems such as fraud detection.

FIGURE 8.6   Sequential learning of XGBoost to combine many weak learners into a strong learner

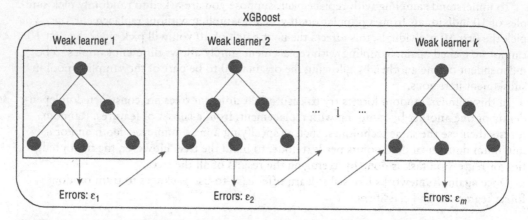

 Given the popularity of XGBoost, you may expect a question or two on the test about the SageMaker implementation. Read the XGBoost documentation in detail to understand the workings of the algorithm, input/output data formats, tunable parameters, and so forth: `https://docs .aws.amazon.com/sagemaker/latest/dg/xgboost.html`.

Textual Data

One of the most common forms of data after tabular data is unstructured text data. This might be documents, social media feeds such as news articles or Twitter feeds, or chats from various chat-based applications.

More and more customers are interested in building models that can understand the natural language in these documents and be used to build intelligent applications such as document classification for front- and back-office jobs in financial services, classification of medical documents for improving medical diagnosis, analysis of sentiment from news and social media feeds, and analyzing chats from customer service applications and routing them to appropriate agents or providing an automated response to the chat by using natural language processing.

In Chapter 1, "AWS AI ML Stack," we discussed a number of AI services that can help users introduce natural language processing and intelligence into their applications such as Textract for document processing, Amazon Comprehend and Comprehend Medical for natural language understanding, and Transcribe to transcribe audio into text. In this section, we will discuss some built-in SageMaker algorithms for NLP.

Document Classification with BlazingText

One of the major breakthroughs in natural language processing using ML came with the release of an architecture called Word2Vec by Google in a series of papers:

- "Efficient Estimation of Word Representations in Vector Space," by Tomas Mikolov, Kai Chen, Greg Corrado, and Jeffrey Dean (2013), *International Conference on Learning Representations*
- "Distributed Representations of Words and Phrases and Their Compositionality," by Tomas Mikolov (2013), *Advances in Neural Information Processing Systems*

Word2Vec is a shallow neural network algorithm that operates in two ways. First, given an input set of contextual words from a prespecified window, represented as tokens, Word-2Vec aims to predict the current word. Here's an example:

The quick brown <token> jumps over the lazy dog.

where the algorithm will aim to predict the word "fox." Another approach is to predict the context, given a word; for example, given an input word, for example, *Paris*, the algorithm predicts "is the capital of France." This is known as the skip-gram method, and the former is called continuous bag-of-words (CBOW).

In either case, the algorithm first requires a fixed vocabulary to be defined, and all the sentences in your corpus (dataset) to be broken up into tokens. A token is simply a mathematical representation of the sentence from the vocabulary that is machine readable. For example, if your vocabulary looks something like this: {quick: 1, the: 5, brown: 6, fox: 25, jump: 14, over: 8, dog: 10}, then you can represent the example sentence in the form of a sequence of numbers that can now be fed into the model as [5, 1, 6, 25, 14, 8, 5, 10].

The actual algorithm uses a neural network to learn embeddings of words. To do so, you have to pass in a training dataset with labeled data, where the labels are either the token or the context in the case of CBOW or skip-gram, respectively. The algorithm then embeds every word into a mathematical vector based on the context of the data it has been trained on—hence the name Word2Vec. At prediction time, these embeddings are used to predict the closest word or set of words (context) that correspond to the input sequence/word.

Word2Vec became highly popular because it was able to preserve the semantic relationships between words. For example, patterns such as "Paris is to France what Washington, DC, is to the United States" were accurately captured. Similarly, the vector representation for the vectors for brother, man, woman, and sister obeys the following relationship:

brother − man + woman = sister

Despite the popularity of this algorithm, Word2Vec suffered from the challenge that it could not effectively be trained on large datasets or using GPUs. Enter BlazingText!

Amazon SageMaker's BlazingText provides highly optimized implementations of Word-2Vec that can run on GPUs, allowing customers to train on billions of words within minutes. Furthermore, by using something called *character embeddings*, it overcomes another limitation of Word2Vec, which is to generalize to previously unseen words, which the original Word2Vec could not do.

BlazingText allows you to use either skip-gram or CBOW methods for document classification on SageMaker or simply extract word embeddings for other downstream tasks, and it supports single GPU training to scale to large datasets.

A lot of the deep learning algorithms we've discussed work by generating some form of vector embeddings of data. For text, you can use the BlazingText algorithm; for images, you can use the image classification and object detection algorithms; and if you want to generate embeddings between *pairs* of objects, you can use the Object2Vec model.

Object2Vec is highly customizable and works on different kind of data inputs. It generates encodings of pairs of inputs and concatenates them into a single embedding vector. This can be useful when you want to compare similar or dissimilar items, extract embeddings of user-item pairs for a recommendation system, or create product-product pairs, customer-customer pairs, or sentence-sentence pairs.

A popular question when deciding on an architecture may be when to use BlazingText versus document classification in Comprehend. Remember that you cannot deploy a Comprehend model outside of Amazon Comprehend since it is a fully managed service. BlazingText models, however, can be hosted as SageMaker endpoints or even deployed outside of SageMaker, so that may be a design consideration to be mindful of.

Custom Algorithms such as BERT

More recently (since 2018), models like Word2Vec have fallen out of favor for a new class of NLP models known as *transformers*, and the most popular of them is called BERT (Bidirectional Encoder Representations from Transformers), first described in this paper: "BERT: Pre-training of Deep Bidirectional Transformers for Language Understanding" by Jacob Devlin, Ming-Wei Chang, Kenton Lee and Kristina Toutanova.

There are several key advances in BERT that go well beyond the scope of this book and the ML Specialty Certification, but the most important ones are the notion of an attention mechanism. Traditional NLP models that leveraged algorithms like RNN or LSTM that we discussed briefly in Chapter 1 suffer from the issue that it is hard for an ML model to understand contextual information. For example, consider the following sentence:

> The company financials are strong, and while *its* shareholders can see a large return on equity in the long term, *they* may not be able to realize gains in the near term.

Although it is clear to a human that *its* refers to the company and *they* refers to shareholders, that can be hard for an ML model. BERT uses a concept called a Transformer architecture.

To understand this better, consider a machine translation task to translate the English "I am a student" to the French "Je suis étudiant."

The encoder block encodes an embedding of an input English token or word as well as its position in the sentence (positional encoding). It then feeds that to an attention network that is a simple transformation, which tells the network what parts of the sentence to pay "attention" to for each word in the sentence.

The mathematical foundations of attention mechanisms are beyond the scope of this book, but BERT introduces another advance: the encoder module encodes attention bidirectionally and attends to words that precede the input word as well as the ones after it.

This encoder block is coupled with a decoder block, which also consists of similar attention layers and LSTM layers that this time encode the French output plus the inputs from the encoder network to predict the next word in the French sentence.

In this way, the model sequentially learns by predicting the next word in the sentence during training. Once the model is trained, it can then be used on arbitrary tasks such as generating text sequences, machine translation, or even using the encodings to then classify documents, summarize text, and so forth.

You will not be expected to understand the BERT architecture for the exam, but given the immense popularity of BERT in NLP, no discussion of algorithms on text data would be complete without at least mentioning BERT.

NLP research is now moving toward larger and larger models that train not on millions but on tens or even hundreds of billions of parameters. Such models don't even fit into the memory of a single GPU instance and need to be spread across multiple instances and can take weeks to train and costs hundreds of thousands of dollars as a result. They belong to the GPT family of models such as GPT-1, GPT-2, and more recently GPT-3, which has now been licensed by Microsoft in partnership with OpenAI. The GPT-3 model, released in 2020, for example, consists of 175 billion parameters compared to BERT in 2018 with roughly 110 million parameters. That is over a 1,000 times increase!

It is worth noting that this encoder-decoder architecture with attention is part of the Sage-Maker Sequence to Sequence (seq2seq) algorithm. Use this built-in algorithm when working on tasks such as machine translation and text summarization or when converting speech to text with SageMaker.

Image Analysis

In the previous chapters we covered Amazon Rekognition, which allows customers to use pretrained object detection or image classification models or train custom image labeling models using transfer learning or from scratch.

On SageMaker, you can use the Image Classification algorithm, which leverages the ResNet algorithm to train an image classification model either from scratch or by using transfer learning, pretrained on the ImageNet database. The image classification algorithm accepts RecordIO or raw images as input and supports training on single or multiple CPUs and GPUs.

ResNet generalizes traditional convolutional neural networks by having residual connections between the layers called *shortcut connections*. These connections improve the gradient flow between layers and prevents gradients from vanishing, improving the model training.

Often the use case is to detect objects within an image instead of classifying an image. In this case, you can use the object detection algorithm, which generates a bounding box around the object in question. Like the image classification algorithm, it can be trained from scratch or fine-tuned using the pretrained model.

> A common design decision is when you should train from scratch versus just fine-tune a pretrained model to your new data and labels. This is also a popular exam topic. If you have a lot of data or a highly custom-ized use case, training from scratch makes sense. If you have only a little actual labeled data, or if your business is looking for quick insights and if the use case does not require highly specialized domain knowledge, using transfer learning is a good solution. Note that fine-tuning is also cost effective since training neural networks from scratch can get quite expensive due to the need for large amounts of labeled data and the infrastructure needs. Fine-tuning only trains the last few layers of the neural network and fixes the rest of the weights, dramatically reducing the number of parameters required to train the model and the cost.

Unsupervised Machine Learning

Another popular paradigm for machine learning is unsupervised learning, where you are building a model to identify patterns or clusters within an unlabeled dataset. Unsupervised learning is also often used as part of a semi-supervised learning strategy, where you have a large amount of unlabeled data but a small number of labels and labeling is prohibitively expensive. We will discuss three common unsupervised learning algorithms for tabular data.

Principal Component Analysis (PCA)

Principal Component Analysis (PCA) is an extremely common unsupervised learning tech-nique for *dimensionality reduction*. Dimensionality reduction refers to reducing the dimen-sionality of a high-dimensional dataset by mapping it to a lower-dimensional vector space. The PCA algorithm aims to do this mapping in a way that retains as much information as possible. The measure of information is given by the covariance matrix.

The principal components are the eigenvectors of the covariance matrix, and each eigen-vector is uncorrelated with one another. The eigenvector with the largest eigenvalue rep-resents the maximal variability in the data, the second largest corresponds to the second largest variability, and so on.

Because PCA is a linear technique (involves linear algebra such as matrix diagonalization) and retains the information in the data but also generates uncorrelated features, PCA is often used to de-correlate a subset of highly correlated features in your dataset. Alternatively, PCA is often applied when you have a large number of features in your data as a way to reduce the data dimensionality prior to ML training.

With Amazon SageMaker's built-in PCA algorithm, you can use either regular or randomized PCA strategies. The regular strategy works for smaller datasets whereas the randomized strategy produces an approximate covariance matrix for large numbers of features. SageMaker's PCA algorithm supports both RecordIO and CSV formats.

 Since PCA is a common technique for dimensionality reduction or de-correlating features, you may also consider PCA as part of your feature engineering process as opposed to actual model training. Generally, PCA is one of the feature engineering steps used prior to model training; however, we include it here as it is an unsupervised algorithm.

K-Means Clustering

One of the most popular unsupervised machine learning algorithms on tabular datasets is k-means clustering. k-means clustering can be used when your data does not have labels but when you are looking to cluster your data points into "similar" groups. Figure 8.7 shows an example of a clustering analysis.

Generally, you may have some upfront business knowledge that tells you how many clusters or groups to expect, or you can run the k-means algorithm multiple times to find the best number of groups. Let's dive into how this may work.

k-means training works by first identifying a random set of k points as the cluster centers. Now for each of the k centers, find a subset of points from the data that are closest to this center using a distance metric such as Euclidean distance. Define the new centroid as the mean vector of all these points. Repeatedly perform these steps until the algorithm converges, that is, the cluster centers do not move past a certain threshold.

FIGURE 8.7 Possible output of a clustering analysis that splits data into three clusters

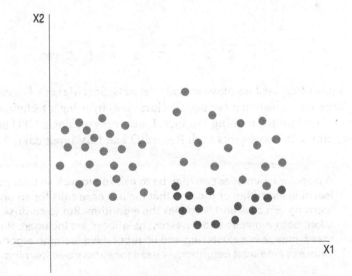

Although in some cases you may have prior business knowledge about the number of clusters, in many problems, that is not usually the case. So, you need to determine the *best* number of clusters or groups in your data.

A common technique for optimizing for the number of clusters is to use an *elbow method*. The elbow method plots the percentage of variance that is explained as a function of the number of clusters. One way to measure this is to look at the ratio of the mean or minimum value of the separation between clusters divided by the max separation within a cluster:

$$Variance = \frac{min\left(Inter\ cluster\ distance\right)}{max\left(Intra\ cluster\ distance\right)}$$

In the elbow method (depicted in Figure 8.8), you plot this quantity as a function of the number of clusters, and it typically has a distinct elbow feature. The right number of clusters is determined by the location of the elbow in the curve.

FIGURE 8.8 Elbow curve analysis of PCA to determine optimal number of clusters, in this case 4 or 5

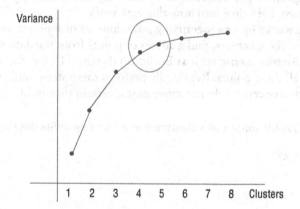

Since clustering is often used on massive-scale datasets, SageMaker's *k*-means algorithm is designed for large-scale clustering (web-scale clustering) by using a technique to directly stream batches of data into the training instance. It also runs on single GPU instances to speed up training times. It also accepts both RecordIO and CSV input data.

A popular exam question may be to ask you to pick an unsupervised learning algorithm or identify that the use case calls for an unsupervised learning use case and then pick the algorithm. But to confuse the test taker, both *k*-means and *k*-nearest neighbors are included. Remember that *k*-means is a clustering and unsupervised learning algorithm, whereas *k*-nearest neighbors is used for supervised learning.

Anomaly Detection with Random Cut Forest

Our last unsupervised learning algorithm is called random cut forest (RCF). RCF works similar to a random forest except that random forest is a supervised learning algorithm. RCF works by first splitting the dataset into random samples, and each random sample is partitioned into a tree known as a k-d tree. A k-d tree, or k-dimensional tree, is a data structure for organizing and clustering points in a k-dimensional space (see Bentley, J. L. (1975). "Multidimensional binary search trees used for associative searching". Communications of the ACM. 18 (9): 509–517. doi:10.1145/361002.361007. S2CID 13091446).

Anomaly scores are then assigned to points that require a large change in the tree complexity required to add that point to the tree, for example, if explaining that point in the tree requires a large change in the tree depth. The anomaly score is then inversely proportional to the tree depth. As in the random forest, the RCF algorithm builds many trees to reduce the overall variance resulting from a single tree and averages the scores of all the trees together. Anomalous points are classified as points that are greater than 3 standard deviations from the mean anomaly score in the dataset.

The RCF algorithm can be used when you have time series data with "spiky" or aperiodic behavior. The RCF algorithm is also designed to scale with large dataset sizes by taking advantage of distributed training, which we will cover in depth later in this chapter. However, it is not designed to work on GPUs.

 Another popular exam question is to make sure you understand the difference between random *cut* forest and random forest. The former is for unsupervised learning, whereas the latter is a common supervised learning algorithm.

Another popular anomaly detection algorithm you may want to consider when building an anomaly detection use case is the isolation forest. We will not cover this algorithm in this book, but you can learn about the scikit-learn implementation here: `https://scikit-learn.org/stable/modules/generated/sklearn.ensemble.IsolationForest.html`.

Topic Modeling with LDA or Neural Topic Model (NTM)

Unsupervised learning can also be applied to unstructured text data. A common use case here is when you are given a set of documents and you want to summarize the documents or identify a set of topics that the documents correspond to.

Summarization is a large topic of research within NLP, and one methodology for summarization is topic modeling. Topic modeling aims to discover a set of topics that represent a corpus of documents. The topics are defined by clusters of similar words and are not known a priori, thus making this an unsupervised technique.

The most common topic modeling algorithm is called Latent Dirichlet Allocation (LDA). LDA uses a Dirichlet distribution to generate a probability model for the distribution of words in a document based on latent or hidden variables. These hidden variables then define the topics. In LDA, the ordering of words does not matter.

LDA is a generative model where, for each word in the document, you pick a topic from a distribution. Then you pick the topic-word distribution and sample another word from the distribution. The goal of the algorithm is to find the topics and the distribution that most accurately "generate" all the words in the document.

Diving into the mathematical formalism behind this algorithm is beyond our scope, but it suffices to understand that this model is used for identifying topics or summarizing documents into topics. It uses a Dirichlet distribution, is unsupervised, and is generative in nature.

Despite its popularity and success, one limitation of this algorithm is that it makes an assumption that the distribution of words in a document follows a Dirichlet distribution. The NTM algorithm relaxes this assumption and aims to learn a latent representation without prior assumptions. Both LDA and NTM algorithms work on GPU and CPU instances to speed up training times. NTM can also run on multiple GPUs, but LDA only supports single instance training.

Another design question is when to choose which algorithm. In general, the NTM algorithm has been shown to outperform the LDA algorithm and is scalable to multinode distributed training. That said, the LDA is conceptually simpler. More details on this can be found here: https://docs .aws.amazon.com/sagemaker/latest/dg/lda.html#lda-or-ntm.

For document summarization in general, other algorithms like BART have started to become popular that can extract accurate summaries of documents instead of just topics. This can be particularly useful in applications where you want to extract a short summary from a corpus of text such as a financial document. However, this is an extractive summarization model—that is, it does not generate new words but simply picks the sentences from the original document it thinks are most important. For more on BART read here: https://arxiv.org/abs/1910.13461.

Reinforcement Learning

We will not cover reinforcement learning in detail in this book, but it is important to understand the difference between reinforcement learning and supervised or unsupervised learning.

Whereas in both unsupervised/supervised learning a model learns patterns from labeled or unlabeled data, reinforcement learning aims to mimic a problem in an environment and consists of an agent that can take a controlled set of actions in that environment. The agent is then rewarded or penalized based on the outcome of the action and can take another action. Over time, the goal is to maximize the rewards and the agent learns an optimal "policy" that maximizes the long-term reward.

Reinforcement learning has a lot of mathematical connections to classical optimization theory, Markov decision processes, and dynamic programming. The Bellman equation gives the principle of optimality, which defines the optimal policy in terms of the rewards and probabilities of taking an action at each step. Although this equation formally defines the problem, in practice, this equation is intractable.

There are many open-source frameworks for RL, such as OpenAI Gym, Ray RLlib, Intel Coach, and frameworks attached to TensorFlow/PyTorch, that you can use on Amazon SageMaker.

> For the test, it is useful to understand the difference among supervised learning, unsupervised learning, and reinforcement learning. Remember that reinforcement learning has an agent trying to learn an optimal policy. There is no notion of policy or agent for supervised/unsupervised learning.

Let's discuss some application of Reinforcement Learning:

- Financial institutions are using reinforcement learning to simulate market dynamics to train an agent to predict stock prices.
- In robotics, you can train agents to perform actions such as pick up and drop off packages in a warehouse like the Amazon warehouse.
- Reinforcement learning could also be used in drone delivery of packages.
- Reinforcement learning has been used to train computers to beat humans at complex games such as Go with AlphaGoZero with no prior knowledge of the game.

Local Training and Testing

Data science is a highly iterative process, and as datasets get large, a natural question arises on how best to train on these large datasets. By *large*, we mean data that typically does not fit on a host instance's memory. Many algorithms (such as XGBoost) require the data to be loaded into memory in order to train, and as your data size grows to hundreds of gigabytes to even terabytes (TB), this becomes impossible.

We will cover distributed training later in this chapter, which can address this big data concern. A second concern relates to the data science process itself; often a data scientist may want to quickly test out their model on a small dataset first for reasons such as the following:

- Finding out if the model can produce good results on a small but representative sample of the data
- Debugging your training code before launching a large training job
- Having the option to iterate with different model algorithms or feature combinations

For all of these reasons, data scientists will first train a model locally on their desktop or laptop either using scripts or even using a notebook interface such as a Jupyter Notebook. Jupyter Notebooks is a highly popular, interactive web application among data scientists for data exploration as well as locally training models. Another popular package is the R framework, and data scientists who code in R tend to use a tool like R Studio. You may also author your code locally using an integrated development environment (IDE) such as Visual Studio Code (VSCode).

To facilitate this data scientist experience, Amazon SageMaker also offers a Jupyter Notebook interface for data scientists to use. The notebooks are linked to Amazon S3 buckets where your data is stored. For remote training, you can either simply run your code on a small dataset on a SageMaker notebook, or even scale *up* your SageMaker notebook to a larger notebook instance to train on a larger dataset.

However, while notebooks are great tools for iteration, when you are ready to train a model on the entire dataset or train in a production setting, you will want to migrate away from notebooks for a few reasons:

- Notebooks can scale up, but not out. You cannot run distributed training on a notebook, and as your data size grows, you may need to train your model over several machines at once.

- It is hard to maintain version control using notebooks. A best practice is to convert your code into a script such as a Python script and upload it to a version control tool such as Git. We will cover this topic in much more detail later in the book in Chapter 12, "Operational Excellence Pillar for ML."

- Your training code may have dependencies on other packages, and you typically do not want to overwhelm the notebook memory by installing a lot of packages. It is preferable to use a separate instance dedicated for training.

For these reasons, SageMaker notebook instances offer a capability for *local mode training*. Rather than storing all your code in notebook cells, with local mode, you can package your training code and all the associated dependencies into a Docker container. To build the Docker container, you can use one of the SageMaker built-in frameworks such as TensorFlow, MXNet, or PyTorch. Local mode does not work with SageMaker built-in algorithms, only with public SageMaker container images.

Local mode uses Docker compose and the NVIDIA Container Toolkit for Docker (https://github.com/NVIDIA/nvidia-docker) to first pull the public SageMaker training images or build a custom training container from scratch. Once the container is built locally on your SageMaker notebook instance, you can run your SageMaker training job as you normally would with the only change being the type of instance the training job is launched on. Instead of specifying a EC2 instance type, you would specify `instance_type= 'local'` or `instance_type= 'local_gpu'`. Note that local mode does not support distributed training, since the training runs on the notebook itself.

Refer to the following GitHub repo for more information on local mode training with different frameworks: https://github.com/aws-samples/amazon-sagemaker-local-mode.

The key benefit of local mode is that you can not only test and debug your algorithm code on a dataset, but also test your training container itself. By packaging all your code and dependencies into a container, you can enforce software development best practices such as version or source control and maintaining container versions.

Remember why you would want to first train locally and the benefits of SageMaker local mode. Note that local mode does not work for Sage-Maker built-in algorithms but allows you to use SageMaker's managed frameworks for TensorFlow, PyTorch, or MXNet as well as bring your own custom container.

Remote Training

Once you are done training locally on a small dataset for development purposes, you will want to launch a training job on the entire dataset. For large datasets, training can take several hours, if not days. For some of the extremely large NLP models we covered in the previous section, such as those in the GPT family with 100+ billion parameters, that training time becomes weeks.

As a best practice, you will want to launch your training jobs not on your notebook or local machine but on a remote cluster, so the model can train in the background while you can continue exploring data, developing other algorithms in your notebook or IDE. To facilitate remote training, Amazon SageMaker offers a Python SDK (or you can also use the lower-level `boto3` AWS Python SDK) to launch a remote training job. SageMaker will run your training job on remote EC2 instances that are hosted in an AWS account. As Sage-Maker is a managed service, these instances will be managed by SageMaker and not visible in your AWS account.

The steps to launch a training job are as follows:

- Store your algorithm code and any associated dependencies in a local folder or in a GitHub repo.
- Pass in the training script as the entry point to SageMaker. This way, SageMaker knows to execute the training script once your code and the training data is loaded into the training container.
- Specify an IAM role. SageMaker training uses EC2 behind the scenes so you will need to pass SageMaker an IAM role along with IAM:PassRole permissions to make EC2 calls on your behalf. These EC2 instances do not live in your account, so you will not see them on the EC2 console.
- Specify the number of instances you want to launch.
- Specify the type of instance you want to launch.
- Specify the output S3 path where you want your model artifacts to be stored.
- Call the `estimator.fit` function by passing in the S3 path to your training data. You can also pass a validation dataset for testing purposes during training.

The following example shows an estimator function for PyTorch framework:

```
# Specifies the git_config parameter. This example does not provide Git
credentials, so python SDK will try
# to use local credential storage.
git_config = {'repo': 'https://github.com/username/repo-with-
                training-scripts.git', 'branch': 'branch1', 'commit':
                '4893e528afa4a790331e1b5286954f073b0f14a2'}


# In this example, the source directory 'pytorch' contains the entry point
'mnist.py' and other source code.
# and it is relative path inside the Git repo.
pytorch_estimator = PyTorch(entry_point='mnist.py',
                        role='SageMakerRole',
                        source_dir='pytorch',
                        git_config=git_config,
                        instance_count=1,
                        instance_type='ml.c4.xlarge')
```

Refer to this documentation for more details on launching remote training on Amazon SageMaker using the SageMaker SDK: https://sagemaker.readthedocs.io/en/stable/overview.html#train-a-model-with-the-sagemaker-python-sdk.

Distributed Training

As machine learning and deep learning models become more complex and data sizes increase, it can take anywhere from multiple hours to weeks to train a model in some cases. Distributed training makes use of parallelism with compute cores in a single instance and across instances to reduce training time. Let's first go over some concepts about training machine learning models before diving deeper into distributed training:

- A subset of the entire training data, called a *mini-batch* of data, is sent for processing to compute units in a single iteration of the training algorithm. But what is one iteration of training?

- A single forward and backward pass performed using a mini-batch of data is called one *iteration*.

- One training cycle through your entire dataset is called an *epoch*. It is common to have multiple iterations per epoch.

- *Stochastic Gradient Descent* (SGD) is a popular optimization algorithm used in deep neural networks that we will use to explain some core concepts of distributed training. Although the details of SGD and other training algorithms are beyond the scope of this book, there are several resources to check if interested. For each epoch in SGD, the algorithm does the following:

1. Initializes weights of the network and splits the data into mini-batches

2. For every sample of data in a mini-batch drawn randomly with replacement, computes the prediction according to the network's current weights

3. Computes the loss using a `loss` function (this is a function of the predicted output and the actual output for that sample)

4. Computes gradients with respect to the loss

5. Updates weights and repeats until you meet some convergence criteria (such as a set number of epochs or non-decreasing loss)

- When the data as well as the model weights can fit in the memory of a single server or instance, all the above steps (1–5) are controlled by a single process that first loads a mini-batch of data and sends it to the GPU to perform these steps.

- When the training data does not entirely fit in the available memory, it is typical to either choose a larger instance with more memory, or perform *data parallel* training; again, first with multiple GPUs on a single instance, and then with multiple instances (with multiple GPUs each, in that order).

- In data parallel training, model replicas are created for each GPU (within an instance or across many instances as applicable), and training is usually controlled with one process per GPU. During each iteration of training, each process loads a mini-batch of data and passes this to a GPU, where gradient calculation is performed. In typical cases (called synchronous data parallel training), the gradients are collected from all GPUs and averaged before updating the model weights. The act of averaging these gradients is done by a worker called a *parameter server*.

- Just as the model training nodes are increased for parallelization, the number of parameter servers can also be increased. However, the ratio of number of parameter servers to training workers is workload dependent because there is a balance to be struck between communication bottlenecks (all parameter servers need to get updates from many/all training workers).

- Lastly, gradient averaging can also be done using the training workers, without the need for separate parameter servers. This is called the *Ring-AllReduce* approach, and is implemented in the popular Horovod Python package that can be used with most popular deep learning frameworks.

- When the model itself is large and complex, such as in the case of many large vision- and language-based models, it may not fit in the memory of a single node. Another strategy in distributed training that helps with this is *model parallel* training. Here, the model itself is partitioned and distributed across many nodes. Then, an execution schedule passes batches of the data across multiple nodes in order for calculating gradients.

- If models are split up, you may ask if certain GPUs are idle until the previous GPU with parts of the model finish processing a batch first, and you are right! In order to maximize GPU utilization, the mini-batch of data we spoke about is further split into several micro-batches—while GPU 1 is processing micro-batch 1, a pipeline execution schedule tells GPU 2 to process micro-batch 2 so that GPU utilization is maximized, and ultimately, your training progresses as quickly as possible.

So when would you use *data parallel* training versus *model parallel* training?

1. If your model can fit in a single instance's memory, you should use data parallel training.

2. If you still think your model doesn't fit in a single instance's memory, check again by gradually decreasing the size of the inputs or batch size and/or changing the model's hyperparameters.

3. If your model still doesn't fit, try mixed-precision training (`https://docs.nvidia .com/deeplearning/performance/mixed-precision-training/index.html`). With mixed precision training, model parameters are represented using different numerical precisions so as to reduce memory consumption and also speed up training. Since reducing the mini-batch size can lead to a higher error rate, it may be beneficial to use mixed precision training to allow for larger mini-batch sizes.

4. If your model still doesn't fit, then use model parallel training.

Now that you know when to use what strategy for distributed training, let's see what this looks like in practice. You can follow along on a terminal with PyTorch installed.

 This code fragment is meant to explain some of the concepts in this section.

Here, we will make use of a toy example from PyTorch. You can use a Jupyter Notebook or your favorite IDE to import the code fragments. First, we import the right modules from PyTorch and initialize a simple model:

```
import torch
import torch.nn as nn
import torch.optim as optim
```

Then, we define a simple, sequential model in PyTorch, involving an input layer, a ReLU (Rectified Linear Unit), and another output Linear Layer. For now, treat these as separate functions f, g, and h, so a "forward pass" through the model with an input x may be thought of as $f(g(h(x)))$.

```
model = nn.Sequential(nn.Linear(5,5), nn.ReLU(), nn.Linear(5,1))
```

Does this model work? Let's try passing in a random tensor to the model:

```
model.forward(torch.randn(5,5))
output
     tensor([[ 0.0093],
             [-0.0814],
             [ 0.0996],
             [-0.0221],
             [-0.0050]], grad_fn=<AddmmBackward>)
```

Great! Now we define the `loss` function and choose the SGD optimizer:

```
loss_fn = nn.MSELoss()
optimizer = optim.SGD(model.parameters(), lr=0.001)
```

Note that `MSE` is the mean squared error and `SGD` is the stochastic gradient descent algorithm that was mentioned in the beginning of this chapter. `lr` stands for the learning rate.

In PyTorch, it is then typical to set gradients of all model parameters to 0. Then we calculate the loss function, backpropagate and calculate gradients using PyTorch's autograd module, and then take one step of the optimizer:

```
optimizer.zero_grad()
outputs = model(torch.randn(20, 5))
labels = torch.randn(20, 1)

loss_fn(outputs, labels).backward()
optimizer.step()
```

These steps are repeated until we reach a total number of *epochs*. What you saw now as steps performed per epoch for a toy model is very similar to most other examples that can be found.

Now, imagine you wanted to use multiple GPU devices on a single instance; the way to implement this on PyTorch would be to use the `DataParallel` module. This parallelizes your model training by splitting inputs into batches. Replicas of the model perform the forward pass (`model(input)`), and during the backward step, gradients are automatically combined from each replica. In code, the only changes you need to make are

```
dataparallel_model = nn.DataParallel(model, device_ids=[0, 1, 2])
```

If you have data that cannot fit in a single instance, you can try distributed training in multiple instances. Without going into the details, you can implement `DistributedDataParallel` like this:

```
from torch.nn.parallel import DistributedDataParallel as DDP

ddp_model = DDP(model, device_ids=[rank])
```

Each GPU device, across the many instances you are training on, has an ID, or a *rank*. Whereas `DataParallel` works on a single instance, controlled by a single process with multiple threads, `DistributedDataParallel` is multiprocess and works on both single and multiple machines. Recall from earlier that if your model is too large to fit on a single GPU, then you can use model parallel training. For this, we first split the model using the `Pipe` command:

```
model = Pipe(model, chunks=8)
```

We can also split the model we have manually by changing the sequential model we had earlier from

```
model = nn.Sequential(nn.Linear(5,5), nn.ReLU(), nn.Linear(5,1))
```

to defining a custom class:

```
class MyModel(nn.Module):
    def __init__(self):
        super(ToyModel, self).__init__()
        self.net1 = torch.nn.Linear(5, 5).to('cuda:0')
        self.relu = torch.nn.ReLU()
        self.net2 = torch.nn.Linear(5, 1).to('cuda:1')

    def forward(self, x):
        x = self.relu(self.net1(x.to('cuda:0')))
        return self.net2(x.to('cuda:1'))
```

The lines that point each layer to a specific device use the to('device') method in the code snippet.

We just walked you through how to use PyTorch library's data and model parallel functions. On Amazon SageMaker's Distributed data parallel library, several optimizations, including faster node-to-node communications and optimal overlapping of the operation on the backward pass, improve GPU utilization and achieve near-linear scaling and, effectively, faster time to train. In some cases, SageMaker's data parallel library outperforms framework-specific implementations; these are tested and reported here: https://docs .aws.amazon.com/sagemaker/latest/dg/data-parallel-intro.html.

SageMaker's Model Parallel library helps you automatically partition your TensorFlow or PyTorch models across several devices with minimal changes to your code. The Model Parallel library in SageMaker also performs scheduled, pipelined executions of operations in parallel where different devices can work on different forward and backward passes with different micro-batches of data. To learn more about SageMaker's Model Parallel training library, please refer to https://docs.aws.amazon.com/sagemaker/latest/dg/model-parallel.html.

Monitoring Training Jobs

AI/ML services on AWS that have a training component like SageMaker can be monitored using services like Amazon CloudWatch. CloudWatch allows you to monitor various processes, including training jobs using real-time logs, metrics, and events. You can also create custom dashboards and alarms that take some action when a specific metric reaches a threshold. Amazon CloudTrail, on the other hand, records individual API calls made by, or on behalf of, entities or services in your AWS account. Lastly, Amazon EventBridge lets you respond to events specific to status changes in training jobs. Let's look at these options in more detail.

Amazon CloudWatch

First, CloudWatch lets you collect and analyze detailed logs from various services. Service-specific logs are found under dedicated "log groups" on CloudWatch. For example, Sage-Maker training job logs can be found under the `/aws/sagemaker/TrainingJobs` log group. This log group contains many "log streams," which look like this: `[training-job-name]/algo-[instance-number-in-cluster]-[epoch_timestamp]`.

For example, you may have a log group in SageMaker for a training job that looks like this: `/aws/sagemaker/TrainingJobs pytorch-training-2021-03-16-17-53-49-690/algo-1-1615917370`. As an aside, SageMaker also pushes logs to log groups corresponding to other features, like notebook instances, processing jobs, and transform jobs.

Many AI services that you have learned about so far that let you train custom models with your own datasets do not have detailed logs of the training that happens behind the scenes. Examples of such services are Amazon Rekognition Custom Labels and Comprehend Custom Classification or Entity recognition. In these cases, the service generates high-level metrics in the service console page, as well as on CloudWatch for you to analyze your model and possibly readjust the data or input parameters and retrain your model. Both Comprehend and Rekognition models emit Precision, Recall, and F1 scores for your custom models that are trained using a dataset that is in your account (most commonly, in an S3 bucket). SageMaker, on the other hand, generates standard as well as custom logs and metrics. When using a notebook instance to start training jobs, real-time logs from the training instance are displayed in the notebook cell output and also sent to CloudWatch. SageMaker publishes several metrics, including for training jobs, processing jobs, transform jobs, and endpoints in a one-minute frequency. Some of the metrics published automatically include `CPUUtilization`, `GPUUtilization`, `MemoryUtilization`, `GPUMemoryUtilization`, and `DiskUtilization`.

Other metrics relevant to features of SageMaker not discussed here are also published, such as from Ground Truth labeling jobs, endpoint invocations, or model-related metrics. An important metric for you to remember from endpoint invocations (model predictions) is `ModelLatency`, which measures the total time taken by a model to respond, including the time taken to send and receive responses from the container (network latency), and the time taken to complete the inference in the container in microseconds. You can find a detailed list of all metrics that are published by SageMaker to CloudWatch here: `https://docs.aws.amazon.com/sagemaker/latest/dg/monitoring-cloudwatch.html`.

AWS CloudTrail

Actions taken by a user, role, or AWS service are recorded by AWS CloudTrail. Detailed visibility into activity in your AWS account is very important for compliance, governance, and operational and risk auditing. CloudTrail allows you to view and analyze up to 90 days of event history in your account, and also gives you the option of archiving these events in Amazon S3 for analysis at a future date, or for compliance reasons. All the services that have been introduced to you so far are supported by CloudTrail; for further reading, we refer you to service-specific topics that can be found in Table 8.1. Note that the table includes both AI/ML services on AWS that were discussed here, as well as some supporting services that help in the architecting of end-to-end solutions for machine learning.

TABLE 8.1   Services relevant to an end-to-end machine learning workflow that are logged by CloudTrail

AWS service	CloudTrail topics
Amazon API Gateway	Log API management calls to Amazon API Gateway Using AWS CloudTrail
Amazon Connect	Logging Amazon Connect API Calls with AWS CloudTrail
AWS Auto Scaling	Logging AWS Auto Scaling API Calls by Using CloudTrail
AWS CloudFormation	Logging AWS CloudFormation API Calls in AWS CloudTrail
CloudWatch Events	Logging Amazon CloudWatch Events API Calls in AWS CloudTrail
CloudWatch Logs	Logging Amazon CloudWatch Logs API Calls in AWS CloudTrail
AWS CodeBuild	Logging AWS CodeBuild API Calls with AWS CloudTrail
AWS CodeCommit	Logging AWS CodeCommit API Calls with AWS CloudTrail
AWS CodeDeploy	Monitoring Deployments with AWS CloudTrail
Amazon CodeGuru Reviewer	Logging Amazon CodeGuru Reviewer API Calls with AWS CloudTrail
AWS CodePipeline	Logging CodePipeline API Calls by Using AWS CloudTrail
AWS CodeStar	Logging AWS CodeStar API Calls with AWS CloudTrail
AWS CodeStar Notifications	Logging AWS CodeStar Notifications API Calls with AWS CloudTrail
Amazon Cognito	Logging Amazon Cognito API Calls with AWS CloudTrail
Amazon Comprehend	Logging Amazon Comprehend API Calls with AWS CloudTrail
Amazon Comprehend Medical	Logging Amazon Comprehend Medical API Calls by Using AWS CloudTrail
Amazon DynamoDB	Logging DynamoDB Operations by Using AWS CloudTrail
Amazon Elastic Container Registry (Amazon ECR)	Logging Amazon ECR API Calls by Using AWS CloudTrail
Amazon Elastic Container Service (Amazon ECS)	Logging Amazon ECS API Calls by Using AWS CloudTrail

AWS service	CloudTrail topics
Amazon FSx for Lustre	Logging Amazon FSx for Lustre API Calls with AWS CloudTrail
Amazon S3 Glacier	Logging S3 Glacier API Calls by Using AWS CloudTrail
AWS IoT Greengrass V2	Log AWS IoT Greengrass V2 API Calls with AWS CloudTrail
Amazon Kendra	Logging Amazon Kendra API Calls with AWS CloudTrail
AWS Lambda	Logging AWS Lambda API Calls by Using AWS CloudTrail
Amazon Lex	Logging Amazon Lex API Calls with CloudTrail
Amazon Polly	Logging Amazon Polly API Calls with AWS CloudTrail
Amazon Redshift	Logging Amazon Redshift API Calls with AWS CloudTrail
Amazon Rekognition	Logging Amazon Rekognition API Calls Using AWS CloudTrail
AWS RoboMaker	Logging AWS RoboMaker API Calls with AWS CloudTrail
Amazon Route 53	Using AWS CloudTrail to Capture Requests Sent to the Route 53 API
Amazon SageMaker	Logging Amazon SageMaker API Calls with AWS CloudTrail
Amazon Simple Notification Service (Amazon SNS)	Logging Amazon Simple Notification Service API Calls by Using AWS CloudTrail
Amazon Simple Queue Service (Amazon SQS)	Logging Amazon SQS API Actions by Using AWS CloudTrail
Amazon Simple Storage Service	Logging Amazon S3 API Calls by Using AWS CloudTrail
AWS Single Sign-On (AWS SSO)	Logging AWS SSO API Calls with AWS CloudTrail
AWS Step Functions	Logging AWS Step Functions API Calls with AWS CloudTrail
Amazon Textract	Logging Amazon Textract API Calls with AWS CloudTrail
Amazon Transcribe	Logging Amazon Transcribe API Calls with AWS CloudTrail
Amazon Translate	Logging Amazon Translate API Calls with AWS CloudTrail

Amazon EventBridge

Amazon EventBridge is a serverless event bus that delivers real-time data from custom applications, supported software-as-a-service applications, and AWS services and sends this data to targets such as AWS Lambda, Amazon SNS, Amazon SQS, Amazon ECS tasks, CodeBuild, CodePipeline, API Gateway, and more. EventBridge *rules* are used to determine which *events* can trigger a *target*. You can create custom events and rules and also have other services react to events from AWS services. In this section, we look at some of the AI/ML services from AWS that emit events that can be detected by EventBridge.

Amazon SageMaker

Amazon EventBridge detects status changes in various SageMaker components such as labeling, processing, training, tuning, inference endpoints, and feature groups. Here are examples of events that EventBridge monitors: AlgorithmStatus, EndpointStatus, HyperparameterTuningStatus, LabelingJobStatus, ModelPackageStatus, NotebookInstanceStatus, ProcessingJobStatus, TrainingJobStatus, EndpointStatus, FeatureGroupStatus.

> For example, if you need to monitor and react to a failed training job, EventBridge publishes an event with the source aws.sagemaker, and other information such as the account, region, training job name, hyperparameters, input and output data configuration, and tags. These events can trigger an AWS Lambda function or send an Amazon SNS notification.

Augmented AI

EventBridge events can be used to detect and react to changes in human review loops in Amazon Augmented AI. When a review loop changes its status to Completed, Failed, or Stopped, Augmented AI can send an event with details, including the human loop name, ARN, status, failure code, and failure reason.

Debugging Training Jobs

Debugging training jobs is generally more difficult than debugging code because it involves the following:

- Longer running times
- The need to debug underlying framework code (e.g., for PyTorch or TensorFlow framework errors)
- Testing locally, as well as in cloud services like SageMaker
- Complex, distributed processing jobs that may run on multiple devices or instances

- Tracking, correlating, and analyzing individual training jobs that can all be part of a single experiment

- Logging and searching through logs from distributed training jobs or hyperparameter tuning jobs

- When architecting ML solutions on AWS, may involve debugging roles, connections between services, and individual service-specific logs

With AI services on AWS, high-level tracking and analysis of results are possible, without details from the underlying algorithms. When using a custom (or built-in) algorithm on Amazon SageMaker, you can debug, monitor, and profile training jobs using a feature called SageMaker Debugger. SageMaker Debugger provides two major functions:

- *Debugging*, for model optimization; this is for deeper analysis of training jobs.

- *Profiling*, for performance optimization; this is for identifying performance issues and providing suggestions to improve resource utilization.

Both these functions are supported by built-in rules (you can also create your own custom rules). When these rules are triggered, you can automate actions such as stopping a training job or sending an SNS notification. For any training job on SageMaker, you can use built-in rules that are related to the following:

- System metrics—CPU bottleneck, I/O bottleneck, low GPU utilization, and overall system usage

- Framework metrics—initialization time, overall framework-level metrics, and outliers detected in step durations

- Model training tensors and metrics—vanishing gradient, exploding tensor, overfitting, overtraining, class imbalance, loss not decreasing, and more

SageMaker Debugger provides an open-source Python library called smdebug that is used to set up built-in and custom rules. Debugger also generates a report that aggregates all of the monitoring and profiling rules. For more details on how SageMaker Debugger works and best practices, please visit https://docs.aws.amazon.com/sagemaker/latest/dg/debugger-how-it-works.html.

Hyperparameter Optimization

Hyperparameter optimization (HPO) involves running multiple training jobs with various input parameters for finding the best model according to some metric. Let's explore this by revisiting the toy example that was used in the section on distributed training:

```
model = nn.Sequential(nn.Linear(5,N1), nn.ReLU(), nn.Linear(N1,1))
```

Here, an extremely simple network is used involving a linear layer, ReLU activation, and another linear layer. The term *N1* is configurable or depends on user input. Later on in the code, we define the optimizer with another configurable input *N2* representing the learning rate.

```
optimizer = optim.SGD(model.parameters(), lr=N2)
```

In this very simple example, we need to run several experiments controlling the values of *N1* and *N2*. These are our hyperparameters, and hyperparameter optimization is the process of finding out the combination of *N1* and *N2* that minimizes a metric we defined earlier, the mean squared error:

```
loss_fn = nn.MSELoss()
```

We define the range (upper and lower bounds) of *N1* and *N2*, and also decide what type of variable *N1* and *N2* are. Here, we decide that *N1* is an integer that can range from a value of 20 to 50, and that *N2* (learning rate) is a float number that can range from 0.0001 to 0.1.

Let's now walk through multiple HPO "algorithms," starting from the simplest experiment you may want to run to more complex ones:

Manual Tuning   Here, you can manually change the values of *N1* and *N2*, rerun the training code, measure the loss, and do several such runs. As you can imagine, this method is time consuming and involves manually deciding what values of *N1* and *N2* to try based on previous experiments.

Grid Search   To speed up manual training, you can write code to automate and search through every possible *N1* and *N2* value. We can do this easily for *N1*, which is an integer number ranging from 20 to 50, but how do you explore all the possible float numbers between 0.0001 to 0.1 for *N2*? This is usually done by "discretizing" the range for *N2*; that is, a graph of points explored for *N1* vs *N2* would look like that shown in Figure 8.9.

FIGURE 8.9   Values of *N1* and *N2* explored with grid search

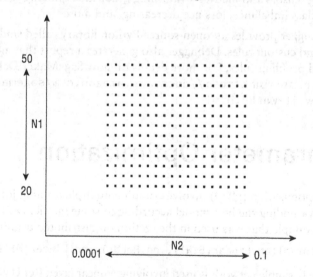

Random Search   Here, we randomly sample *N1* and *N2* from a distribution and use this specific combination of (*N1,N2*) to run an experiment. We can continue to randomly sample points until we reach a set maximum number of experiments or when a desired metric value is reached. On the same graph, points explored using random search would look like Figure 8.10.

FIGURE 8.10   Values of *N1* and *N2* explored with random search

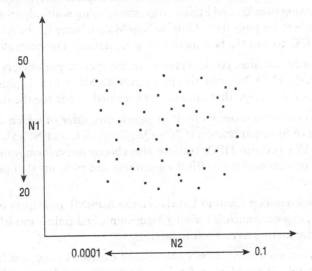

Bayesian Search   Bayesian optimization is a very popular algorithm for efficient, large-scale hyperparameter optimization. In both grid search and random search, no information learned from previous experiments was used to inform subsequent experiments with the aim of reaching a good answer while also reducing the total number of training jobs. With Bayesian optimization, the model's performance according to the metric we chose is modeled as a Gaussian process, which helps answer the question of what parameters (*N1* and *N2*) to try next based on all previous experiments. For more information about Bayesian optimization, you can refer to the following papers: `https://arxiv.org/abs/1206.2944` and `https://docs.aws.amazon.com/sagemaker/latest/dg/automatic-model-tuning-how-it-works.html`.

Multi-algorithm HPO   Until now, we were only changing *N1* and *N2* as they related to one "training algorithm," defined by the network parameters and the training optimizer parameters. It is typical to try solving an ML problem with multiple algorithms, so using a procedure that simultaneously explores multiple training algorithms is also useful.

You can use the AWS console or supported API calls to create an HPO job on Amazon Sage-Maker. These HPO jobs can use random search, Bayesian optimization with single or multi-algorithm cases. For a detailed example on how to run HPO jobs on Amazon SageMaker,

you can refer to this section of the official documentation: `https://docs.aws.amazon`
`.com/sagemaker/latest/dg/automatic-model-tuning-ex.html`.

You can use Amazon SageMaker's HPO functionality to tune your own training runs,
whether it uses one of the 17 built-in algorithms or algorithms that you bring in using
one of the supported frameworks (TensorFlow, PyTorch, MXNet, scikit-learn, etc.) or
your own container. SageMaker Autopilot can be used to automatically infer the type of
prediction problem for your tabular data and then explore several algorithms, including
XGBoost, neural networks, and logistic regression, using multi-algorithm HPO to find
the model that best fits your data. Outside SageMaker, many of the AI services on AWS
can perform HPO to find the best model for your dataset. For example:

- In Amazon Personalize, you can choose recipe-specific parameters or perform
  recipe-specific HPO. You can also perform Auto ML, which explores multiple recipes and uses the recipe that optimizes a specified metric for the final solution.

- Amazon Forecast includes six built-in algorithms, three of which allow for manual
  overriding of hyperparameters (CNN-QR, DeepAR+, and NPTS). CNN-QR
  and DeepAR+ perform HPO. You can also choose to perform AutoML to have
  Amazon Forecast explore multiple algorithms and pick one that performs best for
  your dataset.

- Amazon Rekognition Custom Labels can use AutoML to inspect input images
  and labels, explore multiple training algorithms, and train a model that maximizes
  performance metrics over a test dataset.

- Other services such as Amazon Comprehend Custom Labels, Amazon Fraud
  Detector, Lookout for Metrics, Lookout for Vision, and Lookout for Equipment
  all have the ability to run AutoML (usually involving multiple data preparation,
  training, and exploration strategies to find the best model for your input data).

Summary

In this chapter, we discussed ways that machine learning use cases are categorized—
unsupervised, supervised, and reinforcement learning. We also discussed how training can
be implemented in local and remote instances and the basics of distributed training and
hyperparameter optimization. Lastly, we discussed how training jobs can be monitored and
debugged using appropriate tools on AWS.

Exam Essentials

**Understand the difference between unsupervised, supervised, and reinforcement
learning.**   Learn how to read a use case description and map it to one of these types of
ML categories.

Understand the difference between data parallel and model parallel training.   Refer to the section on distributed training to learn when to use what, as related to the type of distributed training.

Know how monitoring services like CloudWatch can help track training jobs and deployed models from AI/ML services on AWS.   Refer to the section on Monitoring Training jobs to understand the difference between CloudTrail, and CloudWatch and how to use EventBridge.

Understand what hyperparameter optimization is and why it is an essential component of the ML lifecycle.   Hyperparameter optimization is an essential machine learning technique for finding the right parameters that optimize the model's performance relative to a particular metric.

Understand the most common HPO strategies such as random, grid search and Bayesian.   In particular, know that Bayesian search uses the outputs of the previous set of trials to inform the next set of hyper parameters to select in search space.

Review Questions

1. A customer is getting started with using deep learning to classify sports video clips. Video clips are tagged using a voting system open to the public on a website. The customer is confused as to what kind of problem this is. What do you tell the customer?

   A. This is an unsupervised learning problem since the tagging is not supervised by the customer.

   B. This is a supervised learning problem since tags from the community can be used as labels.

   C. This is a reinforcement learning problem since the website can be used as an environment that human agents interact with.

   D. This is a semi-supervised learning problem where the videos are first clustered into similar videos, followed by using a subset of the tags for classification.

2. You are generating an ML model for your team using Amazon SageMaker. Your team has a fixed cost budget on the total number of training jobs you can experiment with, but you still want to explore multiple parameters and deliver the best model to the business. What hyperparameter optimization (HPO) strategy will you use for this?

   A. Since the customer is on a budget, just experiment with a few sets of parameters manually

   B. Random search

   C. Bayesian optimization

   D. Search engine optimization (SEO)

3. You have a sparse dataset with hundreds of feature columns (X) and a predictor column (y) with numbers. The dataset also contains a significant portion of outliers. You have a simple linear regression model that is not performing well, and you think many of the features are not important. One of your colleagues asks you to try regularization. What type of regularization will you try first?

   A. L3

   B. ElasticNet

   C. L2

   D. L1

4. A customer has a dataset with millions of rows and is interested in using XGBoost to predict the value of a target variable. The dataset contains several missing values. What advice will you give the customer before she starts training? (Choose all that apply.)

   A. XGBoost cannot handle missing values.

   B. XGBoost handles missing values by treating each missing value as NaN.

   C. XGBoost supports missing values by default, and branch directions for missing values are learned during the training process.

   D. XGBoost supports missing values by treating missing values as 0 in some cases.

5. You have a dataset containing images of printers placed on tables. What built-in SageMaker algorithm can be used to identify the location of the printer with respect to the table?

   A. Object detection

   B. Image classification

   C. DeepAR

   D. Object2Vec

6. A customer would like to use historical sales data for predicting future sales of several items on their inventory for planning purposes. What services on AWS can help with this problem? (Choose all that apply.)

   A. Amazon Forecast

   B. DeepAR built-in algorithm on Amazon SageMaker

   C. Amazon Personalize

   D. AWS Lambda

7. You have a large language model that needs to be fine-tuned based on a custom dataset. The instances that you have access to cannot fit the model in memory, but you have access to multiple instances. Which of the following distributed training strategies will you use?

   A. Data parallel

   B. Model parallel

   C. Device parallel

   D. Instance parallel

8. Your team currently runs ML training on notebooks with the assumption that running these jobs locally on a notebook gives them access to logs. These logs are useful for fine-tuning and debugging their models. They feel that using a service like SageMaker will prevent them from having access to logs. What advice will you give them?

   A. Continue using the notebook; their assumption is correct.

   B. Training job logs can be obtained by contacting AWS.

   C. SageMaker training job logs can be found in CloudWatch logs.

   D. SageMaker training job logs can be found in CloudTrail logs.

9. Which of the following is the easiest way to react to a training job status change on Amazon SageMaker and trigger an action based on this change?

   A. Use EventBridge.

   B. Poll for the job status using a Lambda.

   C. Poll for the job status using an EC2 instance.

   D. Use SageMaker Debugger.

10. A customer archives news articles produced by major publications and would like to use machine learning to summarize these articles into short sentences. Manually summarizing each article produced so far will be impractical and costly. What built-in algorithm with Amazon SageMaker will you suggest the customer try out for this use case?

A. SageMaker Summarizer

B. SageMaker Sequence-to-Sequence

C. SageMaker NTM

D. SageMaker BlazingText

11. Consider the same use case as in the previous question. You have used Ground Truth to label the helmets on a subset of players. What algorithm would you use next to train a model to detect helmets on players?

A. Object detection using Single Shot Detector (SSD)

B. Image classification using Inception

C. Random Forest

D. ARIMA

Chapter

9

Model Evaluation

THE AWS CERTIFIED MACHINE LEARNING (ML) SPECIALTY EXAM OBJECTIVES COVERED IN THIS CHAPTER INCLUDE BUT ARE NOT LIMITED TO THE FOLLOWING:

✓ **Domain 3.0: Modeling**

- 3.5 Evaluate machine learning models

  - Common metrics related to machine learning

  - Common ways to visualize data, model metrics, and compare different machine learning models

✓ **Domain 4.0: Machine Learning Implementation and Operations**

- 4.2 Recommend and implement the appropriate machine learning services and features for a given problem

  - Details about what machine learning experiment management is about

  - Details about tools that can be used to track machine learning experiments based on the AI/ML service on AWS

Experiment management and model evaluation are important concepts you will use daily in your work with machine learning projects. In this chapter, we cover how experiment management is integrated with several services in the AI/ML stack on AWS and what metrics can be used in your experiments to evaluate ML models that you train.

Experiment Management

Machine learning (ML) practitioners today use experiment tracking solutions to track and compare various experimental trials involving different choices of data preprocessing and training strategies. Over time, manual and automated experimentation can result in many trials, and it becomes increasingly important to track your models and training jobs. With AI/ML services on AWS, the AWS console and corresponding APIs give you a way to track and log model training runs and lists of previous models. First, let's take a look at out-of-the-box tracking that is available for most AI/ML services on AWS that have custom modeling capabilities:

Rekognition Custom Labels Organizes resources in projects; each project can be associated with datasets and models. The describe-projects API action lists and describes all your Custom Labels projects in your account, in that region. These project details can also be viewed on the AWS console. Once you have the Project ARN of the project you are interested in, you can use the describe-project-versions API action; this includes details about training and testing data locations, training results, models generated, and information about hosted models (such as number of inference units).

Comprehend Custom Lets you train custom classifiers and entity recognizers with a custom set of documents. Once you train your custom models, you can use the list-document-classifiers or the list-entity-recognizer API call to receive a paginated list of trained models. Batch detection jobs and endpoints that are part of Comprehend can also be listed in a similar fashion.

Amazon Forecast Uses custom time series datasets to train predictors, which can then be used to create forecasts. All these entities (datasets, predictors, and forecasts) can be listed using the corresponding list-* command, for example list-predictors. This returns a list of ARNs, which can be used in subsequent describe-* calls. These resources can also be seen on the AWS console and are again account/region specific.

Amazon Personalize   Organizes datasets into dataset groups; you then use these datasets to create a solution (train a model), and then create a campaign (deploy the model) to get recommendations. As with Amazon Forecast, each of these resources can be listed and described using the appropriate API calls. The same information is presented in the AWS console.

Amazon SageMaker   Lets you build, train, tune, and deploy ML models at scale. Relevant to this section, you can keep a track of your labeling jobs, training jobs, trained models, and endpoints from the AWS console, or use APIs similar to the ones discussed in this section with other services (`list-` and `describe-`). SageMaker also provides a search API that helps with the following functions:

- List training jobs using properties, performance metrics, and any training job–specific metadata.

- Find the best training job based on some output metric (like validation accuracy).

- Trace a model's lineage by answering the following questions: What training job led to the creation of this model? What hyperparameters were used to train this model? What dataset was used? You can also evaluate models and search for training jobs using the console or the search API.

- SageMaker offers a way to organize your trials using Experiments. Experiments can contain multiple trials, and trials can contain one or more trial components that are each processing, training, or transforming jobs. Amazon SageMaker Studio is an end-to-end IDE for ML that also includes an experiment browser. Here, you can double-click on an experiment to display all the trials in that experiment; you can then look into the trial components in each trial, and then the details of each trial component. One of the most important features of having an experiment management system is the ability to compare and visualize different experiments. You can filter the trial components to show just the training jobs, and then create charts that compare multiple training jobs based on hyperparameters used and metrics generated. For a tutorial on how to do this, visit the following site: `https://docs.aws.amazon.com/sagemaker/latest/dg/experiments-mnist.html#experiments-mnist-compare-trials`.

You may choose to use other experiment management tools that work with AWS ML services like SageMaker or other self-managed ML tools on AWS. TensorBoard, MLFlow, Kubeflow, and Pachyderm are examples of tools that can help with experiment management. It is out of the scope of this book to go over the details of these and other options that exist on experiment management capabilities.

Metrics and Visualization

We described some ways to analyze experiments conducted on AWS AI/ML services, which include charting and visualization on SageMaker Studio experiments, as well as with individual services. In other sections such as the one on distributed training and hyperparameter optimization (HPO), we discussed how metrics that were used in a toy model (mean squared error) can inform how well a particular training job performed or what parameters to try next in an HPO context. In this section, we dive deeper into some of the most popular metrics that you will encounter as an ML practitioner or data scientist, both for models trained using AWS AI services with custom modeling capabilities and for your own algorithms that you can train using Amazon SageMaker.

Let's start with a simple toy example that describes a binary classification problem. Your data consists of only two features, X1 and X2, and you need to classify each data point as either Class 1 or Class 2 based on previous labeled data. In the diagram shown in Figure 9.1, we plot all the training data, with Class 1 represented as a circle (o), and Class 2 represented as an x.

FIGURE 9.1   Data from a toy two-class classification problem

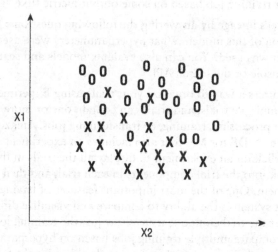

A common algorithm used for these purposes is called a support vector machine (SVM). We outlined this algorithm in a separate section in Chapter 8, "Model Training." As discussed, SVM is used to build a linear or nonlinear decision boundary that separates the two classes of points we have. Let's continue this example using the linear decision boundary case. Here, the algorithm tries to draw a line (decision boundary) that separates the two classes well. As you can see in Figure 9.2, the SVM model does well to classify most of the points correctly; everything above the line is classified as Class 1 (o) and everything below as Class 2 (x). There are, however, some points that are misclassified; that is, there are some Class 2 (x) points above the line, and some Class 1 (o) points below the line. Typically, in this case, a better, nonlinear kernel can be used with SVM, or a more complicated neural network can be used to classify the points using a nonlinear decision boundary. However, we are not going to explore that case. Here, we can use this example to discuss some basic metrics that you will encounter.

FIGURE 9.2   Example SVM hyperplane separating the two classes of data

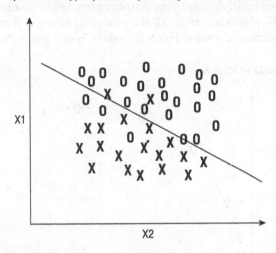

True Positives (TP)   Number of Class 1 (o) points correctly classified as Class 1 (assume for now that Class 1 represents the "positive" class)

True Negatives (TN)   Number of Class 2 (x) points correctly classified as Class 2

False Positives (FP)   Number of Class 2 (x) points wrongly classified as Class 1 (o)

False Negatives (FN)   Number of Class 1 (o) points wrongly classified as Class 2 (x)

These four metrics are useful as is for analyzing your training jobs, but we can derive even more scores and analyses based on TP, TN, FP, and FN, as discussed next.

Confusion Matrix   A table with these four metrics that looks similar to this:

	Class 1	Class 2
Class 1	TP	FP
Class 2	FN	TN

Precision   The percentage of positive predictions that actually belong to the positive class, i.e., TP / (TP + FP).

Recall   The percentage of correct positive predictions relative to the total number of positive examples, i.e., TP / (TP + FN). Recall is also referred to as the true positive rate (TPR).

False Positive Rate (FPR)   The percentage of positive predictions when the true value is negative, i.e., FP / (FP + TN).

F1 Score   The harmonic mean of precision and recall: F1 = 2 Precision × Recall / (Precision + Recall).

ROC Curve The ROC (receiver operator characteristic) curve is a plot of TPR to FPR, usually created from multiple confusion matrices obtained by changing a classification threshold. The ROC plot summarizes all the confusion matrices that you could get by changing the parameters of your decision boundary in one graph. See Figure 9.3.

FIGURE 9.3   Example ROC curve

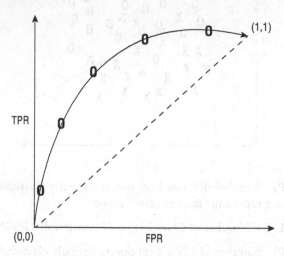

Area under the Curve (AUC) You can use AUC to quickly compare two models that have two separate ROC curves. It calculates the AUC for each ROC graph. In the plot in Figure 9.4, since the ROC curve for model 1 (o) has higher AUC at all thresholds than model 2 (x), we can conclude that model 1 is generally better for our use case.

FIGURE 9.4   Example showing comparison of two ROC curves by calculating the AUC

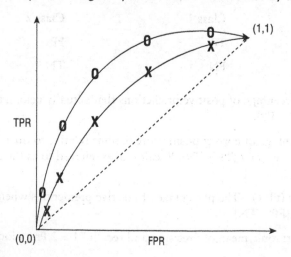

Precision-Recall Curves   Show the trade-off between precision and recall. You can also calculate the AUC for a precision-recall curve. A typical precision recall curve looks like the graph shown in Figure 9.5.

FIGURE 9.5   Example precision vs. recall curve

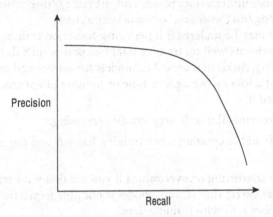

Metrics in AWS AI/ML Services

Although many of the metrics listed above are relevant to classification problems, others are relevant to regression problems, such as mean absolute error (MAE), mean squared error (MSE), and root mean squared error (RMSE).

It is typical to use different metrics for different types of problems; for example, Amazon Forecast publishes RMSE, WQL (weighted quantile loss), and WAPE (weighted absolute percentage error) for all forecast predictors that you train. You can learn more about metrics specific to services on AWS at these sites:

- Amazon Forecast: `https://docs.aws.amazon.com/forecast/latest/dg/metrics.html`

- Amazon Personalize (mean reciprocal rank, normalized discounted cumulative gain, etc.): `https://docs.aws.amazon.com/personalize/latest/dg/working-with-training-metrics.html`

- Rekognition Custom Labels (recall, precision, F1 score): `https://docs.aws.amazon.com/rekognition/latest/customlabels-dg/tr-metrics-use.html`

- Amazon Comprehend Custom classification (accuracy, precision, recall, F1, Hamming loss, etc.): `https://docs.aws.amazon.com/comprehend/latest/dg/cer-doc-class.html`

- Amazon Comprehend Custom Entity Recognizer (precision, recall, F1 score): `https://docs.aws.amazon.com/comprehend/latest/dg/cer-metrics.html`

Amazon SageMaker publishes several metrics for each of the 17 built-in algorithms, as well as newer features relevant to model bias (SageMaker Clarify) and system- or framework-level metrics from SageMaker Debugger and Profiler.

Amazon SageMaker Data Wrangler lets you create visualizations of your training data frame, including histograms and scatterplots, or create your own custom visualizations using your own code. For more information, please visit: `https://docs.aws.amazon.com/sagemaker/latest/dg/data-wrangler-analyses.html`

Your trained model may be underfit if it performs poorly on training data. On the other hand, if your model performs well on training data but poorly on validation data, you may have a case of overfitting. Analyzing most ML models for under- and overfitting involves looking at the graph of a loss metric against time or number of epochs. Your model may be underfit or undertrained if

- The training loss remains flat or is very slowly decreasing.

- The training loss is still decreasing when training has reached the maximum number of epochs.

Your model may be overfitting or overtrained if you see that your train loss curve diverges from the validation loss curve; that is, your model is not able to generalize well with unseen (validation) data but does well with training data.

If your model training is slow, you may want to stop your training job early, change parameters, and trigger another training job. This is important since training jobs can be long and expensive; this is especially true when you are running an HPO job that spawns multiple training jobs. Automatically stopping long-running training can help save on cost, avoid overfitting, and reduce your experiment cycles overall. Amazon SageMaker provides an early stopping capability that can be enabled for HPO jobs; read more about it here: `https://docs.aws.amazon.com/sagemaker/latest/dg/automatic-model-tuning-early-stopping.html`.

SageMaker Debugger provides several built-in rules that can help debug model training data in real time. These include

- Class imbalance

- Stalled training

- Overfitting

- Goodness of a confusion matrix

- Overweighting some features

Summary

In this chapter, we discussed tools used to manage experiments. We also discussed how to evaluate your machine learning models using typical metrics.

Exam Essentials

Understand how to track and manage different trials with experiment management.   AI/ML services on AWS help track datasets, models, training jobs, deployed endpoints, and batch inference jobs on the AWS console or using APIs.

Know how to detect the difference between overfitting and underfitting.   Graphs of your training and validation losses can inform you of how well your model generalizes with unseen data.

Understand how to evaluate common machine learning models using metrics.   Each model may emit one or more metrics that summarize how well the model fits the data. On AWS, different AI services and built-in algorithms on SageMaker provide a metrics dashboard that can be useful for evaluating and visualizing model performance.

Review Questions

1. You are tasked with compiling a list of all training jobs with high-level metrics in a table. What typical APIs would you use to do this for AI/ML services on AWS?

    A. `list-` and `describe-` APIs

    B. `get-` and `describe-` APIs

    C. `getlist-` and `describelist-` APIs

    D. `create-` and `describe-` APIs

2. A customer would like to track and compare different SageMaker trials involving training and batch transform jobs. What SageMaker feature(s) can help with this? (Choose all that apply.)

    A. SageMaker Neo

    B. SageMaker MLtracker

    C. SageMaker Experiment

    D. SageMaker Search

3. A model you trained has the following training (solid line) and validation (dashed line) curves (see the following graphic). What term describes your model correctly?

    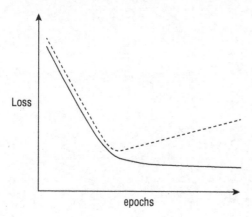

    A. Underfitting

    B. Overfitting

    C. Diverging

    D. None of the above

4. A customer has a time series dataset that is used to train a forecasting model using Amazon Forecast. Which of the following metrics should they choose to evaluate and compare multiple forecasting models? (Choose all that apply.)

   A. Root mean squared error (RMSE)

   B. Weighted quantile loss (WQL)

   C. F1 score

   D. Recall

5. A two-class classification model that you have trained results in the following confusion matrix. You are tasked with calculating the false positive rate since subject matter experts in your company need it to be as low as possible. What is the value of the false positive rate based on this confusion matrix?

	Class 1	Class 2
Class 1	TP = 50	FP = 5
Class 2	FN = 2	TN = 5

   A. 10

   B. 0.1

   C. 0.5

   D. 0.25

6. An image classification algorithm is used to distinguish between benign and malignant tumors detected on X-ray images of patients. Your company wants to correctly detect all patients (100 percent) who actually have cancer. What metric should you use to tune your models?

   A. Accuracy

   B. Squared error

   C. Recall

   D. Precision

7.   A customer has a dataset with two features, X1 and X2. When plotted on a graph, this customer's dataset looks like the following graphic. The customer would like to distinguish two types of rows (labeled as "o" and "x" in the graph) in the dataset by building a neural network. What advice will you give the customer to help with this use case?

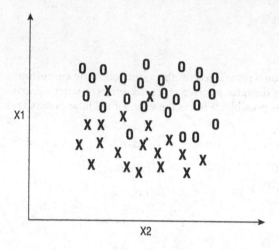

A.   Neural networks can be used for image classification jobs but not for classification of numerical data in a tabular dataset.

B.   Neural networks can only be used for regression and forecasting use cases but not for classification.

C.   Build a random forest classifier using neural networks to classify this dataset.

D.   Neural networks can be used to train this model. Tell the customer to go ahead and try building and training a model.

8.   You want to create a model that can classify fraudulent credit card transactions. What objective metric will you use to determine how good your model is on Amazon SageMaker Autopilot?

A.   AUC (area under the ROC curve)

B.   F1 score

C.   Number of false negatives

D.   Number of false positives

9. A company's employees have recently been receiving many spam and phishing emails. The company has a machine learning team that would like to explore AWS services that can help analyze the subject line and decide whether an incoming email is spam. Spam emails will be immediately deleted and not forwarded to employees. After some exploration, the ML team has decided to try Comprehend Custom for this purpose. What metric should the ML team use to evaluate their model?

   A. Number of spam emails not detected

   B. F1 score

   C. Number of spam emails detected

   D. Number of normal emails detected

10. An ML experiment management system lets you compare multiple training jobs by creating interesting visual plots. You have been using this system to build hundreds of gradient boosted trees using a popular algorithm for the past month and want to look at the impact of changing two hyperparameters—maximum depth and learning rate—on the validation accuracy of the model. To this end, which of the following methods will provide you with the *most* amount of information that can help you analyze your experiments quickly with the least amount of work?

   A. Create a scatter plot with the max depth and learning rate as the axes, and color each point by the validation accuracy.

   B. Create a bubble plot with the max depth and learning rate as the axes and have the size of the bubble represent the validation accuracy.

   C. Create a line plot with two y-axes, one for max depth and another for learning rate; have the validation accuracy on the x-axis.

   D. Create a bar chart for each trial representing the validation accuracy.

Chapter

10

Model Deployment and Inference

So far, we covered what algorithms and services you can use to solve some of your business use cases with machine learning on AWS, how to manage your ML experiments, and how to evaluate if your trained model in fact solves your business use case. The next step usually involves either setting up an API to do real-time inference with your trained model or to apply your trained model to a batch of data (batch inference). In this chapter, we cover deployment features available in AI-level services on AWS, as well as dive deeper into deployment on SageMaker, including deployment and testing strategies.

Deployment for AI Services

In Chapter 1, "AWS AI ML Stack," we explored various AI services offered by AWS, some of which had the ability to train custom models based on your own input data. For example:

- **Rekognition Custom Labels**—Train a model based on a dataset that you label for scene-level classification or finding objects in images.

- **Amazon Forecast**—Trains a forecasting model based on time series data provided with statistical and deep learning–based algorithms and other training-specific parameters such as the frequency of the data and the forecast horizon.

- **Amazon Personalize**—Trains a recommendation system based on user, item, and interaction data for user-user, user-item, and item-item personalization.

- **Amazon Comprehend Custom**—Trains models for custom document classification and custom entity extraction.

- **Amazon Kendra**—Creates an intelligent search interface to an updatable index of documents and lets users receive specific answers to natural language questions.

- **Amazon Transcribe Custom**—Trains custom speech transcription models based on domain-specific vocabularies and audio transcription data.

Apart from these services, other recently announced AI services such as Amazon Fraud Detector, Lookout for Equipment, Lookout for Metrics, and Lookout for Vision also create custom models based on your datasets; however, discussion about deployment of these services is beyond of the scope of this book.

Once you have trained the respective models for the services just listed, trained models are organized within the console as projects, solutions, or classifiers. Generally, before you can start making predictions, you need to first "deploy" or "host" these models.

For AI services, the models are hosted in a managed AWS account that is owned by the service. If you need more control over the hosting container, architecture, security, and autoscaling groups, you can use Amazon SageMaker. In the case of Amazon SageMaker, you have access to the trained model artifact, but the model is hosted in an Amazon Sage-Maker owned account (i.e., not your AWS account). If you require even more control of your hosting infrastructure, you can use other services to deploy your trained model such as Amazon EC2, AWS Lambda, AWS Fargate, or Amazon EKS.

For the AI services just discussed, let's take a look at how you can host models and obtain predictions:

- **Rekognition Custom Labels**—Once you are ready to host your model as an API for use in predictions, you can "start" it using the console or with supported SDKs. While the model is starting, you can check progress using the console or using the `DescribeProjectVersions` API. Once your model has started, you can use the `DetectCustomLabels` API to make predictions.

- **Amazon Forecast**—A forecasting model is called a Predictor in Amazon Forecast. Once you have trained a Predictor, you check Predictor metrics before moving on to using the model using the `CreateForecast` operation. You can then query the forecast using specific `item_id` and date filters using the `QueryForecast` operation.

- **Amazon Personalize**—Training a model in Personalize is called creating a solution. Once a solution has been created, you can host a solution version by "creating a campaign." Once you have successfully hosted your model, you can do one of two things to get predictions:

  - Call the `GetRecommendations` API to make recommendations from a trained model. When you do this, Amazon Personalize generates scores for items in your items dataset based on user interaction data and metadata.

  - Call the `GetPersonalizedRanking` API to get a list of recommended items that are reranked for a specific user. You may also filter results based on custom criteria and perform batch predictions.

- **Amazon Comprehend Custom**—Once you have trained your model, you can create a custom endpoint for Comprehend Custom and do one of two things (based on the model you created):

  - Call the `ClassifyDocument` API to classify the document as one of the classes you defined during training, or

  - Call the `DetectEntities` API to return a list of entities and entity types for a document you input. You can also perform these actions on the AWS console.

- **Amazon Kendra**—Once you have created an index in Kendra with all your documents, you can immediately start using the underlying trained models by querying the index, filtering queries, tuning responses, and providing feedback. Unlike the other services on the list, there is no specific API action similar to creating and hosting a model or creating an endpoint.

- **Amazon Transcribe Custom**—Once you have trained a custom, domain-specific language model for your speech-to-text use case, you can use the `StartTranscriptionJob` API to transcribe your input audio.

Deployment for Amazon SageMaker

We briefly described model hosting in Part I of this book. For completeness, and for readers who may be interested in forming their own learning path, we recap some of the information you already learned here.

Training a model on SageMaker results in a trained model artifact on Amazon S3 (a `model.tar.gz` file). To get predictions from this model, you can do one of the following:

- Host a persistent endpoint for real-time predictions, where SageMaker provides fully managed model hosting services and generates a private HTTPS endpoint, where your model can return prediction outputs.

- Use the SageMaker batch transform APIs to apply model predictions to an entire test dataset, where SageMaker initializes the requested number of compute instances and distributes inference workload involving getting predictions for a large test dataset between these instances.

In this section we dive deeper into what SageMaker endpoints look like under the hood and provide useful variants that you may encounter as a Machine Learning Specialist Solutions Architect.

SageMaker Hosting: Under the Hood

Like training on SageMaker, hosting on SageMaker is dependent on containers, although a deep understanding or the need to build containers before hosting is not necessary. For real-time endpoints, SageMaker uses a trained model artifact (`model.tar.gz` file containing the saved model) from S3 and an inference container from ECR within multiple, auto-scalable instances (Figure 10.1). When a client needs a prediction from this model, a `POST` call (via one of the APIs) is made, which then is directed to one of the instances hosting the model. In the case of multimodel endpoints, each instance can hold multiple models.

FIGURE 10.1   SageMaker real-time endpoints under the hood

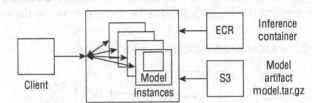

When hosting a real-time endpoint:

- SageMaker uncompresses the provided model artifact into the `/opt/ml/model` path and allows you to access the same model directly from the inference code. Built-in algorithm and framework containers provided by SageMaker are structured in a similar way.

- SageMaker starts serving a model using the following Docker command: `docker run [Image] serve`.

- SageMaker provides an HTTPS endpoint to access your model for predictions via authorized API calls. SageMaker handles authorization with IAM identity-based policies, where you can specify allowed and denied actions and resources, as well as condition keys. To learn more about this, please visit `https://docs.aws.amazon .com/sagemaker/latest/dg/security_iam_service-with-iam.html`.

- SageMaker performs health checks that time out in 2 seconds before hosting the endpoint; a failed endpoint health check will result in your model not being hosted. You can perform custom health checks, and it is routine to load a model successfully during a health check. This health check happens in the `/ping:8080` route.

- Real-time invocations happen in the `/invocations:8080` route and time out at 60 seconds; this means that the model must return a prediction within 60 seconds. It is routine for a model invocation to be much faster than this upper limit of 60 seconds.

- Removing a model artifact after a model is hosted may result in unpredictable results; although the endpoint may continue to provide predictions temporarily, model updates and autoscaling actions may fail.

- Outputs and errors recorded in the container or inference code are sent to CloudWatch logs.

- You can provide a source folder with your inference code and choose a prebuilt container rather than building and pushing a custom container. For more information on this, please see `https://docs.aws.amazon.com/sagemaker/latest/dg/pre-built-containers-frameworks-deep-learning.html`.

- For more information on hosting, please visit the SageMaker documentation page on hosting: `https://docs.aws.amazon.com/sagemaker/latest/dg/how-it-works-deployment.html`.

For SageMaker Batch Transform operations, the dataset is split and sent to multiple instances, where an agent iterates through the dataset collecting inferences; the inferences are then collated before sending results back to S3, where you can access them (Figure 10.2).

FIGURE 10.2   SageMaker Batch transform under the hood

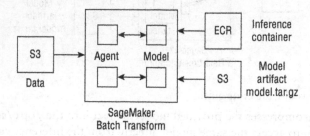

When using SageMaker Batch Transform:

- SageMaker manages the provisioning and deprovisioning of instances that are used for batch transform; you only pay for the time the resources are in use.

- Typically, you first instantiate a `Transformer` class from the trained model and then launch a Batch Transform job using this `Transformer`. For example, if you are using Python code to do this:

```
transformer = xgb_model.transformer(
    instance_count=1,
    instance_type='ml.m4.xlarge',
    output_path=batch_output
)

transformer.transform(
    data=batch_input,
    data_type='S3Prefix',
    content_type='text/csv',
    split_type='Line'
)
transformer.wait()
```

For more information about using Docker with SageMaker for advanced deployments, please visit https://docs.aws.amazon.com/sagemaker/latest/dg/docker-containers.html.

Advanced Deployment Topics

Next, we discuss some advanced deployment–specific topics such as how to implement autoscaling and different styles of endpoint deployment strategies using SageMaker.

Autoscaling Endpoints

Autoscaling SageMaker endpoints, similar to autoscaling EC2 instances, adjusts the number of instances based on your incoming workload or prediction requests (or any metric that is available as a CloudWatch metric; more on this later). Autoscaling can increase or decrease the number of instances that hold your model. As such, there are two ways of setting up the autoscaling action:

- Target tracking scaling (recommended in most use cases): You define a scaling metric and a target value. Application Autoscaling will automatically create a CloudWatch alarm and calculate the adjustment required to serve your predictions in terms of number of instances.

- Step scaling (recommended for advanced users): Apart from defining the scaling metric and target, you also define *how* your endpoint should be scaled when the target threshold is crossed. To do this, you additionally define the lower bound, the upper bound, and the amount by which to scale.

For both types of scaling, we also specify the following parameters using the API for endpoint configuration:

- Target metric (for example, InvocationsPerInstance) and a target value
- Minimum and maximum number of instances for the endpoint
- Cool-down period for scale-in and scale-out activities (which defaults to 300 seconds). You may also disable scale-in if your situation only requires that the endpoints scale out (or add instances).

Let's take a look at a simple autoscaling policy that you might use for one of your SageMaker endpoints:

```
{
    "TargetValue": 70.0,
    "PredefinedMetricSpecification":
    {
        "PredefinedMetricType": "SageMakerVariantInvocationsPerInstance"
    }
}
```

This example uses the `InvocationsPerInstance` metric with a target value of 70; autoscaling will attempt to keep the average invocations per instance at or around a value of 70. Let's take a look at a slightly more involved example using a custom metric:

```
{
    "TargetValue": 50,
    "CustomizedMetricSpecification":
    {
        "MetricName": "CPUUtilization",
        "Namespace": "/aws/sagemaker/Endpoints",
        "Dimensions": [
            {"Name": "EndpointName", "Value": "myendpointname" },
            {"Name": "VariantName","Value": "variant1"}
        ],
        "Statistic": "Average",
        "Unit": "Percent"
    }
}
```

Here, we use autoscaling to keep the average CPU utilization to 50 percent across all instances. Note also how you can target a particular production variant for autoscaling (here, only `variant1` will scale out or scale in according to this metric). You can then apply this autoscaling policy to your SageMaker endpoint using the `PutScalingPolicy` API call in Application Autoscaling.

Deployment Strategies

Similar to traditional application deployment, SageMaker along with other services on AWS support various deployment strategies. Here, we take a look at a few common application deployment strategies and how they apply to SageMaker endpoints for machine learning models. In the following descriptions, assume that you have two models—model A and model B. Also assume that these models can be launched onto endpoint A and endpoint B, or the same endpoint based on the strategy:

Re-create Strategy   Shut down endpoint A and use model B to launch endpoint B. This implies that there is some downtime where model requests are not being served; for this reason, re-create strategy may rarely be used in practice (Figure 10.3). On SageMaker, first stop endpoint A:

delete_endpoint(endpoint_A)

Then, start endpoint B:

create_endpoint(endpoint_B, config_name)

FIGURE 10.3   Re-create strategy showing how to stop endpoint A and start endpoint B

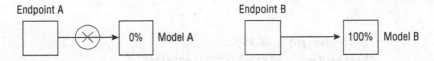

Ramped Strategy   Gradually shift traffic from Production variant A to Production variant B behind the same endpoint (Figure 10.4). To do this on SageMaker, first create a new endpoint configuration and update the variants by passing in a list of `new_production_variants` to the following API call:

`create_endpoint_config_from_existing`

When creating a production variant, set the initial weight of model B to 10% of model A, continue testing, and then gradually increase model B's weight to 100% by using the `update_endpoint` API. When it first receives this request, Amazon SageMaker first sets the status to "Updating." After the change is made, the status returns to "InService" again.

FIGURE 10.4   Ramped strategy showing how to gradually shift from endpoint A to endpoint B

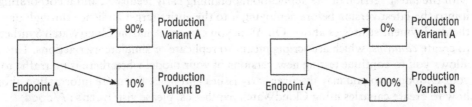

Blue/Green Strategy   When you only need to update the model behind an existing endpoint, use the ramped strategy, since you can point to a new model and gradually shift production traffic to a new variant. On the other hand, when you need to change the instance type and the model behind each production variant, create another production variant and then update the weight of the new variant to 100 after conducting tests. You can use the `UpdateEndpointWeightsAndCapacities` API call to switch the new variant as follows:

```
sm.update_endpoint_weights_and_capacities(
    EndpointName=endpoint_name,
    DesiredWeightsAndCapacities=[
        {
```

```
            "DesiredWeight": 0.25,
            "VariantName": variant1["VariantName"]
        },
        {
            "DesiredWeight": 0.75,
            "VariantName": variant2["VariantName"]
        }
    ]
)
```

Testing Strategies

The strategies mentioned in the "Deployment Strategies" section talk about how you can deploy new versions of your model into a production deployment endpoint. Testing strategies, often confused with some deployment strategies, let you control the target audience/users/clients and compare models with predefined metrics. Furthermore, testing may involve every aspect of your entire machine learning application and not just the model and the hosting endpoint. Here are a few testing strategies:

Canary Testing   Generally, canary testing involves targeting a small set of customers with the latest version of the application, obtaining early feedback, and incorporating it into the latest version before deploying it to the entire target audience through one of the deployment strategies above. On AWS, you can use Amazon CloudWatch Synthetics to create *canaries*, which are scripts meant to replicate or simulate user actions. This allows you to continue testing new versions of your model when there is no traffic to your endpoint, so you may discover early issues and bugs. For more information about how to create canaries using CloudWatch Synthetics, please visit https://docs .aws.amazon.com/AmazonCloudWatch/latest/monitoring/ CloudWatch_Synthetics_Canaries_Create.html.

Shadow Testing   While you can use canary testing and simulations to discover some early issues, you may still not have metrics/feedback from a sufficient number of real users, since newer versions of your application are never made available to a significant portion of users. On AWS, you can route your incoming requests through a Lambda function, which then mirrors traffic from your production application to the shadow application.

A/B Testing   Production variants discussed in the "Deployment Strategies" section can be used to route a fraction of the traffic to two or more back-end models. You can also target a specific variant based on business rules that you evaluate in a different portion of the entire application—for example, the front end or API layer. Routing rules may also involve other contextual data such as geolocation, browser type, application or device type, and user history. Based on the metrics and feedback collected, you can promote one of your production variants to receive 100 percent of the traffic. Apart from pure model metrics, other feedback and metrics may affect your choice. For example, a slower, slightly more accurate model may disproportionately affect the overall user experience and result in more churn from your web front end than a faster model that is slightly less accurate. Of course, the opposite case may also be true; this is why an A/B test of the complete system is important before upgrading one or more parts of your machine learning application, including the trained model itself.

Summary

In this chapter, we discussed how various AI/ML services on AWS allow users to deploy or host models. With Amazon SageMaker, more complex patterns of testing and deployment were covered, including A/B testing, canary testing, and blue/green deployment strategies.

Exam Essentials

Understand how AWS Services organize trained models and hosted endpoints. Most AI/ML services on AWS that give you the ability to train custom models also let you host your model as an endpoint for generating predictions. Amazon SageMaker provides you with a deeper level of control for launching, maintaining, and updating inference endpoints for your own custom models.

Know the difference between A/B testing, canary testing, and blue/green deployment. Know how to implement different deployment and testing strategies using AWS tools from a theoretical level.

Understand the difference between testing and deployment strategies. Testing is usually used to measure how good a new version of the entire machine learning application is, before using a deployment strategy to promote a specific version of the model or entire application code.

Review Questions

1. A customer that is currently exploring Amazon Kendra recently read that Amazon Sage-Maker provides users with several options to host, maintain, and update endpoints. The customer is wondering if Kendra models can be hosted on SageMaker. What advice will you give them?

   A. It is easy to host Amazon Kendra models on SageMaker with one click on the console or with any supported API.

   B. You cannot host Kendra models on SageMaker.

   C. You will first need to export your Kendra models, and import the same in SageMaker for hosting.

   D. SageMaker APIs can connect to various AI-level services, including Kendra.

2. A customer would like to deploy a model trained on one of their on-premises workstations on AWS. What is the easiest way to do this?

   A. Build a model-hosting service using EC2 instances and upload their model to this custom service.

   B. Use SageMaker training to retrain their model on AWS, and then host the same using EC2 instances as an endpoint.

   C. Use SageMaker training to retrain their model on AWS and then host the same using SageMaker endpoints.

   D. Use the trained model as is to deploy an endpoint on Amazon SageMaker.

3. A customer has trained a recommendation system using Amazon Personalize and needs a way to provide engineers on her team with an API endpoint for generating recommendations for users visiting their e-commerce website. What is the easiest way to provide this functionality to her engineering team?

   A. Use a SageMaker endpoint.

   B. Create a Personalize campaign from the trained solution.

   C. Create a Personalize solution from the trained campaign.

   D. Use API Gateway and Lambda.

4. A customer with a production SageMaker endpoint observes that traffic to the endpoint has been increasing rapidly over the past few weeks. What should the customer do to successfully serve users in the weeks to follow? (Choose all that apply.)

   A. Use Production variants.

   B. Use a new endpoint with a larger instance type.

   C. Set up autoscaling.

   D. Block traffic to the new customers.

5. You would like to release a new version of a web application that points to a more accurate machine learning model behind an endpoint. You have selected a small group of 20 beta testers and have also set up a group of simulated users to test out this new functionality. What testing strategy is appropriate to use in this case?

   A. A/B testing

   B. Canary testing

   C. Blue/green testing

   D. Red/black testing

6. You are rolling out a new service for external clients. In order to quickly test and roll back changes, you want to deploy the service to a small subset of servers first before rolling it out broadly to production. You also want this system to provide early alarms before customers are impacted. Which of the following test strategies would you use?

   A. Canary release

   B. Rolling release

   C. Blue/green release

   D. Shadow release

7. You are rolling out major updates to an existing ML-based service for external clients. You have a model in production that is currently serving traffic and a separate model in a different AWS account and environment that you are currently using to run user acceptance testing and QA. Once QA testing is complete, you will switch all traffic to the new model. Which of the following release strategies does this correspond to?

   A. Canary release

   B. Rolling release

   C. Blue/green release

   D. Shadow release

8. Which of the following statements is true regarding SageMaker model hosting?

   A. SageMaker model hosting supports autoscaling to elastically scale in or out depending on the incoming client traffic.

   B. SageMaker model hosting allows clients to make requests over HTTPS.

   C. SageMaker model hosting requires a model.tar.gz artifact in S3 and an inference container in ECR.

   D. All of the above options are correct.

9. Which of the following statements is true regarding SageMaker Batch Transform? (Choose all that apply.)

   A. SageMaker Batch Transform supports autoscaling to elastically scale in or out depending on the incoming client traffic.

   B. SageMaker Batch Transform creates a persistent instance or cluster that remains online even after all the inferences have been computed.

C. SageMaker Batch Transform requires a model.tar.gz artifact in S3 and an inference container in ECR.

D. SageMaker Batch Transform uses an agent to distribute the incoming dataset across multiple hosts and collate the results before sending them back to Amazon S3 for storage.

10. For which of the following services is the model hosting managed by AWS and not controlled by the customer? (Choose all that apply.)

A. Amazon Rekognition

B. Amazon Kendra

C. Amazon Fargate

D. Amazon SageMaker

Chapter 11

Application Integration

THE AWS CERTIFIED MACHINE LEARNING (ML) SPECIALTY EXAM OBJECTIVES COVERED IN THIS CHAPTER INCLUDE BUT ARE NOT LIMITED TO THE FOLLOWING:

✓ **Domain 4.0: Machine Learning Implementation and Operations**

- 4.4 Deploy and operationalize machine learning solutions

  - Details about how to integrate with on-premises systems

  - Details about how to integrate ML models with Cloud Systems

  - Details about how to integrate with Edge Systems

  - Details about how to integrate with front-end systems

Once you have created your ML model (or models), the next step is to integrate it with other systems so that predictions made by the model are utilized in some way. This chapter discusses the following integration patterns:

- Integration with on-premises systems
- Integration with cloud systems
- Integration with front-end libraries

Let's get started!

Integration with On-Premises Systems

Across the ML development lifecycle, we encounter several architectures that involve partly developing on-prem and partly developing on the cloud. We also group this pattern under "hybrid" architectures. Now, why is there a need to develop these ML systems in a hybrid way? Can't you do everything on the cloud? Yes, you can, but some other constraints may prevent you from operating entirely in the cloud:

- Depending on the maturity of the organization on the cloud, some business-critical systems may still be operating on-prem. These systems may satisfy any and all functional requirements even though there may be advantages when migrating these systems to the cloud. As such, due to the lack of a need or permission to migrate these systems, you may still have systems on-prem.

- Data of certain types of institutions (such as financial service or health care) may be extremely sensitive. Although data on the cloud is also extremely secure, customers may not yet be comfortable transferring all their data to the cloud. As always, security is a shared responsibility between the customer and AWS; for more information, start here: https://aws.amazon.com/compliance/shared-responsibility-model.

- Customers may be interested in extending their on-prem data center to the cloud or may be interested in specific use cases like disaster recovery on the cloud.

- Many companies use VMWare virtualization software for systems on-prem and may want to continue using the same skill sets. On AWS, customers can easily lift and shift their applications with VMware on AWS. In these situations, there may still be systems running on the cloud and on-prem depending on each use case. Training and education on cloud-based alternatives of systems that customers have in place on-prem is necessary to begin the process of migration.

- There is a need for very-low-latency local data processing—for example, in the case of ML models at the edge in factories or other locations without Internet accessibility.

AWS provides a broad range of services that help build hybrid applications. Let's go through a few of these services (for a full list, visit https://aws.amazon.com/hybrid/services).

- *AWS Outposts* allows you to use supported services such as Amazon EC2, Amazon EBS, Amazon S3, container-based services such as Amazon EKS, and database services such as Amazon RDS on AWS Outposts and analytics services such as Amazon EMR on-prem.
- *AWS Wavelength* supports low-latency and high-bandwidth applications on the 5G network by allowing 5G mobile services to reach application servers or back-end systems hosted on wavelength zones.
- *AWS Local Zones* places storage, compute, database, and other services close to a large population, industry, or IT center.
- *AWS Snowball Edge* and *Snowcone* are ruggedized edge devices that can be used as a means to migrate data or run edge compute applications.
- *Amazon RDS on VMware* lets you run a managed RDS database on-prem.
- *Amazon ECS* and *EKS Anywhere* let you run containerized applications based on ECS or EKS on-prem.
- *AWS Direct Connect* lets you have a private connection from on-prem to applications running inside a VPC on AWS.
- *AWS Storage Gateway, AWS Backup, AWS DataSync,* and the *AWS Transfer Family of Services* let you store, transfer, and back up data that exists on-prem to the cloud.
- *AWS IoT Family of Services* such as AWS IoT SiteWise, IoT Core, and AWS Greengrass let you run applications, including ML models at the edge.
- *SageMaker Edge Manager* lets you run ML models on fleets of devices and involves an agent that runs on the edge as well as a connection from models trained on SageMaker to the edge. Models are compiled with SageMaker Neo before deploying to the edge.

With this background, let's now discuss primary patterns of integration with on-prem systems when it comes to machine learning applications:

- Train locally and deploy locally, but send logs to the cloud for dashboarding and broader visibility.
- Train locally but deploy on the cloud. In such cases, models trained with popular ML frameworks can be easily uploaded to Amazon S3 and hosted with a single click or a few lines of code with Amazon SageMaker hosting.

- Train on the cloud but deploy locally. In such cases, we can use services like AWS IoT Greengrass and SageMaker Edge Manager to compile and deploy models to the edge for low-latency use cases.

- Train and deploy on the cloud, but with data that has been migrated from on-prem.

- Train on the cloud, test deployment on the cloud, but finally deploy compiled models on mobile devices running Android or IoS.

- Train and deploy using AWS Hybrid services like AWS Outposts and Wavelength.

Integration with Cloud Systems

In this section, we reiterate some common patterns of ML application development that you may have encountered in the previous chapters, specifically on existing connections from ML services to other services on the AWS cloud. As you will notice, integration with existing cloud-based systems and services involves all phases of the ML development lifecycle; some examples are listed below:

- Data preparation for ML on the cloud: Several services are used today to store, manipulate, and prepare data for machine learning on the cloud, including EC2 instances, container services like AWS Fargate and Amazon EKS, Amazon SageMaker Data Wrangler, AWS Glue and Glue DataBrew, Amazon EMR, and database services like Amazon RDS, Amazon Aurora, and Amazon Redshift. Furthermore, labeling services like Amazon SageMaker Ground Truth and other open source labeling tools that run on Amazon EC2 or container services can be used for this stage of the ML development lifecycle.

- Amazon IAM, AWS KMS, and Amazon VPC are essential components to be used in the training and deployment phases to keep your training data, compute, and deployment stacks secure. Read more about this in Chapter 13, "Security Pillar."

- Amazon IAM, AWS STS, and AWS SSO are essential components to help authorize and authenticate access to your ML stack. Again, read more about this in Chapter 13.

- For many services like Amazon SageMaker, Forecast, and Personalize, the primary way to store data is on Amazon S3. However, other sources are also available for certain services; for example, Amazon SageMaker can also train with data on Amazon EFS, FSx for Lustre, and EMR. Other services connect to Amazon SageMaker and help you with various phases of the ML development lifecycle; for example, Amazon Redshift ML lets you train and use models using familiar SQL statements using SageMaker AutoML (see https://docs.aws.amazon.com/redshift/latest/dg/r_CREATE_MODEL.html#r_user_guidance_create_model), and Amazon Athena ML lets you query an already existing Amazon SageMaker model. It is possible to even create your own user-defined functions (UDFs) on Athena using AWS Lambda to connect to various AI/ML services on AWS with simple SQL commands.

For example, this code snippet uses Athena to query an existing endpoint:

- ```
  USING EXTERNAL FUNCTION predict_customer_registration(age INTEGER)
      RETURNS DOUBLE
      SAGEMAKER 'xgboost-model'
  ```

- ```
  SELECT predict_customer_registration(age) AS probability_of_enrolling,
  customer_id
      FROM "sampledb"."ml_test_dataset"
      WHERE predict_customer_registration(age) < 0.5;
  ```

- After training your model, there are several options to deploy these models in production. For a detailed overview, please take a look at Chapter 10, "Model Deployment and Inference." The topics covered in this chapter include deploying models from services like Amazon Forecast, Amazon Personalize, Amazon Comprehend Custom, and Amazon SageMaker. These models are hosted as managed endpoints. SageMaker also allows you to download and deploy the model on the cloud or at the edge using different services such as Amazon EC2, AWS Fargate, AWS IoT Greengrass, or Amazon SageMaker Edge Manager.

- For real-time deployments that are Internet facing, most hosted models using AI/ML services can follow this general pattern: Amazon API Gateway to AWS Lambda, to AI/ML Services on AWS (see Figure 11.1). You can also use Amazon API Gateway mapping templates to directly integrate with endpoints. For example, once you have an Amazon SageMaker endpoint up and running, you can (a) create an AWS IAM execution role for the REST API, (b) create a mapping template for request integration, (c) create a mapping template for response integration, and (d) finally deploy and test the direct connection between API gateway and SageMaker.

FIGURE 11.1 Typical architecture for connecting Amazon API Gateway to AWS Lambda, and then to AI/ML services on AWS. It is useful (but not necessary) to have AWS Lambda for any custom pre- or post-processing.

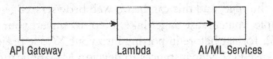

API Gateway   Lambda   AI/ML Services

- Lastly, for logging and monitoring, AI/ML services on AWS integrate directly with CloudWatch Logs and CloudTrail. This was covered in detail in Chapter 9, "Model Evaluation."

Integration with Front-End Systems

In the final section of this chapter, let's talk about integration with front-end systems. By front-end systems, we mean typical tools and services on AWS that support development workflows for React Native, JavaScript, IoS, and Android developers. Front ends are important in various situations where a full-stack application needs to be deployed with one or more ML models in the back end. On AWS, you can use the following:

- *AWS Amplify* allows front-end developers to efficiently create and manage front-end applications; Amplify supports popular frameworks such as JavaScript, React, Angular, Vue, and Next.js, and mobile platforms such as Android, iOS, React Native, Ionic, and Flutter. With Amplify, you can connect to various AI/ML services for use cases such as text translation, speech generation from text, image recognition, natural language understanding, transcribing tests, and connecting to custom models hosted on Amazon Sage-Maker. For more information on AWS Amplify, please visit `https://aws.amazon .com/amplify`.

- *AWS Device Farm* lets you test your web and mobile apps on various desktop browsers and real mobile devices without having to provision and manage any infrastructure. When models are deployed on the edge (in this case, mobile devices), it is important to test compatibility with various configurations before deploying the entire application to production.

- *Amazon Pinpoint* lets you connect with end users using channels like email, SMS, or push notifications. This is useful for communicating ML inference results in real time or aggregate reports based on batch inferences.

- *Amazon Location* services can help you build location-aware ML applications. For example, when recommending products to end users, you can take into account the device's current location or entry and exit criteria based on predefined geofences to deliver relevant predictions and increase user engagement.

- Amazon SageMaker Neo, as mentioned earlier, provides you with the functionality to deploy models on the edge, and this can be on web browsers, edge devices, and mobile devices. For example, you can use SageMaker Neo to convert your existing model into the Apple Core ML format before importing into your XCode project. On a related note, you can also use EC2 Mac instances to develop ML applications for macOS, iOS, iPadOS, tvOS (for Apple TV), and watchOS Apps.

Summary

In this chapter, we outlined how you can integrate your ML models with various on-premises, cloud, and front-end systems when creating a full-stack ML application. We covered various AWS services and integration patterns that are used to architect and develop hybrid, cloud, or edge ML applications.

Exam Essentials

Understand the need for building and maintaining hybrid ML applications.   Due to various constraints that organizations may have, some phases of the ML development lifecycle may have to happen on-prem, with other phases on the cloud using AWS AI/ML services.

Know what tools and services on AWS help with ML model deployment and integration.   When it comes to model deployment, there are various ways to implement ML applications, from deploying models using services like SageMaker hosting or deploying models to the edge, web, or mobile devices.

Review Questions

1. Your client has hired you to take one of their models trained on SageMaker and deploy it on iOS devices. The application is expected to run without any Internet connection on tens of thousands of iPhones. Which of the following steps will you take to achieve this for your client?

    A. You cannot host SageMaker models on iOS devices.

    B. Host the SageMaker model on the cloud and use API calls to get model predictions.

    C. Use SageMaker Neo to create an Apple CoreML model and use this in the iOS application locally.

    D. Use SageMaker Edge Manager to host these models with one click onto tens of thousands of iOS devices.

2. Your team of front-end developers does not have experience with building, training, and deploying ML models but would like to use natural language understanding features. The application needs to run on the web as well as on mobile devices. Which of these options will you ask your team to explore as the easiest first step?

    A. Use SageMaker front-end libraries to create custom NLU solutions.

    B. Use Amplify and built-in NLU functionality with front-end libraries of your choice.

    C. Convert your models to `Tensorflow.js`-compatible ones, and build a Progressive web app to deploy these models.

    D. Train your team on topics around NLU.

3. Your company has sensitive data on-prem that business teams would like to use for machine learning. However, the teams would like to use AWS AI/ML services to deploy these models. Which of these options makes sense to implement for multiple business teams?

    A. Keep the data on-prem; train models using open source frameworks with on-prem compute, and use Amazon SageMaker to host your models.

    B. Amazon SageMaker can connect to all kinds of on-prem data storage solutions. You can keep your data on-prem and train and deploy models on the cloud.

    C. Use Direct Connect to transfer data to Amazon S3; then train and deploy your models using SageMaker.

    D. Use the AWS transfer family to transfer data to Amazon S3; then train and deploy your models using SageMaker.

4. Due to recent changes in security policies, EKS-based ML applications that you were building and using on the cloud have to be migrated to on-prem compute. Which of the following options will you use to migrate these ML applications to on-prem?

    A. Keep the data on-prem; train models using open source frameworks with on-prem compute, and use Amazon SageMaker to host your models.

    B. Use EKS Anywhere and the same EKS tooling on-prem for your ML applications.

    C. Use containers and container definitions with custom tooling on-prem.

    D. There is no way to migrate these applications to on-prem.

5. You would like to expose your SageMaker model as a hosted endpoint to certain end users with registered API keys. Which of the following patterns presents the simplest way to achieve this?

    A. SageMaker endpoints are public by default. You can simply post inference payloads and receive a prediction response.

    B. This is not possible using SageMaker; host your models using AWS Lambda and integrate with API gateway.

    C. Directly integrate API Gateway to SageMaker using custom mapping templates.

    D. Create a CloudFront distribution. Then use a container-based Lambda function and host your SageMaker model using `Lambda@Edge`.

6. Due to the sensitive nature of the data used by your company, you need to host ML models that are trained on such data on premises. The models are trained using Amazon SageMaker on the cloud. What approach would you use to deploy the model on premises?

    A. Use Amazon SageMaker Anywhere to deploy the model locally.

    B. Export the model artifact to your on-premises cluster and host it on premises.

    C. You cannot export the SageMaker Model artifact on premises, so you will have to host the model in the cloud.

    D. Use SageMaker Edge Manager to host the model on premises.

7. In order to build a decoupled architecture, you are hosting your ML model trained on Sage-Maker behind an API gateway. However, the incoming client POST requests need to be transformed to CSV format before the model can make predictions. What AWS service might you use to preprocess the incoming data before calling the endpoint serving API?

    A. Amazon EC2

    B. AWS Lambda

    C. Amazon SageMaker Processing

    D. Amazon EKS

8. You are an ML engineer at a growing SaaS provider and need to host thousands of deep learning models into production on AWS. You have read through a number of different potential options, but a key consideration when hosting these models is the cost of the underlying hosting infrastructure and the low round-trip (under 100 ms) latency for serving. Some of the models need to be hosted on CPUs, whereas others may require GPUs. What hosting architecture might you use to save on cost?

    A. Create thousands of SageMaker endpoints to host your models.

    B. Use a SageMaker multi-model endpoint for hosting your models. You can host multiple models on the same machine, thus lowering cost.

    C. Build a custom hosting service using Amazon EKS. You can use bin packing to efficiently pack multiple containers on the same host, achieving both low cost and lower latency.

    D. Use AWS Lambda to host your models.

9. You are an ML engineer at a growing SaaS provider and need to host a small model that will serve inferences with high throughput in production. Serving latency is a concern, and you would like to avoid cold start. However, you are also concerned with the cost of spinning up a large instance to meet the high-throughput needs for a small model. As the AWS solutions architect, you might propose which of the following architectures? (Choose all that apply.)

   A. Host the small model on a t3.medium SageMaker model hosting endpoint to save on cost.

   B. Host the model on Amazon S3 to save on cost.

   C. Host the model on several small t3.medium SageMaker model hosting endpoints to meet the throughput needs and to keep costs low.

   D. Use AWS Lambda to host the model since it is small, and use provisioned concurrency to avoid cold start.

10. You are the AWS solutions architect for a growing marketing firm that is looking to quickly ingest customer data, segment consumers, and send out personalized content to them via SMS and push notifications. The company is using Amazon Personalize to generate the recommendations. The marketing team is looking for your advice on how to build such a system in the easiest possible way. What solutions would you recommend?

   A. Do nothing. Amazon Personalize offers a service to directly send email and push notifications to customers with recommended content.

   B. Use Amazon SES and SNS to send out emails and push notifications and use AWS Lambda to write customized content for each user segment.

   C. Use Amazon SQS and SNS to send out emails and push notifications and use AWS Lambda to write customized content for each user segment.

   D. Use Amazon Pinpoint to send customized and personalized content to users across multiple communication channels.

Machine Learning Well-Architected Lens

PART

PART III

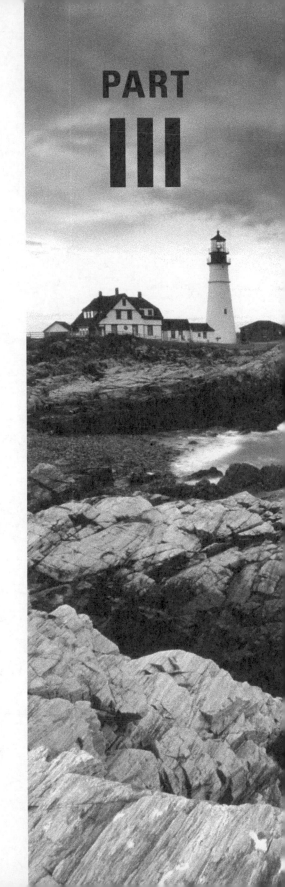

Chapter

12

Operational Excellence Pillar for ML

THE AWS CERTIFIED MACHINE LEARNING SPECIALTY EXAM OBJECTIVES COVERED IN THIS CHAPTER INCLUDE BUT ARE NOT LIMITED TO THE FOLLOWING:

✓ **Domain 4.0: Machine Learning Implementation and Operations**

- 4.1 Build machine learning solutions for performance, availability, scalability, resiliency, and fault tolerance

- 4.4 Deploy and operationalize machine learning solutions

In the AWS Well-Architected Framework, operational excellence means ensuring that your ML systems are designed to operate efficiently in the cloud. In this chapter, we will go over key design considerations and how you can apply practices from DevOps and traditional software development to quickly bring ML workloads to market in a reliable and scalable manner.

Operational Excellence on AWS

As part of other AWS certifications, you may have already be familiar with the AWS Well-Architected framework. In this chapter, we will cover the Operational Excellence pillar of this framework, with a machine learning lens or focus. We will discuss how the standard operational excellence best practices apply to ML workloads and the kinds of tooling you can use to build efficient ML pipelines.

There are five key design principles for operational excellence:

- Everything as Code
- Continuous Integration
- Continuous Delivery
- Continuous Monitoring
- Continuous Improvement

In this chapter, we will cover each of these topics and discuss the AWS AI/ML services you can use to implement these design principles into your ML workloads.

We highly recommend that you read the Operational Excellence section in the AWS Well-Architected Lens for Machine Learning here: https://docs.aws.amazon.com/wellarchitected/latest/machine-learning-lens/design-principles.html.

Everything as Code

One of the main challenges big and small organizations face, albeit sometimes for different reasons, is the ability to reliably reproduce and scale successful workloads and workstreams across the organization. Although some amount of technical debt will naturally be incurred as your organizational practices mature, developing an everything as code strategy is a key methodology to enable you to reproduce pipelines for different workloads, improving the overall team's productivity and allowing you to ship products to market faster.

There are multiple areas in the ML pipeline where you can employ this approach:

- First, ML developers across organizations need an environment that is secure and that meets their organization's security guardrails to experiment, analyze data, engineer features, and train models. This workbench may often consist of notebooks such as Jupyter Notebooks or an IDE for code, along with associated code repositories such as GitHub or AWS CodeCommit. Consider using tools like AWS CloudFormation to build such secure environments for data scientists to quickly get started. For example, this blog shows you how to quickly build a secure ML environment using Amazon SageMaker: `https://aws.amazon.com/blogs/machine-learning/securing-amazon-sagemaker-studio-connectivity-using-a-private-vpc`.

- Although infrastructure as code (IaC) is a way to reproducibly build the underlying infrastructure for ML, you may also need to store and manage configurations, for which you can use AWS Systems Manager (`https://aws.amazon.com/systems-manager`). Runtime parameters used by your IAC tools can be stored in Systems Manager Parameter Store. Wherever possible, store Configurations as Code (CaC).

- In addition to IaC and CaC, pipelines as code (PaC) tools such as AWS CodePipeline, Apache Airflow, Kubeflow, and others allow you to develop pipelines to train and retrain models and deploy ML models to production based on some configurations provided by data scientists.

In Figure 12.1, we show the overall architecture of an ML workflow and where IaC, CaC, and PaC tools can be used to optimize the operations. You can use IaC and CaC tooling to automate the setup of secure ML development, test (or pre-production), and production environments. In many enterprises, this is part of a standard multiaccount strategy where different accounts are spun up for development, testing, and production work. Once these accounts are provisioned, you can use the tools to automate the setup of a secure ML workbench. Once models are ready to be promoted to User Acceptance Testing (UAT), you can use CloudFormation to set up the test infrastructure in the test accounts. It is highly recommended that you at least separate production workloads in their own accounts and minimize human access to production accounts.

FIGURE 12.1   Diagram showing the ML workflow with different ways you can use IaC, CaC, and PaC tools to improve the overall operational efficiency

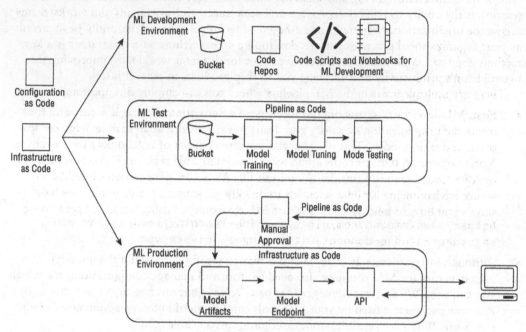

Although the development process is inherently experimental, PaC tooling can be used in the testing or UAT account to train and tune the algorithm specified by the data scientists on the full dataset in a repeatable manner. Once the best-performing model is generated, another pipeline can kick off a human review to approve or reject the model for production. Depending on the human action, this pipeline can then kick off another IaC template to set up the production infrastructure (production endpoints and variants) in the production account and start serving client traffic. We will describe this in more detail in the next two sections.

Continuous Integration and Continuous Delivery

In traditional DevOps, Continuous Integration (CI) is the practice of merging and integrating code routinely and frequently and verifying the integrations with automated builds and unit tests.

As the machine learning practice differs from traditional DevOps in that it is highly experimental, data scientists often do not immediately write production-quality code when they are training and experimenting with models, and it may be challenging to enforce CI best practices. Furthermore, enforcing that all code is always production quality, even during the development stage, can slow down the experimentation and feature engineering process.

In general, AWS recommends that you separate your development and CI environments. Data scientists can engineer features, train models, and write code in notebooks, in a secure development environment such as SageMaker Studio. When they are confident with their model's performance on a smaller dataset, then it is recommended that they check their code into a source control tool such as GitHub or Bitbucket.

Checking code into a code repo enables version control, traceability, reproducibility, and the ability to roll back to prior versions of working code whenever needed.

A second difference between ML and software development is that in addition to code, it is essential to also version the data so that you maintain the lineage of the dataset used to train the models. This is essential both for regulatory reasons and because the ML model performance is highly sensitive to the dataset it is trained on. Additionally, regulators may require you to explain why your model makes certain predictions, especially when dealing with customer data. It may be essential to trace the training data during such an audit.

Data here refers to the raw data; the training, validation, and test data and any engineered features that are essential to your model. Although data may be versioned and stored in Amazon S3, to version and reuse features, consider using a tool like the Amazon Feature Store.

In addition to data versioning, it is essential to version any packages and dependencies you may need for your code to run in the compute environment. A best practice for this is to build containers using tools such as Docker with specific package versions that you need to run your code. Docker containers can be stored and versioned in repositories such as Amazon ECR. Alternatively, package management tools such as Artifactory or AWS CodeArtifact may be used to connect to upstream package repositories such as pip and maven, perform scanning and vulnerability testing on the downloaded packages, and make these approved packages available for use by ML developers.

Continuous delivery (sometimes known as continuous deployment) is the software development practice of using an automated release process to release software into production.

For machine learning models, the software is usually a machine learning model deployed to a production endpoint as a service to serve incoming client requests in real time or as part of a batch process. The process of releasing ML models to production is continuous delivery (CD) for ML.

Once a developer checks in their code to a code repository, this kicks off the CI process of building the model container using the source code and training the ML model. A standard CI tool that can be used here is AWS CodeBuild. CodeBuild can be used to run unit tests against your code. Only once your code has successfully passed the tests can it be packaged into a Docker container deployed to ECR. The container can then be used to train your ML models.

Once the model is trained on the full dataset, the desired accuracy has been achieved on a test dataset, and the model performance meets the outlined business criteria, the model may be deployed to production.

For ML, the deployment process is rarely fully automated, and it is usually recommended that a human ensure that the model indeed meets the business goals. Additionally, a human-in-the-loop may also wish to verify whether the model version has been stored, model hyperparameters documented, and underlying source code, packages, and containers are stored and versioned in a secure repository. In addition to model performance, in certain cases when dealing with sensitive datasets that involve customer data, additional validation steps may be necessary such as a model risk and governance framework analysis. For example, for financial institutions, the Federal Reserve Board has published guidance on model risk management: `https://www.federalreserve.gov/supervisionreg/srletters/sr1107a1.pdf`.

AWS DevOps and Orchestration tools such as AWS CodePipeline and AWS Step Functions allow you to add human verification steps in the pipeline deployment either as a manual approval action or custom Lambda functions that send SNS notifications to appropriate persons and only trigger the next step of the pipeline based on the approval or rejection action. To manage approval actions using CodePipeline, visit `https://docs.aws.amazon.com/codepipeline/latest/userguide/approvals.html`.

FIGURE 12.2 Diagram showing a typical CI/CD workflow that can be used as part of your MLOps lifecycle using AWS native tooling

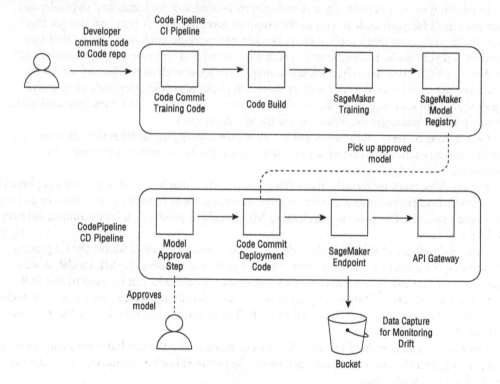

In Figure 12.2, we show a typical CI/CD workflow for ML. Once a developer commits code to a code repo, a CI pipeline is triggered, which first builds the model container using CodeBuild and then triggers model training/tuning on SageMaker. The final model is then registered in the model registry. Once a human approves the model, a second CD pipeline is triggered using CodePipeline, which triggers a second build of any deployment containers and subsequently the SageMaker endpoint. An S3 bucket is also provisioned to capture the data for model monitoring, which is discussed in detail in the next section. Most organizations will have some variations on this overall flow; this diagram captures at a high level what an MLOps workflow looks like.

You can also use SageMaker Pipelines to automate the building and deployment of ML models. SageMaker pipelines run within SageMaker Studio and provide a tool to visualize the ML workflow as a directed acyclic graph (DAG) and monitor the execution steps. You can build a SageMaker pipeline using the `CreatePipeline` API by providing a JSON definition for the pipeline. The `StartPipelineExecution` API can then be used to execute the pipeline. Although a pipeline corresponds to a single ML workflow, to automate pipelines across ML workflows, you can use SageMaker projects, which allows you to package the underlying infrastructure setup and ML pipeline as an AWS Service Catalog product. Data scientists can simply check their code into a source control tool such as CodeCommit and trigger the pipeline release process. For more information on SageMaker projects, refer to the documentation here: `https://docs.aws.amazon.com/sagemaker/latest/dg/sagemaker-projects-whatis.html`.

It is common for customers to use non-AWS tools such as Airflow and Jenkins for pipeline deployment. You should use the tool that best serves your organization's needs.

Continuous Monitoring

Once your software (ML model) is in production, you might wonder, "Am I done? Can I move on to the next use case?" Unfortunately, the answer is no.

The adage "garbage in, garbage out" tells us that ML models are only as good as the data they are trained on. And for many ML use cases, the data is not static over time. A common example of this is recommendation systems that rely on customer clickstream data. As customers' preferences change, they may be interested in different products on your website or app, and this can lead to a drift in the dataset. A second example is fraud detection; as fraudsters get better and better with attempting to hide fraudulent transactions, the ML models must work harder to identify patterns corresponding to fraudulent activity in the data.

Continuous monitoring is the practice of monitoring your incoming data and your downstream ML model performance for any drift. There are two kinds of drift that are relevant to ML models.

The first type is *data drift*. Data drift refers to a change over time in the data, feature, or label distribution. For example, if your model is trained on a particular feature such as income, and over time there is a drift in the distribution of the incomes, that can affect your model quality if that feature is important to the prediction. Monitoring incoming data for data drift against the baseline that the model was trained on is therefore essential to ensuring model quality does not degrade over time.

Sometimes the distribution of the labels may change. For example, imagine a fraud detection model was trained using data in a particular region that had a certain distribution of fraudulent/nonfraudulent labels. If that model was lifted into another region, which had a different label distribution, the model is unlikely to perform well and needs to be retrained on that dataset. This is a form of data drift, which is sometimes also called *concept drift*.

The second type is *model drift*. Model drift refers to a drift in the model quality that may arise as a result of data drift or due to a change in the relationships between the various independent variables. To identify model drift, you should periodically and frequently compare model predictions with actual ground truth derived from human annotators or labelers. To generate human labels, you can use a service such as SageMaker Ground Truth. The labels can then be compared with the model performance to measure any drift in the model accuracy. Data science teams can then be notified if the model performance dips below a threshold to trigger model retraining.

SageMaker has a feature called SageMaker Model Monitor to monitor any drift in data or model performance. Model monitoring works by first identifying a baseline on which the data is trained and deriving statistical distributions for the baseline. The SageMaker model endpoint is then instructed to capture and store a fraction of the incoming data traffic. The distribution of the incoming payload is then extracted and compared against the baseline, and any drift is output to CloudWatch as well as the SageMaker Studio UI.

In addition to monitoring the model performance, continuous monitoring also involves logging the underlying infrastructure itself to ensure that it is healthy to meet your traffic, logging any unauthorized access of production endpoints for security reasons. API calls made to AWS services are logged in AWS CloudTrail, and Amazon CloudWatch can be used to monitor the compute performance of production endpoints for CPU usage, memory usage, and number of invocations. These CloudWatch logs can also be connected to third-party monitoring services such as Splunk or Datadog to visualize the endpoint performance in a centralized manner.

Continuous Improvement

Continuous Improvement refers to the practice of improving your ML model performance during training by experimenting with different algorithms or engineering features or by combining different data sources, as well as triggering model retraining based on any drift that may be detected by the drift detection systems described earlier.

First, let's discuss continuous improvement during training. Often, ML developers will train an ML model, and once it meets a required business threshold, they push the model to production. However, because the ML process is experimental, there are always more features you can engineer, additional data sources you can bring in, and different algorithms you can try based on the latest published research to improve your model performance and derive more business value.

Experiment management refers to the practice of tracking and managing different experiments done by data scientists and storing the associated metadata. This metadata may include timestamps for when the models were trained, the kind of model, model hyperparameters, model performance metrics and graphs, data and feature versions, and so on. These experiments can be stored in a database such as DynamoDB or Aurora. Often data scientists use tools such as TensorBoard to monitor and compare experiments. Other tools include SageMaker Experiments and MLflow tracking.

A key challenge with current experiment tracking systems is the lack of automation. For example, with SageMaker Experiments, users have to manually tag their training jobs as experiments and remember to track certain custom parameters if they are using custom scripts or containers to train ML models. However, as the ML space matures, we expect there to be better automation in the experiment tracking and management area.

Summary

In this chapter, we covered the key pillars of operational excellence: everything as code, CI, CD, and continuous monitoring and improvement in the context of ML workloads.

Exam Essentials

Understand the five pillars of operational excellence. Understand the aspects of operational excellence that are common to most software, and the ML-specific differences. For example, in machine learning, version control refers not only to source code but also data, dependencies, containers, and so on. Similarly, in machine learning, continuous monitoring is also a key step post deployment, and deployments are rarely fully automated.

Understand where you can use infrastructure as code tools to improve the ML workflow. Tools such as Terraform or CloudFormation can significantly help customers reproducibly deploy ML environments and ML infrastructure. Additionally, you can use Service Catalog to convert your CloudFormation templates to products that can be stored in a centralized shared services account in your organization as part of an enterprise multi-account strategy.

Know that you can use CloudWatch to log and monitor infrastructure and CloudTrail to log API calls. The differences between these two services is a popular exam topic across all the AWS certifications and can also arise in the ML context.

Have a broad understanding of the AWS DevOps tools such as CodeCommit, CodeBuild, CodePipeline, and Step Functions.   Note that CodePipeline is a software release tool, and Step Functions is a workflow orchestration tool similar to Airflow to orchestrate an ML pipeline.

Understand how you can use SageMaker pipelines.   SageMaker pipelines is the CI/CD tool developed by SageMaker to build and orchestrate CI/CD pipelines for ML model training and deployment. Read the SageMaker pipelines documentation prior to the test: `https://docs.aws.amazon.com/sagemaker/latest/dg/pipelines.html`.

Familiarize yourself with the SageMaker model monitoring workflow.   The detailed steps in the workflow can be found here: `https://docs.aws.amazon.com/sagemaker/latest/dg/model-monitor.html`

Review Questions

1. Your ML platform team would like to reproducibly deploy ML environments for different lines of business (LoBs) to use in a reliable manner. What AWS tool can be used to build the underlying infrastructure as code (IaC)?

    A. Amazon SageMaker Pipelines

    B. Amazon CloudWatch

    C. AWS CloudFormation

    D. AWS Step Functions

2. Your ML platform team would like to build a manual human approval step into the ML release pipeline to validate that the model performance meets business requirements. What tool can be used to achieve this in the easiest way?

    A. AWS CodeCommit

    B. AWS CodeBuild

    C. AWS Step Functions

    D. AWS CodePipeline

3. Which AWS service would you use to build model containers from source code as part of your CI process?

    A. AWS CodeBuild

    B. AWS CodeCommit

    C. AWS CodeDeploy

    D. Amazon Elastic Container Registry

4. You have successfully deployed an ML model on SageMaker to production that deals with customer clickstream data. Your management is concerned that the model may start to perform poorly over time as customer preferences change. What recommendation would you give them?

    A. Do nothing; ML model accuracy does not degrade over time.

    B. Use Amazon CloudWatch to monitor the underlying compute infrastructure to ensure that the model can service incoming client traffic.

    C. Set up model monitoring on the endpoint to detect data drift. Once the drift passes a threshold, model monitoring will report this in CloudWatch. Set up alarms to be alerted when drift is detected.

    D. Retrain and redeploy your models every week.

5. What are the right steps in the SageMaker model monitoring workflow?

    A. Set up an endpoint with data capture. SageMaker will automatically monitor the endpoint at an hourly frequency and detect drift.

    B. Deploy a SageMaker endpoint with Data Capture ➤ Run a baseline job for model monitoring to generate a baseline of the input feature statistics ➤ Set up model monitoring by passing in the baseline statistics and the endpoint as input and deciding on a monitoring interval (daily, weekly, hourly, etc.).

    C. Deploy a SageMaker endpoint without Data Capture ➤ Run a baseline job for model monitoring to generate a baseline of the input feature statistics ➤ Set up model monitoring by passing in the baseline statistics and the endpoint as input and deciding on a monitoring interval (daily, weekly, hourly, etc.).

    D. Source data ➤ Explore data ➤ Engineer features ➤ Train a model.

6. You are using AWS CloudFormation templates to create and manage the VPC and IAM roles and policies, as well as the SageMaker Studio domain for data scientists to use for development using notebooks. You have created and tested the template and now would like to deploy templates across several target accounts spread across multiple AWS regions. What tool would you use to automate this?

    A. AWS CloudFormation templates can be automatically deployed across regions and accounts. No extra work is needed.

    B. Use AWS CloudFormation StackSets to automate cross-region and cross-account deployments.

    C. AWS does not offer a tool for this. You need to manually deploy the CloudFormation template across different accounts in different regions.

    D. Use AWS CodePipeline to deploy the CloudFormation templates across different accounts.

7. Your company has a new CTO, who has instituted a mandate to leverage infrastructure-as-code tools like Terraform wherever possible to manage infrastructure deployments. Your ML infrastructure team is proficient in programming languages like Python but less familiar with expressing intent directly using JSON/YAML. What AWS tool might you use to simplify the creation of infrastructure-as-code templates using familiar programming languages?

    A. Use Jupyter Notebooks to author the templates.

    B. Use AWS Lambda to author the templates.

    C. Use AWS Cloud Development Kit (CDK) for Terraform (`cdktf`).

    D. You cannot author Terraform templates using CDK. You need to use JSON/YAML.

8. Your ML engineers are training hundreds of small models across different platforms (Sage-Maker, EC2, ECS, EMR, etc.) that need to be reliably deployed to production. Errors in deployments must be caught, the deployment needs to be retried or rolled back, and users have to be notified. Administrators and engineers also require a visual tool to view the execution of the pipeline to quickly identify and visualize failed steps. What deployment tool might you recommend that the customer use?

   A. Use AWS Step Functions.

   B. Use AWS SageMaker Pipelines.

   C. Use KubeFlow pipelines.

   D. Use AWS CodePipeline.

9. You are using SageMaker Pipelines to train, tune, and deploy a SageMaker model. Which of the following steps would you use to test whether the model performance exceeds a previous threshold and branch out the action based on the output?

   A. Transform Step

   B. Training Step

   C. Callback Step

   D. Condition Step

10. Which AWS service would you use to check in and check out code, set up version control, maintain commits, and trigger pipelines in response to code commits made to a main-line branch?

   A. AWS CodeBuild

   B. AWS CodeCommit

   C. AWS CodeDeploy

   D. Amazon Elastic Container Registry

Chapter

13

Security Pillar

THE AWS CERTIFIED MACHINE LEARNING (ML) SPECIALTY EXAM OBJECTIVES COVERED IN THIS CHAPTER INCLUDE BUT ARE NOT LIMITED TO THE FOLLOWING:

✓ **Domain 4.0: Machine Learning Implementation and Operations**

  ▪ 4.3 Apply basic AWS security practices to machine learning solutions

Organizations need to ensure that the machine learning environments in which data scientists and ML developers operate, as well as the ML lifecycle itself, meet their enterprise security requirements. Even if you are a small business, especially once you deal with consumer data you may be required to operate under certain regulatory guidelines, and the ML models you build may need to follow those guidelines. In this chapter, we will cover the basic principles of AWS security and how they apply to ML workloads. We will describe how you can secure your ML environment using Amazon SageMaker.

Security and AWS

As you may already know from previous certifications, the AWS Cloud is architected to be one of the most secure cloud computing environments today. AWS operates with a shared responsibility model with customers, where AWS handles the security of the cloud and AWS customers are responsible for the security of the applications and data in the cloud.

The diagram in Figure 13.1 shows how the AWS shared responsibility model operates (https://aws.amazon.com/compliance/shared-responsibility-model). AWS manages the security of the infrastructure, the facilities that house the infrastructure, and the hardware, software, and networking associated with them. Customers are responsible for the security depending on the AWS services they use. For example, if you build your ML models using Amazon SageMaker versus Amazon EC2, your responsibility will differ. With EC2, you will be responsible for updating and patching of the guest operating system, such as maintaining the firewalls. On a managed service like Amazon SageMaker or an AI service, AWS manages the infrastructure layer, the operating system, and the firewalls on the compute instances used for training, processing, and notebooks. Customers are still able to control how their data is accessed by these services by using tools like Amazon Virtual Private Cloud, AWS Key Management System, and AWS Identity and Access Management.

Since this is an ML certification guide, we will focus on how security applies to machine learning workloads. We highly recommend that you read this AWS Security Whitepaper to develop a broad understanding of AWS security fundamentals: https://docs.aws.amazon.com/whitepapers/latest/introduction-aws-security/introduction-aws-security.pdf.

When designing for security, consider these five key design principles:

- Data protection
- Isolation of compute

- Fine-grained access controls
- Audit and logging
- Compliance scope

FIGURE 13.1   Diagram showing the AWS shared responsibility model. Understand this model in depth prior to sitting any of the AWS certification tests.

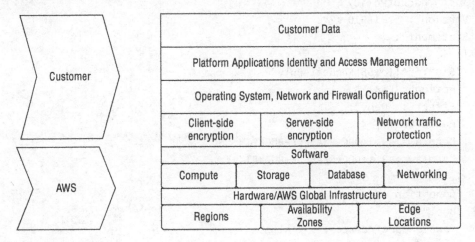

Data Protection

Data is the key to any machine learning workload, and organizations are increasingly realizing that data is their most valuable asset. Data, whether it is internal corporate data, first-party data about your customers, or third-party data you may have collected from other data sources, needs to be protected and secured. You must ensure that you limit access to data to only those who really need it. In addition to users, data is accessed by the compute services that will actually train the ML models themselves.

AWS recommends that you encrypt your data wherever possible and provides you with tools for doing so. Since most data for ML workloads on AWS is stored on S3, it is helpful to review the different data protection options you have on Amazon S3. You can encrypt your data client side, where the data is encrypted prior to being sent to AWS, or server side, where the data is encrypted at the destination.

For server-side encryption of data using Amazon S3, you have the option of encrypting data with S3 managed keys, customer master keys (CMKs) stored in AWS KMS, or customer-provided keys that are managed by the customers. For client-side encryption, you can either use the AWS encryption SDK or use a CMK stored in AWS KMS to first encrypt the data prior to sending it to AWS. To learn more about encryption on S3, read the following document: https://docs.aws.amazon.com/AmazonS3/latest/userguide/UsingEncryption.html.

In addition to encryption at rest, you should consider encryption in transit. All network traffic between AWS data centers is encrypted, as is traffic between VPCs peered across AWS regions. For the application layer, customers have a choice about whether to use an encryption protocol like Transport Layer Security (TLS). All AWS service endpoints that you use to access AWS services support TLS. Refer to the whitepaper on logical separation in AWS for more details: https://docs.aws.amazon.com/whitepapers/latest/logical-separation/encrypting-data-at-rest-and--in-transit.html.

You can also enforce encryption in transit using IAM condition keys on any data movement in and out of your S3 buckets using the following bucket policy:

```
{
    "Id": "BucketPolicy",
    "Version": "2012-10-17",
    "Statement": [
     {
      "Sid": "AllowSSLRequestsOnly",
      "Action": "s3:*",
      "Effect": "Deny",
      "Resource": [
       "arn:aws:s3:::DOC-EXAMPLE-BUCKET",
       "arn:aws:s3:::DOC-EXAMPLE-BUCKET/*"
      ],
      "Condition": {
      "Bool": {
       "aws:SecureTransport": "false"
      }
     },
     "Principal": "*"
     }
    ]
}
```

Isolation of Compute

Another key security consideration is to isolate your compute environments from the public Internet. By placing your resources in a VPC, you can launch resources in a virtual network dedicated to your account. This book will not cover details of VPC, which you should already be familiar with from your prior certifications. If not, we highly recommend that you have a fundamental understanding of VPC prior to taking the test (see https://docs.aws.amazon.com/vpc/latest/userguide/what-is-amazon-vpc.html).

In order for resources in your VPC to communicate with AWS services such as Amazon S3 buckets or Amazon SageMaker, many AWS services support VPC endpoints. VPC endpoints enable you to privately connect to these services without requiring an Internet gateway and a NAT gateway in your VPC. When you use a VPC endpoint, traffic between your VPC and AWS services does not leave the Amazon network. For regulated customers such as financial services, the availability of VPC endpoints is often a prerequisite for a service to be enabled within that organization. In the next section, we will discuss how a managed service like SageMaker integrates with VPC endpoints.

Fine-Grained Access Controls

AWS recommends using the principle of least privilege to limit who has access to what data. AWS IAM can be used to apply fine-grained access control based on a user's role or job function. This is often called role-based access control (RBAC). By creating IAM roles such as data scientist roles or MLOps roles and assigning policies to those roles, you can restrict the kind of access you provide to data scientists. Similarly, you can also define permissions on attributes via tags. This is shown in Figure 13.2 and is known as attribute-based access control (ABAC). For example, say you tag a particular bucket to be used by a certain team such as the "Finance" team. By tagging the bucket with the proper attribute, using a bucket policy, you can ensure that only a principal from the Finance team can access the bucket. For more details on how to do this, see https://docs.aws.amazon.com/IAM/latest/ UserGuide/tutorial_attribute-based-access-control.html.

For ML workloads, your admins will need to ensure that the environments that data scientists operate in are secure and that only approved users are authorized to use them. One approach is to create different AWS accounts, which serve as a logically isolated boundary between different projects and teams. However, this can lead to a proliferation of AWS accounts, which is hard to manage. Alternatively, you can create accounts for your lines of business (LoBs) and put different workloads in that account for each LoB. In this case, by separating data scientist roles from MLOps roles or by creating project-based tags, you can prevent different teams from accessing each other's projects or S3 buckets.

FIGURE 13.2   Diagram showing tag-based controls that can be applied using attribute-based access controls

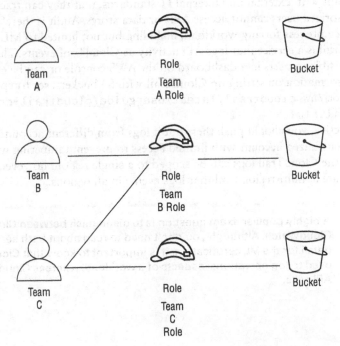

Audit and Logging

Logging of ML workloads may mean two things:

- Developers may want to view logs of the jobs they are running in order to debug them, identify performance bottlenecks, and so on.

- Admins may want to view logs of the usage history, such as which APIs or S3 buckets were called or accessed by whom, or have logs to monitor idle running applications so they can be notified.

Amazon CloudWatch is a service that allows users to monitor their AWS applications and services in real time. CloudWatch enables you to monitor for application performance or health. In the context of machine learning, this applies to the performance of training jobs or processing jobs or the health of your deployed model endpoints. With CloudWatch, you can set up alarms that trigger whenever a metric goes above or below a certain defined threshold. A common best practice is to set up alarms for monitoring your deployed endpoints, which we cover in Chapter 12, "Operational Excellence Pillar for ML."

It is helpful to think of the user personas for whom logging is useful. They can be both developers and admins. By contrast, many large firms will have audit teams, whose sole responsibility is to ensure governance and auditability for workloads both on premises and on the cloud.

Auditing workloads is typically a governance function and mainly has to do with which principal is calling an API. Auditing is usually required by companies to demonstrate that they are compliant with external and internal IT standards, that they can track user access, and that unauthorized users cannot access APIs or data stores. Audit is therefore a key part of the governance process for any workload, including but not limited to ML workloads.

AWS CloudTrail is a service that logs API activity as CloudTrail events. These events are then made visible to users in a dashboard on the AWS console or can be exported to S3. For more information on setting up CloudTrail with S3 buckets, see https://docs.aws.amazon.com/awscloudtrail/latest/userguide/cloudtrail-create-and-update-a-trail.html.

As a best practice, you should push these audit logs from different accounts to a separate S3 bucket in a centralized account with limited access to prevent tampering with audit logs. Remember that the CloudTrail logs can be scoped to a single region; however, as a best practice, you can create a multi-region trail that logs events in all regions.

A highly popular exam question is to distinguish between CloudTrail and CloudWatch. Although you don't need to read about both services in detail for the ML certification, it is important to know that CloudWatch is used to log operational aspects of a workload, whereas CloudTrail logs API calls.

Note the difference between CloudTrail logs and VPC flow logs, which you should be familiar with from prior AWS certifications. If not, remember that VPC flow logs monitor IP traffic from network interfaces within your VPC. CloudTrail logs, on the other hand, log API user access.

Compliance Scope

In addition to logging and monitoring user activity using CloudTrail or monitoring services for operational reasons, you may be required to periodically audit and monitor AWS services for any configuration changes that may occur. A simple example may be that your organization requires all EBS storage volumes attached to EC2 instances to be encrypted at rest or requires continuously monitoring any changes that occur to security groups tied to certain applications.

AWS Config is a service that provides a list of predefined and managed rules, and allows users to create custom rules using Lambda functions to perform detective and preventive controls on their AWS environments. These ensure that either any non-compliant resources are proactively terminated or admins are notified whenever resource state changes occur that put their systems out of compliance. For more information on AWS Config rules, see https://docs.aws.amazon.com/config/latest/developerguide/evaluate-config_use-managed-rules.html.

You may be wondering whether AWS has a service that not only logs and captures API calls but also automatically identifies potential threats from all the different logging tools such as CloudTrail logs and VPC flow logs for logging network access, among others. Amazon GuardDuty is such a service; it uses machine learning algorithms such as anomaly detection to automatically look for anomalies from different logs in your AWS environment. Popular threats include users accessing your underlying instances for cryptocurrency mining and making API calls to or from known malicious IP addresses.

Note that GuardDuty uses machine learning to detect anomalies and for threat intelligence. The other services we've discussed so far (CloudTrail, Config, CloudWatch) do not use ML but rather can log actions taken in your ML environments.

Finally, if you are working in a regulated industry such as financial services or healthcare, you may need to ensure that the AWS services you use are in compliance with different regulations such as the Payments Card Industry (PCI) or Service Organization Controls (SOCs). AWS Artifact is a service that provides access to such compliance documentation. Remember the shared responsibility model here; customers are still required to ensure that any applications they build on top of AWS services meet the compliance and regulatory requirements they are subject to. For more details on AWS Artifact, refer to this documentation: https://docs.aws.amazon.com/artifact/latest/ug/what-is-aws-artifact.html.

A popular exam question is to distinguish between AWS CloudTrail, AWS Config, and Amazon CloudWatch. It is important to have high-level familiarity with these services, although the ML certification does not get into the details about these services.

Secure SageMaker Environments

Since Security is one of the most important pillars and value propositions for moving workloads to the AWS Cloud, the ML certification test expects you to have a working knowledge of security for Amazon SageMaker. In this section, we will cover the different elements of building a secure ML workload on SageMaker and the various capabilities that SageMaker provides from a security perspective. We will approach this topic from the lens of the previous section, dividing it up into the five themes we discussed in the previous section.

We highly recommend that you read the Security section of the Sage-Maker documentation prior to taking the test: https://docs.aws.amazon.com/sagemaker/latest/dg/security.html.

Authentication and Authorization

There are two ways to authenticate users into SageMaker. You can use either AWS IAM or AWS Single Sign-On (SSO). IAM authentication is something you should be familiar with from your previous AWS certifications. You can use the concept of IAM users to correspond to physical users in your organization. Users can be grouped into IAM groups. For example, you can have a group called Data Scientists, ML Engineers, or ML Administrators.

Although IAM groups and users are specific to an account, SSO allows you to manage users and access across all your AWS accounts in a centralized way. You can also use groups in SSO to assign permissions based on roles or job functions. Additionally, SSO integrates with many third-party authentication tools such as Okta, Ping Federate, Microsoft Active Directory (AD), and Azure AD. For more information on AWS SSO, refer to the documentation here: https://docs.aws.amazon.com/singlesignon/latest/userguide/what-is.html.

SSO authentication is only supported for SageMaker Studio. SageMaker Notebook instances support IAM-based authentication only.

While creating IAM users is one way to manage persistent identities in your AWS environment, many organizations may only want to retain a single store of identities on premises using an identity provider (IdP) built on Active Directory or LDAP. If the corporate IdP is compatible with Open ID Connect (OIDC) or Security Assertion Markup Language (SAML) 2.0, then you can use identity federation to avoid creating IAM users.

Suppose a user wanted to access the AWS console (Figure 13.3). The user first browses to your organization's portal and selects the option to go to the AWS console. The portal is backed by the IdP, which verifies the user is indeed part of the organization and returns a SAML assertion that can include preconfigured metadata such as the session duration to the client. The client browser can then be redirected to AWS SSO, which in turn calls AWS STS to obtain temporary credentials. The temporary credentials are retrieved along with a sign-in URL that allows a user to sign into the AWS console. The SAML authentication response can include one or more roles that a user can select to perform actions in the console. The federated user then assumes the role in AWS, without needing to be an IAM user.

FIGURE 13.3 Authentication flow using SAML 2.0 to access the AWS console

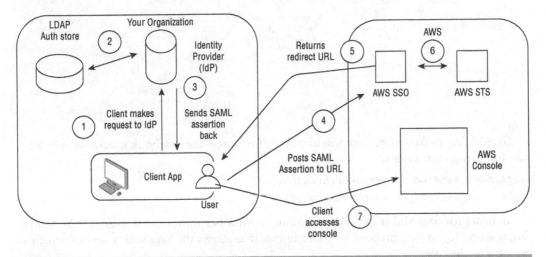

You can also directly call AWS STS without going through the SSO end-point if you are not enabling AWS console access but rather want a user to simply assume a role to perform certain actions such as get or put an object in an S3 bucket. For more information on this flow, refer to the diagram here: https://docs.aws.amazon.com/IAM/latest/UserGuide/id_roles_providers_saml.html.

Once a user is authenticated, SageMaker works with AWS IAM roles to grant users permissions to perform actions. SageMaker is a managed service, so it requires an execution role to perform actions on a user's behalf. As a result, a data scientist may not need explicit permissions to create training or processing jobs. The data scientist simply needs permissions to access the SageMaker notebook instance or Studio user profile (via a PresignedURL), and the notebook or user-profile execution role will perform actions on their behalf. See Figure 13.4 for an illustration.

FIGURE 13.4   Different IAM roles applicable to SageMaker

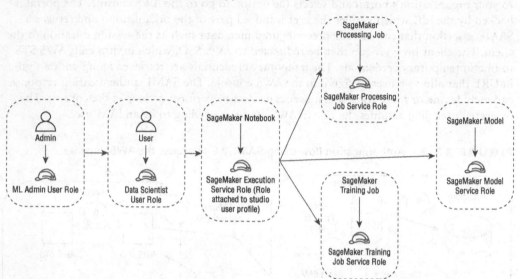

SageMaker Python SDK also provides an API to access the notebook execution role, as the following code shows:

```
sagemaker_session = sagemaker.Session()
role = sagemaker.get_execution_role()
```

In order for SageMaker to perform actions on your behalf, you need to attach the following trust policy to the notebook's execution role that allows the SageMaker service principal to assume the role:

```
{
    "Version": "2012-10-17",
    "Statement": [
        {
            "Effect": "Allow",
            "Principal": {
                "Service": "sagemaker.amazonaws.com"
            },
            "Action": "sts:AssumeRole"
        }
    ]
}
```

Additionally, your notebook execution role must have iam:PassRole permissions in order to run training and processing jobs on your behalf.

With these minimal permissions in place, you can now provide access to specific APIs depending on what you want to do. For example, if you want to run SageMaker Training jobs, the `CreateTrainingJob`, `ListTrainingJobs`, `DescribeTrainingJob`, and `StopTrainingJob` permissions may be relevant. The full list of SageMaker APIs is available here: `https://docs.aws.amazon.com/sagemaker/latest/APIReference/Welcome.html`.

> When constructing IAM policies for a SageMaker notebook execution role, always follow the principle of least privilege by only granting permissions that are needed for that role or job function. A common example is in organizations that have ML engineers who build CI/CD pipelines and data scientists who run model training and model tuning jobs. In this case, the data scientists may not need permissions to access DevOps tools or permissions to deploy models as endpoints, and similarly, the ML engineers may not need permissions to create training or hyperparameter tuning jobs.

Data Protection

Data protection consists of encrypting your data at rest and in transit. For encryption at rest, SageMaker notebooks, SageMaker training jobs, and processing jobs use AWS managed customer master keys (CMKs) by default to encrypt data at rest. However, you can specify customer managed CMKs if you wish to do so.

For SageMaker training jobs, there are two kinds of CMKs you can use—a volume KMS key to encrypt the attached EBS volume, and an output KMS key to encrypt any model artifacts before they are stored in your output bucket. You need to specify these keys when calling the `CreateTrainingJob` API.

The same controls apply to SageMaker processing jobs, SageMaker hyperparameter tuning jobs, and SageMaker AutoML jobs using AutoPilot. When serving a model using SageMaker endpoints, you can encrypt the EBS volume attached to the hosting instance.

For notebooks, if you are using SageMaker notebook instances, you can encrypt the attached EBS volume. For SageMaker Studio notebooks, you can encrypt the attached EFS volume and the EBS volume attached to the host instance using the same CMK. Studio notebooks allow you to share notebooks among users in a Studio domain via an intermediate S3 bucket. You can also encrypt this S3 bucket.

Data is automatically encrypted in transit for internetwork data using TLS (Transport Layer Security protocol) 1.2. Some intra-network data in transit within the Amazon service platform is unencrypted, such as traffic between nodes during distributed training or processing jobs, and communication between service control plane and training jobs. You can enable internode traffic encryption for your training and processing jobs for added security.

NOTE

Enabling internode encryption will increase the training times and therefore the cost. You should be aware of this if you choose to enable internode encryption as an added security measure.

You also need to enable UDP and ESP 50 IP protocols from port range 500 inbound and outbound in your security group for this to work. Read more about encryption in transit here: `https://docs.aws.amazon.com/sagemaker/latest/dg/train-encrypt.html`.

Network Isolation

SageMaker notebooks and Studio notebooks are Internet enabled by default. This can provide a route for unauthorized access to your data. By launching Studio and SageMaker notebooks inside a private VPC (and additionally disabling Direct Internet Access for SageMaker notebook instances), you can control network traffic and data movement to and from your SageMaker environment to flow within your VPC.

A natural next question is how you can then enable SageMaker to access data in your S3 buckets or how you can enable data scientists or applications (such as your containers or Lambda functions) from making control plane API calls to SageMaker APIs. SageMaker uses VPC endpoints to allow users to securely make SageMaker API calls. These VPC endpoints are powered by AWS PrivateLink, and therefore allow you to access SageMaker service without requiring a public IP address, an Internet gateway, or a NAT device. Figure 13.5 shows how SageMaker Studio can use elastic network interfaces (ENIs) to connect to other services inside your VPC. When you create a SageMaker Studio domain in your private VPC, SageMaker will stand up ENIs, which will enable secure and private communication to other AWS services via VPC endpoints, as shown in Figure 13.5.

FIGURE 13.5   Private network traffic to SageMaker Studio

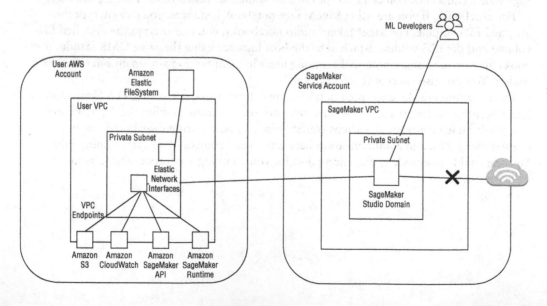

During processing, training, and hosting, SageMaker can also use ENIs to access data in your S3 buckets without traversing the Internet. In order to do so, you need to specify a VpcConfig when you call the CreateProcessingJob API, as shown here (reproduced from https://docs.aws.amazon.com/sagemaker/latest/dg/process-vpc.html):

```
VpcConfig: {
    "Subnets": [
        "subnet-0123456789abcdef0",
        "subnet-0123456789abcdef1",
        "subnet-0123456789abcdef2"
    ],
    "SecurityGroupIds": [
    "sg-0123456789abcdef0"
    ]
```

During hosting, SageMaker endpoints require high availability by default, so you have to specify a minimum of two subnets in different availability zones. For training or processing jobs, you can specify only a single subnet since training and processing jobs are transient. SageMaker tears down the underlying resources once the jobs are complete, so customers don't have to manage idle or unused resources.

Logging and Monitoring

SageMaker training, processing, transform, and endpoints are logged and monitored by CloudWatch logs. For example, logs published during training such as training metrics can be used to debug SageMaker training jobs. You can find them in AWS CloudWatch under the /aws/sagemaker/TrainingJobs namespace. Similarly, if you are using SageMaker endpoints, you can monitor the performance of the endpoint using CloudWatch. You can also publish CloudWatch metrics to other services such as DataDog or Splunk. Alternatively, you can set up alarms to notify you when certain thresholds are surpassed during model hosting.

SageMaker endpoint metrics are available at a minimum frequency of 1 minute.

For training, batch transform, processing jobs, and endpoint instances, the following metrics are available:

- CPUUtilization
- MemoryUtilization
- DiskUtilization
- GPUUtilization
- GPUMemoryUtilization

If you are using multiple CPUs on an instance, you may see a CPU utilization higher than 100%. This is because SageMaker reports the CPUUtilization for a single instance between 0 and 100 multiplied by the number of CPUs. For multiple instances, it reports the average CPU utilization across all instances.

For SageMaker endpoints, the following metrics are automatically collected by SageMaker, at a 1-minute frequency.

- Invocation4XXErrors
- Invocation5XXErrors
- Invocations
- InvocationsPerInstance
- ModelLatency
- OverheadLatency

Model latency corresponds to the time it takes for the model to respond. Overhead latency is the additional time taken for the round-trip request depending on the payload size and authentication/authorization, among other factors.

SageMaker API calls are also logged in CloudTrail for audit reasons so that admins can trace user actions or actions taken by SageMaker. With the exception of the `InvokeEndpoint` API call, all API calls are logged in CloudTrail.

The following code snippet, reproduced from https://docs.aws.amazon.com/sagemaker/latest/dg/logging-using-cloudtrail.html shows an example of a CloudTrail Log when the `CreateEndpoint` API is called:

```
{
    "eventVersion":"1.05",
    "userIdentity": {
        "type":"IAMUser",
        "principalId":"AIXDAYQEXAMPLEUMLYNGL",
        "arn":"arn:aws:iam::123456789012:user/intern",
        "accountId":"123456789012",
        "accessKeyId":"ASXIAGXEXAMPLEQULKNXV",
        "userName":"intern"
    },
    "eventTime":"2018-01-02T13:39:06Z",
    "eventSource":"sagemaker.amazonaws.com",
    "eventName":"CreateEndpoint",
    "awsRegion":"us-west-2",
    "sourceIPAddress":"127.0.0.1",
```

```
    "userAgent":"USER_AGENT",
    "requestParameters": {
        "endpointName":"ExampleEndpoint",
        "endpointConfigName":"ExampleEndpointConfig"
    },
    "responseElements": {
        "endpointArn":"arn:aws:sagemaker:us-west-2:123456789012:endpoint/
exampleendpoint"
    },
    "requestID":"6b1b42b9-EXAMPLE",
    "eventID":"a6f85b21-EXAMPLE",
    "eventType":"AwsApiCall",
    "recipientAccountId":"444455556666"
}
```

Compliance Scope

AWS Config has a set of predefined rules for SageMaker that continuously monitor your SageMaker environments for compliance. For example, the following Config rule (`https://docs.aws.amazon.com/config/latest/developerguide/sagemaker-notebook-no-direct-internet-access.html`) monitors SageMaker notebooks to make sure they are not enabled with Internet access.

For a full list of all the predefined rules, see `https://docs.aws.amazon.com/config/latest/developerguide/managed-rules-by-aws-config.html`. The ones that start with the *sagemaker-* prefix apply to Amazon SageMaker. In addition, you can always create custom rules using AWS Lambda functions.

AI Services Security

The exam does not test the security for the AI services in great detail. Furthermore, though the pillars of Security remain the same for the AI services, you need to refer to each service in order to determine whether certain API calls allow encryption or whether network traffic can be isolated to your VPC.

Generally, AI services have synchronous (sync) and asynchronous (async) APIs. For example, if you are creating a custom Comprehend model, that is an async API call (`CreateDocumentClassifier`). However, if you are just calling the Comprehend pre-trained API to detect sentiment in your text (`DetectSentiment`), that is a sync API. Sync APIs do not store any customer data, so they do not require encryption at rest using customer-managed CMKs. By contrast, async APIs may require CMKs as they often store customer data to process a batch of data or train a custom model, if your security policies require you to encrypt data using CMKs.

A common concern from customers using fully managed software-as-a-service (SaaS) applications such as AI services is whether the service uses customer data to improve the underlying algorithms and models that they are trained on. You can opt out of specific services, doing so either at a service level or as a blanket requirement for all AWS services using AWS Organizations–managed policies. When this is done at an AWS Organizations level, it applies to all accounts within that organizational unit and globally across all regions. For more details on opting out of AI services storing customer data, refer to the following documentation: `https://docs.aws.amazon.com/organizations/latest/userguide/orgs_manage_policies_ai-opt-out.html`.

> For the exam, you just need to know that opting out is available for many AI services such as Amazon CodeGuru Profiler, Amazon Comprehend, Amazon Lex, Amazon Polly, Amazon Rekognition, Amazon Textract, Amazon Transcribe, and Amazon Translate.

Summary

Security is considered to be job zero at AWS, and the AWS ML certification expects that you have a working knowledge of security from prior certifications, as well as security on SageMaker. You can expect at least three to four exam questions on security, so we highly recommend that you deep dive in the SageMaker security section of the documentation (`https://docs.aws.amazon.com/sagemaker/latest/dg/security.html`) prior to taking the test.

Although the documentation takes a product-centric view, in this chapter we have taken a different view of security focused on the pillars of authentication and authorization, data protection, compute isolation, audit and logging, and compliance. This approach is motivated by numerous interactions the authors have had with security teams at various regulated companies, large and small.

Exam Essentials

Understand the AWS shared responsibility model.   Services like SageMaker and the AI services are higher-level services, so customers don't need to worry about patching and hardening the underlying infrastructure. However, they are responsible for encrypting their data and setting up network configurations where applicable for private networking.

Know the difference between Amazon CloudWatch, AWS CloudTrail, and AWS Config.   This is a popular exam question even in the ML certification. You don't need to be an expert in these services, but you need to know the difference.

Know that GuardDuty uses machine learning under the hood. GuardDuty, unlike Config, CloudTrail, and CloudWatch, detects anomalies from a number of different sources such as CloudTrail logs, VPC logs, and DNS logs.

Read the SageMaker security documentation in detail before taking the exam. Security is really job zero at AWS, and for ML, that means knowing SageMaker security well.

Understand how SageMaker connects to a VPC. It is helpful to know that SageMaker uses ENIs to connect to resources in your VPC. Also know how you can provide network configuration settings during training.

Know the different metrics reported to CloudWatch during training and during hosting. The training metrics are simply standard EC2 metrics whereas for hosting, Invocations and Model Latency is also reported.

Understand how SageMaker works with KMS. Carefully read the details of the section: https://docs.aws.amazon.com/sagemaker/latest/dg/encryption-at-rest.html to understand how SageMaker uses KMS to provide data protection at rest and how you can customize options for added security.

Review Questions

1. Which of the following is AWS's responsibility when it comes to security of Amazon Sage-Maker? (Choose all that apply.)

    A. Patching of the instances used to run SageMaker Training jobs

    B. Applying OS-level updates to the instances used to run SageMaker notebooks

    C. Managing the S3 bucket where SageMaker publishes the model artifacts after training the model

    D. Managing the network of your VPC, which grants SageMaker access to your AWS resources

2. Which of the following is the customer's responsibility when using Amazon Comprehend?

    A. Patching the EC2 instances that host the Comprehend custom model

    B. Managing the EBS volume attached to the training instances used to train the Comprehend custom classifier

    C. Managing the health of the endpoint used by Comprehend `DetectSentiment` API

    D. Providing customer-managed CMKs to Comprehend to encrypt any data stored by the service at rest

3. Which AWS service would you use to view performance metrics from your SageMaker endpoint and set alarms and appropriate thresholds to autoscale the SageMaker endpoint if they are surpassed?

    A. Amazon Inspector

    B. Amazon CloudWatch

    C. AWS Config

    D. AWS CloudTrail

4. Which AWS service would you use to log API calls made by users to Amazon SageMaker in their machine learning environments for audit purposes?

    A. AWS GuardDuty

    B. Amazon CloudWatch

    C. AWS Config

    D. AWS CloudTrail

5. You have a requirement to use customer-managed CMKs for all training jobs launched by the user to encrypt the EBS volume attached to the SageMaker training instance. What setting is missing from the following API call that the data scientist needs to include?

```
sagemaker.estimator.Estimator(
    image,
    role,
    instance_count=1,
```

```
    instance_type='ml.m4.xlarge',
    max_run=3600,
    output_path='s3://{}/{}/models'.format(output_bucket, prefix),
    sagemaker_session=sess,
    max_wait=3600,
    encrypt_inter_container_traffic=False
)
```

A. Nothing; SageMaker automatically uses a customer-managed CMK to encrypt attached storage.

B. Add an `output_kms_key` parameter and pass in your customer-managed CMK.

C. Add a `volume_kms_key` parameter and pass in your customer-managed CMK.

D. SageMaker does not support customer-managed CMKs for encryption at rest.

6. You have a requirement to only launch SageMaker training jobs inside your VPC because your S3 buckets are not accessible over the public Internet. What setting is missing from the following API call that the data scientist needs to include?

```
sagemaker.estimator.Estimator(
    image,
    role,
    instance_count=1,
    instance_type='ml.m4.xlarge',
    max_run=3600,
    output_path='s3://{}/{}/models'.format(output_bucket, prefix),
    sagemaker_session=sess,
    max_wait=3600,
    encrypt_inter_container_traffic=False
)
```

A. Provide your network settings using the `security_group_ids` and `subnets` parameters.

B. Provide your network settings using the `security_group_ids` and `subnets` parameters. A minimum of 2 subnets in different AZs are required.

C. Expose your S3 bucket to the public Internet since there is no other way for SageMaker to access it.

D. SageMaker can automatically connect to your S3 buckets via the AWS network without any additional configurations on your part.

Chapter
14

Reliability Pillar

THE AWS CERTIFIED MACHINE LEARNING SPECIALTY EXAM OBJECTIVES COVERED IN THIS CHAPTER INCLUDE BUT ARE NOT LIMITED TO THE FOLLOWING:

✓ **Domain 4.0: Machine Learning Implementation and Operations**

- 4.1. Build machine learning solutions for performance, availability, scalability, resiliency, and fault tolerance

Although a lot of our discussion of the ML lifecycle thus far has focused on the iterative and experimental nature, once an ML model is deployed into production, or once your ML environments are set up, you will want to ensure that they are resilient and fault tolerant against failures, that they can scale up and down elastically to meet your demands dynamically, and that you can quickly mitigate any service disruptions. In this chapter we will consider some best practices for ensuring that your ML environments are reliable.

Reliability on AWS

As you may already know from the AWS Well-Architected principles (https://docs.aws.amazon.com/wellarchitected/latest/reliability-pillar/wellarchitected-reliability-pillar.pdf) or from prior certifications, the Reliability pillar on AWS refers to designing your architecture to be resilient to changing business needs and to possible failures or disruptions that may occur. In this chapter, we will revisit the themes of change management and failure management in the context of your ML workloads.

For your own reading, we recommend that you read the "Reliability Pillar" section in the AWS Well-Architected Review, Machine Learning lens: https://docs.aws.amazon.com/wellarchitected/latest/machine-learning-lens/reliability-pillar.html.

Change Management for ML

Change management refers to the practice of anticipating, preparing for, and testing your applications to adapt to changing conditions, whether it is changing software such as upgrading model versions; deploying the latest version or rolling back to an older version; or changing business needs, such as ensuring that your application architecture can scale to meet growing or declining customer demand.

🌐 Real World Scenario

Change Management

You are a streaming media company that has built an ML model that recommends content to viewers based on their viewing history, their ratings of past content, and other similar viewers. For this first model, your primary customer base is about 100,000 users, mainly based out of the midwestern United States. However, as you collect more content on your website, the number of customers is growing rapidly, and your management expects that you will cross 1 million viewers by the end of the year and expand your user base to the entire United States. Your data scientists have trained the ML model and stored the model artifacts in S3, and the ML engineers are working to deploy this model into production. In the remainder of this chapter, we will discuss how to build a reliable architecture to meet your changing business and infrastructure needs.

There are three key pillars when it comes to change management:

- Manage change as code
- Monitor everything
- Test your environment in a production-like setting before deployment

The first pillar refers to ensuring that when changes occur, you can quickly roll those changes forward or backward as needed via automation and using CI/CD pipelines. The everything-as-code pillar we discussed in Chapter 12, "Operational Excellence Pillar for ML," refers to using automation wherever possible. Using infrastructure-as-code tools such as CloudFormation and pipeline-as-code tools such as SageMaker Pipelines and CodePipeline, you can automate your CI/CD workflows for ML.

For ML workloads, data scientists can check their model code into a code repository like GitHub or Bitbucket. This allows the changes made by data scientists to be versioned and tracked. Engineers can then pick up the branch, run unit tests to check for code quality, before merging the code into the mainline. Once merged, an automation pipeline can trigger the deployment of the model in a test environment. Integration testing may also be required to ensure that the code runs more complex user stories before code is deployed into production.

In addition to the code, make sure that the model artifacts located in S3 are versioned and tagged appropriately. Similarly, any containers used to package your training or inference code and dependencies should be versioned and persisted in a store such as Amazon ECR. For model artifacts that are designed for production use, using a tool such as AWS S3 Object Lock to prevent objects from being deleted (write-once-read-many [WORM]) is a recommended practice.

The second pillar refers to having instrumentation to monitor your ML workloads in production. Just like airplanes are instrumented with different sensors to monitor air temperature, wind speed, and air pressure, ML models that are serving production traffic should be instrumented to monitor the average invocation latency, the number of invocations received, the underlying CPU/GPU memory and disk utilization, and so on, because your ability to serve your customers reliably is dependent on the model performing as expected.

The third pillar refers to testing your models in a test environment under production conditions prior to deploying them to production. This will allow you to anticipate potential failure points and design your application to be resilient to those failures. Let's see how this applies to our earlier case study.

The ML engineers in our case study have created a separate AWS account for testing and production. This is a recommended practice because, by separating test and production accounts, you can limit who can access those accounts and provide a security boundary, as well as ensure that if something fails, it will not affect other production systems and have limited impact or blast radius. They have also pushed the model artifacts, containers, and code into a centralized shared services repository where it can be versioned, tracked, and persisted.

The engineers have now deployed the model in a test account environment using Amazon SageMaker. Here they will test the model endpoints for the expected payload in production and for availability, following the best practices outlined in Chapter 10, "Model Deployment and Inference."

For change management, they have also built a pipeline to perform A/B deployment using SageMaker so that when the data scientists upgrade the model to a new version, they can test the new version with a limited amount of traffic, assess the model performance, and switch over to the new model only if the new model's performance beats the previous model in production.

To test the model endpoints in the test environment, the engineers plan to use Amazon Cloud-Watch metrics to monitor the SageMaker endpoint for the number of invocation requests and latency. Given that the business anticipates that the number of users will grow tenfold by the end of the year, the engineers are testing the model for the future expected number of requests once the user base grows. During this testing, they find that the endpoint latency starts to increase as the number of incoming requests grows. This can result in a poor customer experience.

To solve this, the engineers consider using SageMaker Autoscaling. Autoscaling dynamically adjusts the number of instances serving your model to meet your demand. When the demand grows, more instances will come online to meet the demand, and they will scale down when the demand falls. However, it is important to realize that it is up to the user to test the autoscaling limits before putting their models in production.

Autoscaling requires you to specify an autoscaling policy based on a predefined (`InvocationsPerInstance`) or custom metric (e.g., `CPUUtilization`) on which to dynamically scale.

We highly recommend that you then load-test your endpoint first in production-like conditions to understand the kind of load your endpoint can handle. This will be contingent on the size of the instance, the kind of payload, and other factors. During load testing, monitor your endpoint using Amazon CloudWatch for the desired metric. For example, if you care about the invocation latency, you can monitor the average inference time as the load increases. Once that goes above a desired threshold, it means you have reached peak load capacity and need to scale up. By running tests on a single instance and understanding its limits and knowing your peak traffic requirements, you can determine the desired autoscaling policy. A popular Python-based load testing framework used in machine learning is Locust: `https://locust.io/`.

We recommend that you refer to the SageMaker documentation on load testing (https://docs.aws.amazon.com/sagemaker/latest/dg/endpoint-scaling-loadtest.html) and on autoscaling (https://docs.aws.amazon.com/sagemaker/latest/dg/endpoint-auto-scaling.html) to help you design a fault-tolerant architecture with SageMaker.

Having performed detailed testing, determining the best autoscaling policy, the engineers feel confident that they can deploy their model to production. A CloudFormation template is used to create the necessary SageMaker endpoint and production variants based on the configuration (instance type, autoscaling policy, etc.) determined during testing. After the model is pushed to production, the engineers have used CloudWatch Alarms to notify them in case the model performance dips below the threshold so that they can trigger a rollback to a prior working version of the model.

It is important to realize that there is no one-size-fits-all for change management. The level of change management and instrumentation you need to implement depends on the AWS services used. For AI services such as Comprehend/Textract, AWS fully manages the autoscaling of endpoints to meet customer demand, as well as the management of different underlying model versions. For Amazon SageMaker models, you need to manage the SageMaker model versions, the model artifact version in S3, the container versions in ECR, and so forth.

Failure Management for ML

Although the automation via CI/CD pipelines, the collection of metrics and logs to monitor endpoints, and the testing prior to deployment will allow you to anticipate and react to failure, it is important to ensure that your architecture is designed in a way such that it is fault tolerant.

Like any software, a trained ML model should be recoverable in case of failure or loss. To prevent accidental deletions, using S3 Versioning or S3 Object Lock to store model artifacts intended for deployment is a good practice. Similarly, separating production environments into their own accounts and minimizing any human access to production accounts as much as possible using automation for model deployment will limit any tampering and secure your production environments.

Returning to our case study, noting that the bulk of the customers were in the Midwest, the engineers deployed the model in the Ohio region. Furthermore, to ensure high availability, they deployed the model on multiple underlying instances. SageMaker automatically tries to distribute the instances across AZs for high availability: https://docs.aws.amazon.com/ sagemaker/latest/dg/best-practices.html.

Once again, depending on the underlying architecture used, you will need to consider whether the model is fault tolerant. In the case of AI services, AWS manages the endpoints and their availability on behalf of the customers. If you are deploying models via EC2 or ECS/EKS, you will need to ensure that you are deploying them across AZs for high availability.

When designing your architecture, it is important to anticipate changing business needs. In the case of our example, the engineers deployed the model in Ohio, but as the number of customers grew, particularly in California, customers began to notice an increased latency in the model response. It turns out the engineers had only tested their inference from a single region and did not notice this latency during testing.

Fortunately, since they had developed CI/CD pipelines and diligently versioned all their model artifacts and code, they were quickly able to redeploy an identical SageMaker endpoint infrastructure in the California region as well. By routing traffic using geolocation, they were able to route the requests coming from their California customers to the endpoints in that region and use the Ohio endpoints for the rest of the traffic. A second benefit of this is disaster recovery (DR). Now, in the unlikely event of a regionwide event, their ML model will still be able to serve customers by failing over to the healthy region.

Although multi-region ML deployments may not always be needed, it is important to consider where your customers are located and the desired serving latency. For business-critical applications, AWS recommends that you plan for disaster recovery.

Summary

As your ML applications mature and your ML models serve growing client traffic, it is important to ensure that these applications are fault tolerant and can be recovered in case of failure. Enforcing change management by versioning model artifacts, container artifacts, and source code; tracing model lineage from source to deployment; and implementing automation and instrumentation via monitoring can help you anticipate failures. Rigorous testing under production conditions in a test environment is a recommended best practice before putting any models into production. Implementing monitoring and setting up notification alerts will help you quickly identify the root cause in case of a failure and respond to it in a timely manner. Finally, if needed, consider a multi-region deployment for disaster recovery.

Exam Essentials

Understand the key components of the Reliability pillar.   We recommend that you read the Reliability pillar of the AWS Well-Architected Pillars Whitepaper to get a good understanding: https://docs.aws.amazon.com/wellarchitected/latest/reliability-pillar/wellarchitected-reliability-pillar.pdf.

Understand that different services require different levels of change and failure management.   For AI services, AWS manages service endpoints and model versions on your behalf, whereas if deploying on SageMaker or EC2/ECS/EKS, you need to implement them yourself.

Read the AWS Deployment Best Practices documentation for SageMaker.   The document can be found here: https://docs.aws.amazon.com/sagemaker/latest/dg/best-practices.html.

Review Questions

1. Which of the following AWS services can you use to discover when the `Invocations-PerInstance` metric of the SageMaker endpoint exceeds the desired threshold?

   A. Amazon CloudWatch Logs

   B. Amazon CloudWatch Metrics

   C. Amazon CloudTrail

   D. AWS Config

2. You are part of an ML engineering team tasked with deploying a fault-tolerant ML application. Which of the following best practices might you consider for storing model artifacts to aid in recovery and failure management? (Choose all that apply.)

   A. Consider using S3 Object Lock to implement a WORM model.

   B. Store model artifacts in S3 and implement a bucket policy that only allows certain IAM principals to access the bucket.

   C. Use S3 versioning and MFA delete to require multifactor authentication (MFA) when deleting an object version.

   D. Store model artifacts in an EBS volume attached to the host instance for deployment.

3. You are part of an ML engineering team tasked with deploying a highly available ML application on Amazon SageMaker. Which of the following best practices might you consider for ensuring high availability while also enforcing low cost?

   A. Deploy the model endpoints using multiple instances for high availability in multiple regions and in an active-active configuration for disaster recovery.

   B. Deploy the model artifacts in a single region but using multiple instances. In the case of failure, SageMaker will automatically attempt to redistribute instances across availability zones (AZs).

   C. Deploy the model artifacts in a single region but using a single instance. In the case of failure, SageMaker will automatically attempt to restart the instance in a different AZ.

   D. SageMaker endpoints are not highly available. Deploy on EC2 instead and use multiple instances in different AZs for high availability and low cost.

4. Which of the following services can you use to deploy ML infrastructure using infrastructure-as-code practices?

   A. AWS CloudFront

   B. AWS Elastic BeanStalk

   C. AWS CodePipeline

   D. AWS CloudFormation

5. Which of the following are advantages of separating production workloads in their own AWS account? (Choose all that apply.)

   A. AWS recommends deploying dev, test, and production workloads in the same AWS account to save cost.

   B. Fault isolation; separating production workloads in their own account can reduce the possibility of a failure in one system affecting other production systems.

   C. Accounts are a hard security boundary in AWS. By separating production workloads in their own account, you can implement least privilege and minimize human access to production workloads.

   D. It simplifies disaster recovery when an application fails.

6. You are part of an ML engineering team tasked with deploying a highly available ML application on Amazon SageMaker. Which of the following best practices might you consider for ensuring high availability while also enforcing low cost?

   A. Deploy the model on two or more instances across multiple availability zones (AZs) for high availability and use SageMaker spot pricing to lower cost.

   B. Deploy the model artifacts in a single region but using an `infl` instance. In the case of failure, SageMaker will automatically attempt to restart the instance in a different AZ, and `infl` instances are lowest-cost instances for inference on SageMaker.

   C. Deploy the model artifacts in a single region but using multiple instances. In the case of failure, SageMaker will automatically attempt to redistribute instances across AZs.

   D. SageMaker endpoints are not highly available. Deploy on EC2 instead and use multiple instances in different AZs for high availability and low cost.

7. You are part of an ML engineering team tasked with storing production ML model metadata and lineage for reproducibility, auditability, and traceability. Your company has wasted dev cycles trying to trace back code associated with production models serving external client traffic when the models were audited externally. Which of the following ML artifacts would you consider storing as part of an ML lineage or metadata management service?

   A. Data the model was trained on.

   B. Dependencies used to build the model training and hosting containers.

   C. Commit ID or hash to the code used to train the algorithm and deploy the model.

   D. All of the above options are correct.

8. You are part of an ML engineering team tasked with storing production ML model metadata and lineage for reproducibility, auditability, and traceability. Your company has wasted dev cycles trying to trace back code associated with production models serving external client traffic when the models were audited externally. Which of the following ML artifacts are likely not useful for storing as part of the lineage service?

   A. Data the model was trained on.

   B. Jupyter notebooks used for data exploration and model training.

   C. Commit ID or hash to the code used to train the algorithm and deploy the model.

   D. Hashes to the containers containing stable dependencies and packages used to produce the model.

9. In deploying a new ML model to production, you want to test the new model on a control group of customers to measure any uplift in your business key performance indicators (KPIs) before rolling the model out in production to all customers. What testing strategy might you use to achieve this?

    A. A/B testing

    B. Blue/green testing

    C. Canary testing

    D. Rolling deployments

10. Which of the following AWS services would you use to view logs from SageMaker Processing jobs?

    A. SageMaker Studio

    B. SageMaker Profiler

    C. AWS CloudWatch

    D. AWS CloudTrail

Chapter

15

Performance Efficiency Pillar for ML

THE AWS CERTIFIED MACHINE LEARNING (ML) SPECIALTY EXAM OBJECTIVES COVERED IN THIS CHAPTER INCLUDE BUT ARE NOT LIMITED TO THE FOLLOWING:

✓ **Domain 4.0: Machine Learning Implementation and Operations**

- 4.1 Build machine learning solutions for performance, availability, scalability, resiliency, and fault tolerance.
- 4.4 Deploy and operationalize machine learning solutions.

In the AWS Well-Architected Framework, the Performance Efficiency pillar focuses on efficient use of computing resources to satisfy design requirements. This covers data preparation, training, hosting, and end-to-end pipelines.

Performance Efficiency for ML on AWS

In this chapter, we will cover the Performance Efficiency pillar of the framework with a focus on machine learning. We assume that you have read the Performance Efficiency pillar of the AWS Well-Architected Framework that can be found here: https://docs.aws.amazon.com/wellarchitected/latest/performance-efficiency-pillar/welcome.html.

As a recap, let's first start with some highlights from design principles that you will find on the overall Performance efficiency paper under the Well-Architected Framework that also apply to ML. Later, we will dive deeper into some strategies of Performance Efficiency that apply specifically to machine learning workloads on AWS:

- Make adoption and use of ML easy for your team by using managed services for ML, especially ones that have serverless architectures implemented on your behalf; this lets the team focus on actual product development versus infrastructure management.

- Go global in minutes: think of how your global customers will benefit from deploying your ML workload in multiple AWS regions. The "everything as code" concept that we spoke about in Chapter 12, "Operational Excellence Pillar for ML," is extremely relevant here.

- Experiment often and decide what architecture and compute resources work best for your ML workload.

In this chapter, we will cover each of these topics and discuss the AWS AI/ML services you can use to implement these design principles into your ML workloads. Specifically, we will go over how you can use the following areas to achieve performance efficiency on the cloud; where relevant, we will talk about services and features that will help you perform these tasks:

- Selection
- Review
- Monitoring
- Trade-offs

When discussing each of these areas, we will go over multiple phases of the ML lifecycle. Let's begin!

Selection

As with optimizing the performance of any AWS architecture, use a data-driven approach to inform your decisions on what compute, storage, database, and network selections provide you with the maximum performance. To do this, you must first understand the wide variety of services available on AWS that can help you meet your technical requirements. Understanding the services available lets you compare, benchmark, or load-test your workloads and finally decide on the architecture that will be deployed in production for that particular workload. In the case of ML workloads:

- Chapter 1, "AWS AI ML Stack," discussed several AWS services in the AI/ML stack; familiarize yourself with these services and perform experiments to compare services that do have an overlap in functionality. For example, if you have a forecasting problem, consider testing Amazon Forecast, built-in algorithms within SageMaker, and your own algorithms for forecasting written using popular frameworks and implemented using Amazon SageMaker. Also consider cost alongside performance when evaluating these options.

- Benchmark your current implementation so that you can report on performance improvement (or degradation). This applies to all stages of the ML lifecycle. For example, when trying out a new technology for ETL or data preparation like Apache Spark or Dask, benchmark and record the time it takes to prepare your data, along with time taken for intermediate steps. When benchmarking training, you have several factors to consider, including training code–specific optimizations, GPU versus CPU optimized code, single GPU versus multi-GPU training, single instance versus multi-instance training, choice of using spot fleets, and when it comes to distributed training, considerations of communication and aggregation strategies implemented within existing ML frameworks or in specialized libraries like Horovod. Consider running the training job on self-managed compute or in a fully managed service like Amazon SageMaker. Finally, several aspects of deployment were discussed in Chapter 10, "Model Deployment and Inference," including selection of the inference stack, instance type, and choice of service when deploying your model in production. When considering cost-to-performance ratios, understand that the cost of training a model with 10 instances may be very similar to training with 1 instance, considering linear scaling (i.e., depending on the algorithm and other training specifics, you can theoretically train 10 times faster with 10 instances). In practice, although the cost for achieving this performance may not be identical in both cases, the difference may be negligible.

- Specifically for training, use SageMaker Debugger and Profiler or similar tools that can surface framework-level metrics and system-level metrics. SageMaker Debugger also automatically identifies issues such as I/O bottlenecks, underutilized GPUs, and other bottlenecks during training. Remember that better utilization of resources like GPUs may lead to both better performance and lower cost, thus leading to a better cost-to-performance ratio for your training phase.

▪ Specifically for deployment, it is important to use strategies discussed in Chapter 10 such as shadow and A/B testing along with model monitoring to capture the impact of your choices of instance type or model serving stacks. This will help you identify bottlenecks or excess capacity. Finally, we also covered autoscaling your model deployment with an appropriate scaling strategy so that you can scale out and scale in based on incoming demand. On AWS, you can match supply with demand using multiple approaches, including demand based, buffer based, or time based. Refer to the cost optimization section in the Well-Architected Framework for more information on this topic (https://aws.amazon.com/architecture/well-architected).

▪ When benchmarking and load-testing, use infrastructure-as-code (IaC) to run your tests in parallel with multiple copies of the testing environment; doing so lets you complete your test faster and keep the costs the same.

▪ Amazon SageMaker also lets you train your models with data residing on various storage services. Typically, data from Amazon S3 is copied over to the training instance before training commences. Although you don't pay for the time it takes for this transfer, this may add significant time to your experimentation and slow down your progress, especially with large datasets that take time to transfer. In these cases, you can evaluate the use of Amazon EFS or FSx for Lustre during training with SageMaker. Although with EFS, there is still an initial (and then, occasional) download to the EFS volume from S3, FSx for Lustre can automatically sync with S3 as a data source. Both EFS and FSx add cost to your evaluation, but you may be greatly improving application performance when compared to training on Amazon S3, especially when training with a large number of files or extremely large files. EFS and FSx also let you fine-tune performance using different models. With EFS, you can choose either the general-purpose performance mode or max I/O performance mode. With FSx, you can control the throughput by choosing a larger storage volume. When it comes to evaluating various storage options, use metrics such as throughput, input/output operations per second (IOPs), and latency.

▪ If you use a database that already has a managed ML training capability (like Redshift ML), consider testing and comparing this capability in terms of functionality offered, as well as performance efficiency and the total cost of ownership with respect to a bring-your-own ML framework offering.

▪ Finally, reevaluate your choices over time. Compared to what was initially observed, your system may be more memory-intensive, compute-intensive, or network-intensive. This gives you the opportunity to reoptimize your system with a focus on performance.

Review

The Review section of the Performance Efficiency pillar encompasses two major use cases:

▪ Review your existing choices over time as requirements change.

▪ Review your existing choices over time as new services become available.

In both cases, performance review of your ML workload should consider the following:

Everything as Code:

- Chapter 12 included a section titled "Everything as Code." This section talked about the main challenges that organizations of all sizes face: the ability to reproduce, test, and scale workloads across the organization. For ML workloads, we can define CloudFormation templates to build environments for ML teams that extend through all phases of the ML development lifecycle. The section also talked about using Systems Manager to store and manage configurations, specifically runtime parameters that are used by your CloudFormation templates. This can be considered configuration as code (CAC) for your CloudFormation Templates (IAC). Lastly, pipelines as code (PaC) tools such as CodePipeline, Airflow, Kubeflow, and others allow you to develop pipelines to train and retrain models and deploy ML models to production based on configurations provided by data scientists.

- Chapter 12 also talked about CI/CD (continuous integration/continuous delivery) for ML, including sections that compared and contrasted with traditional DevOps practices. CI/CD for ML also enables you to version your source code, data, notebooks, and pipelines and deploy in a repeatable and consistent way.

Metrics and Visualization:

- Chapter 9, "Model Evaluation," talked about metrics and visualization, two very important best practices under the Review section of the Performance Efficiency pillar. In order to test reliably, well-defined metrics are required to be identified up front so that comparisons can be made with respect to the right metric across experiments and across time.

- Use analytics and visualization to dig deeper into generated logs and metrics. This lets you know where performance issues are occurring throughout your ML workload.

Performance Review:

- Lastly, remember that this performance review can be done using an automated process along with your deployment pipeline. For example, with training, use SageMaker Debugger and Profiler rules to automatically stop training jobs when certain conditions are met; for example, overtraining, vanishing or exploding gradients, low resource utilization, or custom rules that you define.

- For deployment, canary testing that replicates typical loads can be used to test uptime and overall performance before updating or changing the configuration of a current model. As mentioned in the Well-Architected paper for Performance Efficiency, implementing a performance review process will allow you to apply Deming's Plan-Do-Check-Act (PDCA) cycle to drive iterative development (`https://en.wikipedia.org/wiki/PDCA`). This will let you evolve your ML workload over time as new requirements, options, features, and/or services emerge.

Monitoring

Previous chapters on model evaluation (Chapter 9) and the Reliability pillar (Chapter 14) talked about how to generate, aggregate, process, and visualize metrics. Specifically, we talked about how many AI/ML services automatically use services like CloudWatch to log and visualize primary metrics around training and deployment and what change management for ML refers to:

- Managing change as code
- Monitoring everything
- Testing your ML workload in a production-like setting before deployment

For both training and deployment, you should monitor your workloads to ensure that they are performing as expected or as planned. This is, once again, no different than monitoring any workload on AWS, and involves the following:

- Recording performance-related metrics (read about the built-in and custom metrics that the service you choose uses)
- Analyzing metrics when events or incidents happen
- Using features that help generate alarm-based notifications (see use of SageMaker Debugger and Model Monitoring for this)
- Reviewing metrics regularly; also consider reevaluating the metric definitions to see if you are measuring the right thing
- Proactively addressing performance issues; where possible, using automated alarms and triggering automated actions

Trade-offs

You can use trade-offs to improve performance of your ML workload. Trade-offs to increase performance often include increased costs and increased complexity of your architecture; this may further introduce the need to do more load testing and benchmarking. Let's take a look at a few scenarios where improvement in performance introduces changes in cost, complexity, consistency, and durability of your ML workloads:

- Using a pipeline for data preparation rather than preparing data ad hoc increases complexity, increases the need to test these ETL pipelines, and increases the need to test various alternatives to perform this ETL using AWS services. For example, data can be prepared with various database and analytics services on AWS such as Redshift, Athena or other database services, Glue, EMR, SageMaker Processing, SageMaker Data Wrangler, or Glue Data Brew. On the other hand, defining the data preparation step as one of these options gives you the opportunity to automatically test these steps and integrate them with the larger ML pipeline, thereby improving performance efficiency.

- For training, increasing the number of training instances and using the right setup for distributed training (in cases where distributed training is applicable) can greatly improve performance efficiency. In some cases, it is not practical to train your model with a single instance; these cases include data parallel or model parallel training, which are covered in Chapter 8, "Model Training." Here, the trade-off to be considered is performance versus cost. Note that since training typically runs faster with distributed training while using a greater number of instances, the cost may remain comparable to running the job on a single instance for longer.

- Performing hyperparameter optimization using Amazon SageMaker for your own models, as well as built-in HPO and AutoML features for other services like Amazon Personalize or Forecast, lets you explore various model hyperparameters and choose the model that maximizes a particular accuracy metric as the model to be used in production. The trade-off here is the ability to find more accurate models with higher cost.

- For model deployment, increasing the number of instances manually or through auto-scaling will let you serve more users or calling entities, generally with higher cost. In these cases, focus on the overall performance improvement to your ML workload, and capture user interaction and satisfaction scores as a function of time.

- In some cases, model deployment may need to happen at the edge; these are cases where model latency needs to be very low or where Internet availability is limited or nonexistent. Compiling a model, managing a fleet of edge models, and monitoring models at the edge require additional features or services, and this increases complexity. Features like Amazon IoT Greengrass and SageMaker Edge Manager aim to simplify this end-to-end application. In fact, deploying models at the edge may both increase performance and reduce cost, with an increase in complexity of your end-to-end ML stack.

Summary

In this chapter, we have covered various measures to improve the performance efficiency of your ML application, with a focus on selection, review, monitoring, and trade-off options. Use a performance review process that includes a data-driven strategy to continuously improve the performance efficiency of your ML workload. Using infrastructure as code, configuration as code, and pipelines as code helps you continuously evolve your architecture as requirements and metrics change and as new services and features become available that can add value to your ML use case.

Exam Essentials

Understand the various design principles for performance efficiency of your ML workloads. Use selection, review, monitoring, and trade-offs to completely evaluate the performance of your ML workload, across various experiments and across time.

Understand that performance improvements need to be made across all phases of your ML development lifecycle. From data preparation to training, testing, and deployment, evaluate your ML workload with well-defined and carefully selected performance metrics, while trading off against ease of use, ability to experiment and iterate, consistency, durability, global presence, cost, and complexity.

Review Questions

1. You work for a media company where you are building a computer vision neural network model to identify objects from images. You notice the model is taking a very long time to train even a single epoch on a single CPU. What are some approaches you can take to boost model training speed without sacrificing model performance?

   A. Switch to a larger CPU with more memory.

   B. Reduce the amount of data sent to the model and train the model on a smaller dataset.

   C. Reduce the number of layers in your deep neural network to reduce the number of training parameters.

   D. Switch to a P3 GPU instance type.

2. You have trained a deep learning model on a P3.8xlarge GPU and are now ready to deploy the model to production. However, you have noticed during testing that GPU usage during inference is quite low and that 3.8xlarge instances are quite expensive. What are some ways to optimize your hosting workloads to maintain the high throughput but lower the inference costs? (Choose all that apply.)

   A. Consider running your inference on lower-cost GPUs such as the G4 instance family.

   B. Compile your model using the AWS Neuron SDK to be able to run on EC2 Inf1 instances powered by AWS Inferentia.

   C. Switch to using CPUs instead. CPUs will maintain the throughput but significantly lower the cost.

   D. Run inference on AWS Lambda for lowest cost.

3. You have deployed an ML model to production using SageMaker but have begun to notice that during certain times of the day, the inference latency is starting to spike. The spike corresponds to an increase in traffic to the SageMaker endpoint. What is the recommended way to scale your endpoints while maintaining optimal performance and maintaining low costs?

   A. Manually deploy the model on a second SageMaker instance and use an application load balancer to route traffic to either endpoint in a round-robin manner.

   B. Switch to a larger instance type to handle the extra demand during certain hours.

   C. Use SageMaker Autoscaling to handle demand during peak hours. SageMaker will automatically scale down when the demand drops.

   D. Switch from SageMaker hosting to hosting your models on Fargate, and employ ECS autoscaling on Fargate to handle the increased demand during peak hours.

4. You are training a deep learning model using PyTorch on a large dataset that spans several hundred gigabytes. In order to train on the large dataset, you have switched to using distributed training across several GPUs. However, you are beginning to notice a significant drop in performance and are experiencing longer training times. How can you improve the training performance without sacrificing model performance?

   A. Training performance is slowing down due to I/O between nodes. It is expected when doing distributed training.

   B. Switch your framework to TensorFlow, which is known to have better performance than PyTorch.

   C. Modify your training code to use PyTorch Distributed Data Parallel (DDP).

   D. Modify your training code to use SageMaker's Distributed Data Parallelism library.

5. You are working for an ad-tech company and have deployed an ML model to production for real-time bidding. Your application uses ML to decide the best ad to show upon receiving a bid request. Due to the real-time nature, your application has very stringent inference latency requirements in the single-digit milliseconds. What is the best solution for model training and deployment when faced with this requirement?

   A. Train your model on premises but deploy your model using AWS Lambda in the cloud, fronted with an API gateway for low-latency serving.

   B. Train and deploy your model on Amazon SageMaker. SageMaker round-trip inference latency is already in the single-digit milliseconds.

   C. Train your model in the cloud but deploy the model at the edge (at the bidding location) for real-time, low-latency inference.

   D. Train and deploy your model on Amazon EC2. EC2 instances does not have the overhead of managed services like AWS Lambda and SageMaker and can be customized to meet your latency needs.

6. You have deployed an ML model in production that has a high throughput requirement for serving incoming client traffic using Amazon SageMaker. You have instrumented your endpoint to monitor the CPU utilization and the memory utilization. What other metric might you consider monitoring in order to ensure that you meet the incoming demand?

   A. InvocationsPerInstance

   B. ModelLatency

   C. GPUUtilization

   D. GPU Memory

7. You have deployed an ML model in production that has a high throughput requirement for serving incoming client traffic using Amazon SageMaker. The application is highly latency sensitive, and you need to set up proper thresholds for autoscaling in order to meet the service level objectives (SLOs) for your end customers. During testing, you have instrumented your endpoint to monitor the CPU utilization and the memory utilization. What other metric might you consider monitoring in order to ensure that you correctly set up your autoscaling policy in production?

   A. InvocationsPerInstance

   B. ModelLatency

     C. GPUUtilization

     D. GPU Memory

8. You are a machine learning engineer training deep learning models on expensive GPU instances on Amazon SageMaker. Leadership is concerned about the rising compute costs and would like to quickly instrument a system to reduce cost for long-running training jobs by shutting them down if the model performance has not improved after a certain time period. What AWS service might you consider to build such a system?

     A. Have your model code write the loss after each epoch to a STDOUT and store the results in a file. Use AWS Lambda to read the latest results from the file and if the loss has not decreased past a set threshold, have the Lambda function stop the training job.

     B. SageMaker is a managed service and as such imposes cost premiums. To lower cost, switch to a self-managed option such as EC2.

     C. Use SageMaker Debugger. SageMaker Debugger has built-in rules to monitor algorithm metrics such as loss and can automatically shut the job down if the loss is not decreasing.

     D. Use SageMaker Model Monitor. SageMaker Model Monitor has built-in rules to monitor algorithm metrics such as loss and can automatically shut the job down if the loss is not decreasing.

9. You are part of a large team of machine learning scientists, all of whom need to develop, train, and evaluate ML models. The scientists commit their code to GitHub once they are happy with their algorithm. As the engineering lead supporting these scientists, you are interested in building an automated pipeline where scientists can simply pass in some inputs and run at the click of a button that will train and evaluate the model on the provided dataset so that other scientists can quickly and reliably reproduce each other's results. What services might you consider to build such a pipeline? (Choose all that apply).

     A. AWS CodeBuild

     B. AWS CodePipeline

     C. KubeFlow

     D. AirFlow

10. As part of your enterprise cloud migration, you are starting to test training some models on Amazon SageMaker. However, your enterprise is using Airflow for CI/CD, as currently they are operating in a multicloud or hybrid environment. They are reluctant to migrate away from this because Airflow is used in many applications within the company. The customer is concerned that SageMaker as a managed service will not run using Airflow. As their trusted AWS solutions architect, you would give which of the following advice to the customer to build MLOps pipelines?

     A. The customer is correct. SageMaker does not run on Airflow, but it does run on Kube-Flow. Switch to KubeFlow to still use open-source technology, and use SageMaker Operators for Kubernetes instead.

     B. The customer is correct. SageMaker does not run on Airflow, but it does run on Kube-Flow. Switch to KubeFlow to still use open-source technology, and use SageMaker Kube-Flow pipeline components instead.

     C. The customer is correct. SageMaker does not run on Airflow, but it does run on Sage-Maker pipelines. Switch to SageMaker pipelines for your MLOps needs.

     D. Use SageMaker operators for Airflow.

Chapter 16

Cost Optimization Pillar for ML

THE AWS CERTIFIED MACHINE LEARNING (ML) SPECIALTY EXAM OBJECTIVES COVERED IN THIS CHAPTER INCLUDE BUT ARE NOT LIMITED TO THE FOLLOWING:

✓ **Domain 4.0: Machine Learning Implementation and Operations**

- 4.4 Deploy and operationalize machine learning solutions

  - Details about how to measure and keep track of cost implications of changes to your ML model

  - Strategies on how to reduce cost while maintaining performance of your ML model

Cost Optimization
Pillar for M

A cost-optimized ML workload meets the functional requirements of the application that involves one or more ML
models at the lowest possible price point. The ML Lens builds
over concepts that are explained in the Cost Optimization whitepaper on AWS that you
can read here: https://docs.aws.amazon.com/wellarchitected/latest/cost-
optimization-pillar/welcome.html.

In this chapter, we reiterate patterns outlined in the Cost Optimization whitepaper with
a focus on ML workloads. Finally, we end with a list of strategies to reduce cost when
designing your ML workloads.

Common Design Principles

Design principles discussed here are common to ML and non-ML workloads and are
directed at achieving business outcomes while minimizing cost. Before we move on to
ML-specific design principles and strategies, let's briefly go over common design principles:

- Invest in a team that is responsible for maintaining a culture of cost-awareness. This is
  absolutely essential as teams, such as analytics and data science teams, iterate quickly on
  the cloud while experimenting with massive-scale workloads. This increases both cloud
  usage and costs. You can use AWS Cost Explorer to forecast cost based on your historical costs.

- Implement cost-awareness in all internal processes; use services like AWS Cost Explorer
  and AWS Budgets to report on cost optimization improvements. Also, implement alerts
  based on spikes in cost usage so that the right teams will be notified and can act quickly
  to remediate the changes that caused the increase in spend.

- Develop and implement cost goals and targets for your team and/or organization.
  Consolidated billing in AWS Organizations lets you isolate and distinguish cost across
  different teams, groups, or functions within your company.

- Set up cost controls using organization service control policies, AWS Config, AWS Systems Manager, and AWS Budgets and SNS notifications. You can use IAM permissions
  to grant users or groups permissions to perform operations (like viewing billing- and
  budget-related information) on billing and cost management resources.

- Identify and attribute costs to different workloads and departments using tagging.
  Implement tag policies to define how tags can be used in AWS Organizations. Learn
  more about how to use cost categories here: https://aws.amazon.com/aws-cost-
  management/aws-cost-categories.

- Learn to autoscale and deprovision resources based on reduced usage to reduce cost. Learn more about which services can be used with AWS Autoscaling here: `https://aws.amazon.com/autoscaling`.

- When evaluating services to be used in your architecture, consider using serverless services, manager services to reduce operational overhead, and open source packages to reduce licensing costs.

- Select the right type, size, and number of the resource you are using. On AWS, you can do this using performance-cost modeling, based on historical metrics, or automatically using autoscaling.

- Select the right pricing model that works for the resources used in your architecture. Consider on-demand versus spot instances, and learn about savings plans and reserved instances.

- Finally, optimize cost constraints over time, and consider the previous bulleted items as your requirements change and as AWS releases new services.

As you can see, all of these points apply to machine learning projects as well. In the next section, we apply the ML lens and add on to these points.

Cost Optimization for ML Workloads

This section discusses cost optimization principles specific to ML workloads on AWS.

Design Principles

With the previous discussion on general cost optimization best practices in mind, here are additional principles designed specifically for ML workloads from the machine learning lens (`https://docs.aws.amazon.com/wellarchitected/latest/machine-learning-lens/design-principles-4.html`):

- Use managed services to reduce your total cost of ownership on AWS. For example, setting up and maintaining infrastructure to do machine learning may give you additional control and flexibility but may also be a heavy burden in terms of the effort required. Instead, consider using a managed service that lets you focus on building and maintaining ML models rather than maintaining infrastructure.

- Experiment with a small dataset, training for a few epochs, and deploying locally before training with the full dataset and deploying on an endpoint, especially when working with Amazon SageMaker.

- Right-size your instances when training and deploying. Start with smaller instances, scale to large instances, and then scale to an even larger number of instances. When training using GPUs, first move up to an instance type with a greater number of GPUs, to increase the number of instances.

- Optimize for cost by using spot instances, elastic inference on Inf1 instance types, and mixed precision training on instances with Tensor cores like P3 or G4.

- Consider which models are needed for real-time predictions and which ones are needed for batch inferences. Having a real-time endpoint up and running 24/7 can be unnecessary and costly.

Common Cost Optimization Strategies

First, there are several features that are built into managed AI/ML services that eliminate the need for you to build these services for yourself from scratch. In several AWS whitepapers, you will see managed services helping with this "undifferentiated heavy lifting." Take Amazon Forecast as an example. Forecast is a managed service that gives you access to various high-performance forecasting algorithms that you can make use of, with the ability to perform multi-algorithm hyperparameter optimization as well as host your forecasting model as an API—all this in a pay-as-you-go service. Another example is Amazon Sage-Maker, where several features related to security and compliance (like fine-grained access, VPC support, CloudWatch logging, end-to-end encryption at rest and transit) as well as features related to storage, network, and compute (such as remote training; training from S3, EFS, and FSx; managed projects; experiments; pipelines; solutions; and pretrained models) are built in; these features take time and resources to develop and maintain. Opting for a fully managed service may reduce your total cost of ownership compared to building the same functionality.

During the build stage, there are several strategies that you can follow. As examples, we provide four strategies that are relevant to workloads created using SageMaker components:

Strategy 1   Delete idle notebooks and apps. For SageMaker Notebook instances, you can use a lifecycle configuration script to automatically detect and shut down these instances. On SageMaker Studio, you can use a script to detect and delete running apps. For both Notebook instances and Studio, you can use a combination of CloudWatch events or Amazon EventBridge with AWS Lambda to shut down Notebook instances or running apps, respectively. An EventBridge rule can trigger a Lambda function that lists and stops running notebook instances or running Apps on SageMaker Studio. For more examples of how to achieve this, please take a look at this blog: `https://aws.amazon.com/blogs/machine-learning/right-sizing-resources-and-avoiding-unnecessary-costs-in-amazon-sagemaker`.

Strategy 2   Consider moving notebooks running on SageMaker Notebook instances to SageMaker Studio. On SageMaker Studio, the ability to switch quickly to another instance type and run multiple notebooks on several instance types allows you to right-size your development workload. Furthermore, you can use several features of Sage-Maker Studio such as experiments comparison, as well as view notebooks and reports for free, while other features are pay-per-use.

Strategy 3   When labeling your data with Amazon SageMaker Ground Truth, use both assistive labeling features and auto-labeling where high-confidence data is auto-labeled based on an active-learned model. This saves on labeling costs by allowing you to label more data in less time.

Strategy 4   Use SageMaker Data Wrangler to quickly build data preparation workflows in a visual way; then, export this pipeline as a notebook, as a processing job, or into a feature store. Sharing features and data preparation pipeline both increases productivity and reduces the number of repeated transformations done by separate teams to create the same features for various ML models.

In the Training phase, here are four more strategies that can help you optimize on costs:

Strategy 1   Use managed spot training on Amazon SageMaker. If a spot instance is interrupted, Amazon SageMaker automatically obtains adequate spot capacity again and resumes the training job.

Strategy 2   Use the right instance types for the right models; simple models may not train faster on larger instances since resources are not being fully utilized.

Strategy 3   Use SageMaker Debugger and Profiler rules to view system- and framework-level metrics. You can stop a training job when a specific condition based on a rule is met; also, you can view the automatically created reports to right-size your training instances.

Strategy 4   Use SageMaker's Bayesian optimization algorithm for HPO rather than performing costly grid or random search methods to tune your model.

When deploying a model, the following strategies will help optimize on costs:

Strategy 1   Use Autoscaling with Amazon SageMaker for scaling up and down your endpoints based on demand.

Strategy 2   Use multimodel endpoints where appropriate; for example, rather than creating 10 model endpoints, consider hosting the 10 models using the same endpoint. You can read about multimodel endpoints on SageMaker here: `https://docs.aws .amazon.com/sagemaker/latest/dg/multi-model-endpoints.html`.

Strategy 3   Use elastic inference (EI) for deep learning models. Test with different combinations of instance types and EI accelerator types to make sure you choose the right setup for your ML application.

Strategy 4   Use a combination of Neo compiled models with instance types that provide good performance-to-cost ratios like the g4dn.xlarge instance.

Strategy 5   Use Inferentia where possible; start with a inf1.xlarge and test your model's performance-to-cost target. For more information about AWS Inferentia, see `https:// aws.amazon.com/machine-learning/inferentia`.

Summary

In this chapter, we discussed various best practices around cost optimization on AWS while listing various strategies to save on cost for your ML workloads while maintaining performance targets.

Exam Essentials

Understand best practices and design principles for cost optimization.   Understand general design principles for optimizing your ML workloads for operating at a lower cost point, including setting up a practice for cost optimization, using managed services to speed up time to market, and using spot instances.

Familiarize yourself with common strategies to cost-optimize your ML workloads.   Learn about strategies that can be used in each stage of the ML lifecycle, including building, training, tuning, and deploying your ML models.

Review Questions

1. Your team currently runs a weekly HPO job and uses grid search for finding optimal hyper-parameters for a model. The team realizes that this is very costly. What strategy will you suggest to get to the same or better level of accuracy with a lower cost?

    A. Tune a model while changing only half the parameters.

    B. Tune a model with random search on SageMaker.

    C. Tune a model with Bayesian optimization on SageMaker.

    D. Tune a model on a notebook instance with grid search.

2. You want to use spot training on Amazon SageMaker but notice that sometimes the TensorFlow training job is interrupted and you lose progress. Although this happens rarely, you want to continue using spot training without losing work. Which of the following steps will you take?

    A. Stop using spot instances and use on-demand instances.

    B. Detect when the training job stops due to spot instance interruption and start an on-demand training job.

    C. Detect when the training job stops due to spot instance interruption and start a spot training job.

    D. Use checkpointing and continue progress with training in the new instance that SageMaker launches.

3. You want to label 100,000 images with the least cost and time on AWS. Which of the following options will you use?

    A. Use an open source labeling tool hosted on AWS and labeling.

    B. Use SageMaker Ground Truth with the auto-labeling feature with a Mechanical Turk workforce.

    C. Use Rekognition custom labels to label your images.

    D. Use Amazon Textract to automatically label your images.

4. A SageMaker Debugger report for one of your training jobs indicates that you have low GPU utilization. Which of the following strategies will likely increase your performance while lowering cost?

    A. Try a smaller GPU instance type.

    B. Try a larger CPU instance type.

    C. Try a larger GPU instance type.

    D. Try a smaller CPU instance type.

5. A company trains several models—one per ZIP code in the country—and is concerned that hosting these models on AWS will be very expensive. Which of the following will let the company easily host these models with minimum cost?

    A. Use SageMaker spot endpoints.

    B. Use SageMaker on-demand endpoints.

    C. Use SageMaker multimodel endpoints.

    D. Use one low-cost EC2 instance per model.

6. You are training large PyTorch-based deep learning models using a p3.16xlarge GPU on SageMaker. As the training time grows, training cost is rapidly starting to become a concern for leadership. What solution would you recommend to lower cost while still being able to train deep learning models with the least amount of code change and without impacting training times?

    A. Use TensorFlow 2 instead. TensorFlow models train faster than PyTorch models.

    B. Switch to training on EC2 to avoid the cost premiums imposed by managed AWS services.

    C. Switch to training on a single p3.2xlarge instead.

    D. Use SageMaker spot instances for training.

7. You are serving large PyTorch-based deep learning models using a p3 GPU instance. Since the serving infrastructure needs to be always on, costs are starting to grow. However, you have noticed that the GPU utilization during serving is not necessarily high but that serving on CPUs leads to increased latency and lowered inference throughput. How could you lower inference costs while still maintaining inference latency and throughput with little to no code change?

    A. Refactor your model and inference code to run using TensorFlow. TF serving is more performant than TorchServe.

    B. Switch to a g4.dn instance that is designed for inference.

    C. Switch to an r5 instance that is designed for inference.

    D. Use SageMaker Inferentia to deploy models using a custom chip for reduced inference costs.

8. As your data science team grows, as an administrator you are concerned about rising costs associated with keeping SageMaker notebook instances open and running. Furthermore, you have noticed that while scientists sometimes require GPU-based notebooks, at other times the GPU usage is extremely low as the scientists are primarily exploring data or writing algorithm code. What solution might you consider to lower costs while also maintaining a good customer experience and avoiding long instance startup and switch times?

    A. Package IPython and the notebook environment into a container and deploy it on EC2. Have scientists switch between different EC2 instances based on whether GPU or CPU is required.

    B. Switch to SageMaker Studio, which provides fast-start GPU-and CPU-based notebooks. Scientists can quickly switch between them in a couple of minutes and optimize cost by dynamically choosing the right instance for their tasks.

C.   Switch to Glue Studio, which provides fast-start GPU- and CPU-based notebooks. Scientists can quickly switch between them in a couple minutes and optimize cost by dynamically choosing the right instance for their tasks.

D.   Switch to EMR Studio, which provides fast-start GPU- and CPU-based notebooks. Scientists can quickly switch between them in a couple minutes and optimize cost by dynamically choosing the right instance for their tasks.

9.   As your data science team grows, as an administrator you are concerned about rising costs associated with keeping SageMaker notebook instances open and running. To lower costs, you would like to automatically shut down idle notebooks. What approaches can you use to do this?

A.   Create an AWS Lambda function that calls the `StopNotebookInstance` API using boto3. Manually call the Lambda function every day at a certain time.

B.   Create an AWS Lambda function that calls the `StopNotebookInstance` API using boto3. Create an EventBridge Rule to trigger the Lambda function at a set time.

C.   Specify an idle time and use SageMaker lifecycle config to install a script that calls the Jupyter API periodically to determine if there is any notebook activity in the specified idle time. If not, the script calls the `StopNotebookInstance` API and stops it.

D.   SageMaker notebooks cannot be stopped, only terminated. Save all the notebook data to S3 and terminate the notebook.

10. You have successfully used Amazon Rekognition for building image classification models, but you are getting concerned with the growing costs associated with the fully managed AI service. While you can retrain the model using another AWS infrastructure service, you are still interested in benefiting from pretrained models and fine-tuning them instead of training from scratch. You also want to leverage a managed service for hosting instead of developing your own model inference architecture. What approach could you use to lower cost while still retaining some benefits of managed AWS services?

A.   Use Rekognition Custom Labels to still benefit from pretrained models and fine-tune them. Extract the trained model artifacts to S3 and deploy them yourself using EC2.

B.   Use Rekognition Custom Labels to still benefit from pretrained models and fine-tune them. Extract the trained model artifacts to S3 and deploy them yourself using SageMaker.

C.   You cannot train a model on Rekognition and deploy it elsewhere. Use pretrained image classification models available on TensorFlow Hub for fine-tuning and host them on a custom hosting service built on EKS.

D.   Use SageMaker's built-in image classification algorithm to fine-tune the model and use SageMaker hosting.

Chapter

17

Recent Updates in the AWS AI/ML Stack

THE AWS CERTIFIED MACHINE LEARNING SPECIALTY EXAM OBJECTIVES COVERED IN THIS CHAPTER INCLUDE BUT ARE NOT LIMITED TO THE FOLLOWING:

✓ **Domain 1.0: Data Engineering**

- 1.1 Create data repositories for machine learning.
- 1.2 Identify and implement a data-ingestion solution.
- 1.3 Identify and implement a data-transformation solution.

✓ **Domain 2.0: Exploratory Data Analysis**

- 2.1 Sanitize and prepare data for modeling.
- 2.2 Perform feature engineering.
- 2.3 Analyze and visualize data for machine learning.

✓ **Domain 3.0: Modeling**

- 3.2 Select the appropriate model(s) for a given machine learning problem.
- 3.3 Train machine learning models.
- 3.5 Evaluate machine learning models.

✓ **Domain 4.0: Machine Learning Implementation and Operations**

- 4.2 Recommend and implement the appropriate machine learning services and features for a given problem.
- 4.4 Deploy and operationalize machine learning solutions.
  - Details about recent updates, features and service launches in AWS related to AI and ML.
  - Details about how you can make use of recently announced features for operationalizing ML.

Ninety percent of the roadmap for new or updated features and services on AWS is a direct result of customer requests and feedback. Consequently, AWS announces many feature and service updates throughout the year, generally concentrated around December, in time for their annual event, re:Invent: https://reinvent.awsevents.com.

In this chapter, we focus on recently announced updates, features, and new services in the AWS AI/ML stack and describe how these updates may be used in actual workloads. These may not be included directly in the current version of the certification exam but may be relevant for two reasons: (1) future versions of the exam may include these topics, and (2) our aim for writing this book is also to prepare you for becoming an effective Solutions Architect, Data Scientist, or Specialist in AI/ML space, with a focus on AWS services. Let's get started!

New Services and Features Related to AI Services

In this section, we cover recently announced AI services and new features related to existing AI services.

New Services

Over the past year, AWS announced several new AI services. Here is a brief overview of these services.

Amazon Monitron

Amazon Monitron is a service that uses machine learning to detect abnormal behavior in industrial machinery such as pumps or gear boxes using vibration and temperature data. The service uses sensors that can be set up and monitored using a mobile application that sends data to AWS for training specialized ML models. Amazon Monitron lets you register equipment that needs to be monitored, add one or more sensors to the equipment, and configure the Amazon Monitron Gateway so that sensors can securely send raw data to the user's AWS account. When Amazon Monitron detects abnormal behavior, users receive push notifications on their mobile app. Visit this link for more information on Amazon Monitron: https://aws.amazon.com/monitron.

Amazon Lookout for Vision

Amazon Lookout for Vision is a service that allows users to train custom machine learning models for visual detection of anomalies in images. Manufactured products that have visual defects may generally cause customer satisfaction or safety-related issues, and as such, it is important to detect these defects as soon as possible in the manufacturing process. Lookout for Vision can be used for detecting defects in products (for example, scratches on a car door in the manufacturing line) or for detecting missing components in a product (for example, a missing resistor in a mass-manufactured circuit board). Lookout for Vision lets users get started with as few as 30 images, trains a model, and allows users to create an endpoint for setting up prediction APIs. For more information on Amazon Lookout for Vision, please visit `https://aws.amazon.com/lookout-for-vision`.

Amazon Lookout for Metrics

Amazon Lookout for Metrics is a service that uses machine learning to detect anomalies in business or operational data. For example, assume you are tracking sales revenue; a sudden drop compared to the average trend in sales revenue can be detected by Amazon Lookout for Metrics. Additionally, Lookout for Metrics has ready-made connectors to popular storage services like Amazon S3, Redshift and Relational Database Service (RDS), and popular tools like Salesforce and ServiceNow. Lastly, Lookout for Metrics ranks anomalies by severity, and groups anomalies that may be related to the same root cause. For more information on Amazon Lookout for Metrics, please visit `https://aws.amazon.com/lookout-for-metrics`.

Amazon Lookout for Equipment

Amazon Lookout for Equipment is a service that uses machine learning to detect early warning signs that could lead to machine failures. Amazon Lookout for Equipment ingests time series data from any sensors attached to your equipment (e.g., for measuring temperature, pressure, flow rate), trains a custom model based on your data, and lets you continuously monitor this data for abnormalities. Lookout for Equipment can ingest data coming in from up to 300 sensors, and it can analyze close to 28,000 algorithm combinations to come up with the most accurate model for your predictive maintenance use case. You can run inference in real time or by triggering a scheduled analysis based on your business requirements. For more information on Amazon Lookout for Equipment, please visit `https://aws.amazon.com/lookout-for-equipment/features`.

AWS Panorama

AWS Panorama is a device that can be used to deploy vision-based deep learning models at the edge. AWS Panorama can be installed in factories or on-premises where there are visual monitoring or inspection use cases, and it can be used for typical computer vision use cases like object detection or activity recognition. AWS Panorama lets you add and stream images from IP cameras in your network that are Real-Time Streaming Protocol (RTSP)-enabled. A single Panorama device can connect to multiple incoming camera streams, and it can host multiple ML models. The device uses an NVIDIA Xavier GPU, and it is water- and dust-proof; as such, it is ruggedized for use in any environment. The corresponding Panorama SDK provides the software stack and APIs that can be used to easily deploy models at the edge. For more information about the AWS Panorama device and SDK, please visit `https://aws.amazon.com/panorama`.

 Real World Scenario

Rekognition Custom Labels, SageMaker Models, and Amazon Lookout for Vision

When dealing with real-world use cases, you may have to combine more than one service to solve the problem at hand. For example, imagine a factory with a single manufacturing line that is producing knives. The business may be looking at identifying the root cause of scratches that appear on the handle of these knives. In order to locate the position of these scratches (think of object detection or segmentation tasks), you can build a solution using (1) Rekognition Custom Labels or SageMaker models, and (2) Amazon Lookout for Vision. Rekognition Custom Labels or SageMaker models can be used for finding the location of the defect (like a bounding box), and Amazon Lookout for Vision can be used for determining whether the identified Region of Interest (RoI) represents an anomaly.

Amazon DevOps Guru

Amazon DevOps Guru is a service that uses ML to detect operational issues in applications. DevOps Guru uses application metrics, logs, and events to detect operational issues such as code or configuration changes that might result in anomalies such as underutilized compute or memory leaks. Insights provided by Amazon DevOps Guru can help detect and fix issues. DevOps Guru gets information from multiple sources, including Amazon CloudWatch, AWS Config, AWS CloudTrail, AWS CloudFormation, and AWS X-ray. Amazon DevOps Guru is also integrated with Amazon SNS and AWS Systems Manager OpsCenter for helping users quickly react to detected issues in applications running on AWS. For more information on Amazon DevOps Guru, please visit `https://aws.amazon.com/devops-guru`.

Amazon HealthLake

Amazon HealthLake is a Health Insurance Portability and Accountability Act (HIPAA)-eligible service that helps health-care companies to store, transform, and analyze health data at massive scale. Examples of health-care data include clinical notes, insurance claims, medical images, and other sensor data like EEGs. Amazon HealthLake organizes and structures patient information and saves this information in an easy-to-access, secure, and compliant manner. HealthLake uses ML models to transform unstructured data and provides powerful search and querying capabilities. Structured data is used to understand relationships between features and identify trends. For more information about Amazon HealthLake, please visit `https://aws.amazon.com/healthlake`.

New Features of Existing Services

Several ML features were added recently to services that already existed in AWS. Here are some recent announcements and updates that you may be interested in:

Amazon EMR Studio   This is a feature of EMR that lets admins set up managed notebooks for their analysts and data scientists. Any kernels or notebooks created within EMR Studio run on EMR clusters, which you can discover right from EMR Studio. Furthermore, notebook code can run on EMR clusters that use either an EC2 or an EKS backend. EMR Studio also lets you switch between multiple backend clusters, debug using the Spark UI, set up workflows using Apache Airflow, and automatically schedule or run parameterized versions of notebooks in production. For more information on EMR Studio, please visit `https://docs.aws.amazon.com/emr/latest/ManagementGuide/emr-studio.html`.

Amazon Redshift ML   Amazon Redshift is a managed data warehouse for querying and analytics over petabyte-scale data. With Redshift ML, users can use SQL queries to train and deploy ML models using data in Redshift. Under the hood, Redshift ML uses Amazon SageMaker Autopilot to automatically preprocess data and run hyperparameter tuning jobs to train the best model for your use case. Users can also use XGBoost and have deeper control of hyperparameters to train custom models for tabular data on SageMaker. To create a simple model using Redshift ML, your SQL query may look like this:

```
CREATE MODEL model_name
FROM { table_name | ( select_statement ) }
TARGET column_name
FUNCTION function_name
IAM_ROLE 'iam_role_arn'
[ MODEL_TYPE { XGBOOST | MLP } ]
[ PROBLEM_TYPE ( REGRESSION | BINARY_CLASSIFICATION | MULTICLASS_CLASSIFICATION ) ]
[ OBJECTIVE ( 'MSE' | 'Accuracy' | 'F1' | 'F1Macro' | 'AUC') ]
SETTINGS (
    S3_BUCKET 'bucket')

CREATE MODEL model_name
FROM { table_name | ( select_query ) }
TARGET column_name
FUNCTION prediction_function_name
IAM_ROLE 'iam_role_arn'
```

```
SETTINGS (
  S3_BUCKET 'bucket',
  [ MAX_CELLS integer ]
)
CREATE MODEL model_name
FROM { table_name | (select_statement ) }
TARGET column_name
FUNCTION function_name
IAM_ROLE 'iam_role_arn'
AUTO OFF
MODEL_TYPE XGBOOST
OBJECTIVE { 'reg:squarederror' }
HYPERPARAMETERS DEFAULT EXCEPT (
    NUM_ROUND '10',
    ETA '0.2',
    NUM_CLASS '10',
    (, ...)
)
PREPROCESSORS 'none'
SETTINGS (
  S3_BUCKET 'bucket',
  KMS_KEY_ID 'kms_key_id', |
  MAX_CELLS 100000
)
```

For more information on Redshift ML, please visit https://docs.aws.amazon.com/
redshift/latest/dg/machine_learning.html.

Amazon Kendra Features   Amazon Kendra announced new features and improvements
recently, and we mention a few of these features here. The Kendra UI allows users to
provide feedback for results that they see for their search queries. Using feedback from
queries, Kendra uses incremental learning to improve ranking algorithms that then
improves subsequent search results. Users can provide feedback visually on the AWS
console using a JavaScript library or using Kendra APIs. Two types of feedback can be
provided: counts of how many times a result was clicked, and marking the result as "relevant" or "not relevant." Amazon Kendra also added features for connecting to Google
Drive and ingesting documents from Google Docs and Google Slides. The Google
Drive connector is a new addition to a list of existing connectors to AWS services (like
Amazon S3 and RDS), as well as external connectors like Microsoft OneDrive and
SharePoint, Salesforce, and ServiceNow. Lastly, Amazon Kendra added the ability to use
custom synonyms to improve the accuracy of search results. Adding a synonyms file can
help improve results in cases where there are domain-specific or business-specific words
in the documents provided. For more information on Amazon Kendra, please visit
https://docs.aws.amazon.com/kendra/latest/dg/what-is-kendra.html.

Amazon Neptune ML   Amazon Neptune is a managed graph database that helps users create sophisticated graph applications. With Amazon Neptune ML, users can easily build Graph Neural Network (GNN)-based models using the open-source Deep Graph Library (DGL) on Amazon SageMaker. With this feature, users can train GNNs using standard Neptune queries with ease. Typical use cases like product recommendation or fraud detection can be set up as node classification, node regression, edge classification, edge regression, or link prediction problems.

Training a model is as simple as using a `Curl` command that looks like this:

```
curl \
  -X POST https://(neptune-endpoint)/ml/modeltraining
  -H 'Content-Type: application/json' \
  -d '{
        "id" : "(model-training-ID)",
        "dataProcessingJobId" : "(data-processing-id)",
        "trainModelS3Location" : "s3://(bucket)/neptune-model-graph-
autotrainer"
      }'
```

It is common to use Jupyter Notebooks to run Gremlin queries against a graph database. On a notebook, Neptune ML provides helper commands to simplify the process of preparing the data for ML, training ML models, and performing inference on these trained models. For example, the following commands will start a training job from a notebook that has been configured correctly to use Neptune ML:

```
 training_params=f"""
--job-id {training_job_name}
--data-processing-id {training_job_name}
--instance-type ml.p3.2xlarge
--s3-output-uri {str(s3_bucket_uri)}/training """
```

```
%neptune_ml training start --wait --store-to training_results {training_params}
```

For more information about Neptune ML, please visit `https://docs.aws.amazon.com/neptune/latest/userguide/machine-learning.html`.

PennyLane on Amazon Braket   Amazon Braket is a managed quantum computing service that helps users build, run, and test quantum algorithms on AWS. With respect to machine learning, quantum computers can be used as coprocessors, and hybrid algorithms that run some steps on classical compute resources and other steps on quantum computing resources can be created. PennyLane is an open-source Python library that provides interfaces to common ML libraries like TensorFlow and PyTorch so that quantum circuits can be trained like ML models. Much like GPUs that you are aware of, quantum computers can be used as coprocessors to classical computing resources. PennyLane comes preinstalled on Amazon Braket notebooks and can be readily imported using the following command:

```
import pennylane as qml
```

Models that are defined in familiar frameworks like PyTorch can be modified using layers that are defined using PennyLane (using qml that was imported earlier). For example, assume that you load a pretrained ResNet model from PyTorch:

```
model_hybrid = torchvision.models.resnet18(pretrained=True)
```

You can then change the final fully connected layer of the model you loaded to quantum ML layers that you define using PennyLane, as shown here:

```
model_hybrid.fc = DressedQuantumNet()
```

Once you have defined your hybrid quantum-ML network, you can use Amazon Braket to train this model using a combination of classical and quantum compute. For more information about PennyLane and Braket support for the library, please visit the following sites: https://pennylane.ai and https://docs.aws.amazon.com/braket/latest/developerguide/hybrid.html.

Amazon QuickSight Q   Amazon QuickSight is a managed service on AWS for dashboarding and business intelligence. QuickSight Q allows business users to create visualizations out of their data using natural language questions. For example, "What is our customer churn rate by segment this year?" This results in a graph of churn rate in the current year categorized by customer segment. QuickSight Q is trained using data on sales, marketing, financial services, and healthcare data. This lets business users build visualizations with ease without any technical training on creating dashboards or analyzing data. For more information on QuickSight Q, please visit https://aws.amazon.com/quicksight/q.

Amazon Connect Features   Amazon Connect is an end-to-end, managed contact center for providing customer service at low cost on the cloud. Amazon Connect released a feature called Contact Lens in 2019 that used ML to analyze sentiment in transcriptions and compliance in conversations. Recently, this functionality was extended to work in real-time scenarios, enabling this ML-powered analysis to happen live, during calls. Based on these new features, contact center supervisors can be alerted when a customer support call includes specific language, sentiment, volume levels, or gaps in conversation. Additionally, calls can be automatically categorized based on categories defined up front by supervisors. Lastly, languages supported using Contact Lens was extended to 18 post-call and 4 real-time options. Amazon Connect also added Voice ID, a feature that creates a unique digital voiceprint of a user's voice that can be used to automatically authenticate the user when they call back into the call center. For more information about Amazon Connect, please visit https://aws.amazon.com/connect.

New Features Related to Amazon SageMaker

Amazon SageMaker announced several new feature improvements recently. This section provides you with an overview of these features.

Amazon SageMaker Studio

Amazon SageMaker Studio is an Integrated Development Environment (IDE) for machine learning. Apart from providing a centralized, fully managed Jupyter Lab environment for performing standard data science tasks on notebooks, SageMaker Studio also lets you track experiments, create projects, author and run pipelines, and more. SageMaker Studio is a centralized IDE that includes multiple features such as the following:

- Ability to organize multiple users with granular permissions within a SageMaker Studio domain
- Start multiple notebooks, kernels, and supported SageMaker applications within the same domain
- Notebooks that run built-in or custom container images with your packages and requirements
- Ability to change the underlying compute instance that runs each notebook and application on Studio with a few clicks
- Create and share notebooks with peers that share the same Studio domain as snapshots that include the notebook as well as the environment
- Visually pull, commit, and push changes to code and project folders using the visual Git workflow
- Discover Amazon EMR Spark clusters and use PySpark to run end-to-end data preparation workflows using notebooks

For more information on SageMaker Studio, please visit `https://aws.amazon.com/sagemaker/studio`.

Amazon SageMaker Data Wrangler

Amazon SageMaker Data Wrangler is a visual data preparation and feature engineering tool that currently supports adding steps to process tabular data. Data Wrangler provides over 300 built-in data processing steps, as well as the ability to add custom steps using Python,

SQL, or PySpark. You can import data from Amazon S3, Amazon Athena, Amazon Redshift, AWS LakeFormation, and Snowflake. Once you import your data, you can use one of many built-in data transformation steps in sequence to prepare your data. Here are some examples of these steps:

- Join data frames using various join types—inner, full outer, etc.

- Encoding data with one-hot encoding, label, or text encoding.

- Convert columns to different data types—text, numeric, date, etc.

- Process text data—pad, strip, capitalize, etc.

- Detect and remove outliers.

- Drop or impute missing values.

- Sort or shuffle rows.

- Assemble or flatten vector columns.

- Scale numeric columns using standard operations from Spark—for example, use the Standard Scaler or the Min-Max Scaler.

- Search, find, and replace strings in a column.

- Once your data transformation pipeline is built, you can export the pipeline as a stand-alone Data Wrangler Processing job, a SageMaker Python Notebook, or a Feature Store (see the next section).

- And more! For additional information on Data Wrangler, please visit the documentation page on AWS: https://docs.aws.amazon.com/sagemaker/latest/dg/data-wrangler.html.

Amazon SageMaker Feature Store

Amazon SageMaker Feature Store is a fully managed solution for storing, updating, retrieving, and sharing ML features. Features can be thought of as columns in your dataset. You spend several hours carefully preparing these features from a source dataset, without realizing that someone else on your team may need to prepare the same feature in exactly the same way. You may also need to reuse the same prepared feature in a different model that solves a different use case. Storing these features in a common, accessible repository of data is the main purpose of a feature store. With SageMaker's Feature Store, you can store and retrieve features for real-time or batch cases using simple APIs. Primarily, Feature Store lets teams browse through a catalog of available features, ensures that multiple team members are using standardized features with common metadata, and is useful in training (offline mode) as well as real-time (online mode) or batch inference use cases. Once a Feature Store is created, accessing data is as simple as querying the Feature Group using Athena SQL statements. These queries can also be run inside a notebook, where you can conveniently receive query results as a data frame. For example, you can run the following SQL query that joins two tables to form your training dataset.

First identify the two tables you want to join—in this case, imagine we had an identity table and a transactions table that need to be joined:

```
identity_query = identity_feature_group.athena_query()
transaction_query = transaction_feature_group.athena_query()

identity_table = identity_query.table_name
transaction_table = transaction_query.table_name
```

Then form the query string:

```
query_string = (
    'SELECT * FROM "'
    + transaction_table
    + '" LEFT JOIN "'
    + identity_table
    + '" ON "'
    + transaction_table
    + '".transactionid = "'
    + identity_table
    + '".transactionid'
)
```

Run and wait for the query to complete:

```
identity_query.run(
    query_string=query_string,
    output_location="s3://" + default_s3_bucket_name + "/" + prefix + "/query_
results/",
)
identity_query.wait()
```

Finally, load results into a dataframe on your notebook:

```
dataset = identity_query.as_dataframe()
```

To view and run the complete example shown here, please visit https://sagemaker-examples.readthedocs.io/en/latest/sagemaker-featurestore/sagemaker_featurestore_fraud_detection_python_sdk.html.

For more information about Amazon SageMaker Feature Store, please visit https://aws.amazon.com/sagemaker/feature-store/.

Amazon SageMaker Clarify

Amazon SageMaker Clarify is a feature of SageMaker that lets you detect bias across the various stages of machine learning. An example of bias is where your dataset does not have data from a particular demographic group. Imagine building a model that is used to predict whether a loan should be sanctioned to a particular individual. Bias in the dataset could cause the model to consistently reject a certain demographic. This is an active area of research in the field of machine learning. Bias can be detected before and after training on datasets. Once you have trained models, you can also monitor endpoints after deployment for bias. Clarify provides you with a mechanism to first analyze your dataset with various metrics even before you start training your dataset. Some of these metrics are class imbalance, difference in proportion of labels, and the Kullback-Leibler divergence score. More information about each of these pretraining bias metrics can be obtained here: `https://docs.aws.amazon.com/ sagemaker/latest/dg/clarify-measure-data-bias.html`.

Amazon SageMaker Clarify is integrated with Data Wrangler. You can specify columns in your dataset that need to be analyzed for bias (like age or gender), and Clarify will generate a report after analyzing your dataset with many standard bias metrics. More information about how you can generate reports using SageMaker Clarify can be found here: `https://docs.aws.amazon.com/sagemaker/latest/dg/clarify-data-bias- reports-ui.html`.

Amazon SageMaker Clarify also helps detect post-training bias. With post-training bias metrics, you can detect whether the data or algorithms used for training have introduced bias into your final model. Most of the metrics include comparing predicted labels with proportions of certain groups or facets in the dataset, or comparing actual and predicted labels. Some post-training bias metrics that are included in SageMaker Clarify are Disparate Impact and Difference in Conditional Rejection. For more details around post-training bias metrics, please visit `https://docs.aws.amazon.com/sagemaker/latest/dg/ clarify-measure-post-training-bias.html`.

Amazon SageMaker Clarify also provides you with a tool that helps explain your model predictions. After model deployment, there are several techniques that allow you to explain why a model made a particular prediction. One of the most popular methods for explaining model predictions is Shapley values, or SHAP. SHAP assigns a feature importance score for each prediction. SageMaker Clarify uses a scalable implementation of SHAP to generate feature importance scores. For more information on how to use SageMaker Clarify for your models, please visit `https://docs.aws.amazon.com/sagemaker/latest/dg/ clarify-model-explainability.html`.

SageMaker provides a container image with Clarify for running SageMaker processing jobs that can analyze your data or models for bias. The processing job saves the analyses conducted within the Clarify container in the Amazon S3 location that you specify. For more information about how Amazon SageMaker Clarify works, please visit `https:// docs.aws.amazon.com/sagemaker/latest/dg/clarify-configure-processing- jobs.html#clarify-processing-job-configure-how-it-works`.

Amazon SageMaker Autopilot

Amazon SageMaker Autopilot is an AutoML capability that automatically prepares features, and trains and tunes models with your custom tabular dataset for typical classification and regression tasks. Autopilot also generates a notebook that you can use to edit the individual steps that are used to build your model. To get started with SageMaker Autopilot, you simply point to a tabular dataset on S3 (for example, as a CSV file), select the target column, and start Autopilot. Autopilot then provides you with a dashboard that tracks the progress of the AutoML job, provides you with a leaderboard of all the models explored, and gives you the ability to compare different trials and deploy selected models to SageMaker endpoints. For more information on Amazon SageMaker Autopilot, please visit https://aws.amazon.com/sagemaker/autopilot.

Amazon SageMaker JumpStart

Amazon SageMaker JumpStart provides users with hundreds of pretrained models in the natural language processing (NLP) and computer vision space, as well as readily available solutions for various use cases in the form of CloudFormation templates. Pretrained models that are available from JumpStart can be deployed directly as endpoints, and some models can be fine-tuned with your own datasets, all from a single visual interface. Apart from models, solutions that demonstrate the use of SageMaker components along with other AWS services such as predictive maintenance, credit risk prediction, or demand forecasting are also available for you to explore. To learn more about Amazon SageMaker JumpStart, please visit https://docs.aws.amazon.com/sagemaker/latest/dg/studio-jumpstart.html.

Amazon SageMaker Debugger

Amazon SageMaker Debugger is a feature in SageMaker that allows you to debug and profile training jobs in real time or as a generated report. SageMaker Debugger can look into data that is flowing through your training jobs in real time and apply this data to built-in or customized rules. Some conditions that can be detected using the functionality of SageMaker Debugger are as follows:

- CPU bottleneck, GPU memory usage, I/O bottlenecks, or overall system usage
- Overall metrics for the framework used (e.g., TensorFlow or PyTorch) such as initialization time, and forward and backward pass–related statistics
- Detection of outliers in the duration taken for each step
- Specialized reports for XGBoost models, including saving loss values, feature importance scores, and predictions and labels for every five steps
- Detection of conditions related to deep learning models such as vanishing gradient, exploding tensor, class imbalance, overtraining, and stagnating loss function

With Amazon SageMaker Debugger, you can also create custom rules outside the set of provided built-in rules, and then trigger certain actions when these rules are detected, such as sending an email or an SMS or stopping the training job. This can help save on costs when certain conditions are met, especially when there is little to no benefit of continuing the training job. You can also create custom actions based on rules with the help of AWS Lambda Functions. For more information about Amazon SageMaker Debugger, please visit https://docs.aws.amazon.com/sagemaker/latest/dg/train-debugger.html.

Amazon SageMaker Distributed Training Libraries

Amazon SageMaker provides distributed training libraries for two major use cases: data parallel training and model parallel training. Parallelizing training jobs by splitting the dataset across multiple instances is called *data parallel training*. Parallelizing training jobs by splitting large models across multiple instances is called *model parallel training*. Diving deeper into the details of SageMaker distributed training libraries is out of the scope of this book. For more details on this topic, please visit https://docs.aws.amazon.com/ sagemaker/latest/dg/distributed-training.html.

Amazon SageMaker Pipelines and Projects

Amazon SageMaker Pipelines allows you to author, run, and monitor ML directed acyclic graphs (DAGs) that run individual steps, like processing, training, tuning, or model deployment, in a particular order. Since SageMaker Pipelines comes integrated with the SageMaker Python SDK, you can author your pipeline completely in Python. This makes it easy for data scientists, who are generally familiar with Python, to create end-to-end workflows for ML. Once you've created the pipelines, you can view and monitor them visually within Amazon SageMaker Studio. For more information on SageMaker Pipelines, please visit https:// docs.aws.amazon.com/sagemaker/latest/dg/pipelines-sdk.html.

Amazon SageMaker Projects give users the ability to create a CI/CD (continuous integration/continuous delivery or deployment) template to build, train, and deploy models. A SageMaker Project template is essentially a CloudFormation template that is managed as a product in AWS Service Catalog. A SageMaker Project is associated with several ML-related entities such as datasets, Git repositories, pipelines, model versions, and deployed endpoints. SageMaker provides users with several built-in templates that use different flavors of Git repositories and different pipeline choices, all as Service Catalog products. A typical setup includes triggering a pipeline when you commit a new version of the training or processing code. For example, an AWS CodePipeline or Jenkins pipeline is used to run the workflow you created using SageMaker pipelines, every time you check in code to a particular branch in your repository that may be created using AWS CodeCommit or GitLab. For more information on SageMaker Projects, please visit https://docs.aws .amazon.com/sagemaker/latest/dg/sagemaker-projects.html.

Amazon SageMaker Model Monitor

Amazon SageMaker Model Monitor can be used to detect whether models have deteriorated over time (also known as model drift), or when the data that was used to train the model is significantly different from the data that is being used for prediction. SageMaker Model Monitor can continuously monitor your models in production, and it's also integrated with SageMaker Clarify to detect model bias. For more information on SageMaker Model Monitor, please visit https://aws.amazon.com/sagemaker/model-monitor.

Amazon SageMaker Edge Manager

Amazon SageMaker Edge Manager is a software agent that runs on edge devices and provides edge inferencing capabilities. Models trained on Amazon SageMaker can be compiled using SageMaker Neo for the right target architecture and deployed onto the edge with Sage-Maker Edge Manager. SageMaker Edge Manager also provides a centralized dashboard to monitor models deployed to the edge, and it collects a sample of input and prediction data for monitoring, relabeling, and retraining. For more information on Amazon SageMaker Edge Manager, please visit https://aws.amazon.com/sagemaker/edge-manager.

Amazon SageMaker Asynchronous Inference

Amazon SageMaker Asynchronous Inference processes an incoming series of inputs to an endpoint and processes these predictions asynchronously. It is useful when you have large payload sizes, where it may take a long time to process incoming requests, and where there is a requirement to autoscale this real-time endpoint to zero instances when there are no incoming requests. To use SageMaker Asynchronous Inference, you point the endpoint to a payload placed in S3. The endpoint then processes the inputs provided in S3 and saves predictions back to a different S3 location. For use cases where there are erratic incoming requests of large sizes with small latency requirements, SageMaker Asynchronous Inference can be used to save on cost. For more information on Amazon SageMaker Asynchronous Inference, please visit https://docs.aws.amazon.com/sagemaker/latest/dg/async-inference.html.

Summary

In this chapter, we discussed various new AI/ML services, along with new features added to existing AI/ML services on AWS. Knowledge of these new services can simplify the design of your solutions to real-world problems when there is a good fit, so apply these new services and features when helping your customers with their AI/ML workloads on AWS. When there are new updates to Amazon SageMaker or AI services, you can expect launch announcements, additions to the documentation on AWS, and blogs detailing how to use these new features. Note that you will not need in-depth knowledge of these (and other forthcoming) announcements and new features for the current version of the exam, but you may need this knowledge to be effective in a role that expects you to be up-to-date with the latest from AWS.

Exam Essentials

Familiarize yourself with new services and features in the AI/ML space on AWS.   Although the content covered here may not be immediately useful for you in the exam, it may be useful in future versions of the exam, as well as in the real world when solving business use cases with services on AWS.

Appendix

Answers to the Review Questions

Chapter 1: AWS AI ML Stack

1. B. Although option C is also correct, you are looking for the easiest option in the list, which is option B.

2. D. This option involves the least effort since SageMaker trained models can be used on custom devices on the edge.

3. B. Amazon SageMaker allows the customer to use the same open source algorithm, with the same libraries and dependencies, but on the cloud.

4. A. When using SageMaker Studio, customers can create, view, and run pipelines without leaving the Studio console. This is the easiest way to orchestrate all manual steps that are being done in Studio notebooks.

5. B. Given the availability of the Spark processing feature on SageMaker, this is the solution that requires the least effort and maintenance to use, while also integrating with other steps in the ML pipeline.

6. D. Amazon SageMaker GroundTruth allows for custom UI templates; this is well suited for the current audio classification use case that is not directly supported by a built-in template.

7. B. Rekognition APIs support all of the customer's requirements and should be explored first before trying out any other solution given that the company does not have a lot of machine learning expertise.

8. A. Lex can be used for the chatbot experience, and Translate can be used for providing other language services.

9. D. Option C is incorrect because Amazon ETS does not have an item metadata option and will not solve the accuracy issue. Option B is incorrect because the company has a concern with the ARIMA performance. Option A is a potential answer, but the MAPE loss does not distinguish between over- and understocking, and you will need to use a weighted quantile.

10. D. DeepRacer allows you to learn about reinforcement learning using a physical race car that can be programmed and used for such a scenario.

11. A. Weighting the quantiles differently allows you to penalize under- versus overprediction. The other loss metrics use absolute values and are identical for over- versus under-predictions.

12. C. You should use Amazon Forecast, which is a managed service for time series forecasting. However, the DeepAR+ algorithm requires that related time series data be available in the prediction interval. So, option C is correct.

13. B. Only Amazon SageMaker Ground Truth is a data labeling service.

14. C. SageMaker Inference Pipeline lets you deploy a model sequentially by first deploying a processing container followed by the model inference container in the same host.

15. B. Although you can develop an entity detection model on SageMaker, doing so requires ML expertise. With Amazon Comprehend you can use pretrained models out of the box, so option B is correct. Be careful not to select Kendra, which also uses natural language understanding but for different use cases.

16. A. Remember that both Kendra and Comprehend provide NLU/NLP services but that only Kendra is an intelligent search service based on natural language.

17. B. Textract is a service for extracting text from documents. Be careful not to confuse Textract with Comprehend and Kendra, which are services for performing downstream tasks on text.

18. B, C. TimeStream and Clarify cannot process PySpark or Scala code.

19. A, B. Both AWS Step Functions and SageMaker Pipelines can be used to define custom MLOps workflows.

20. B. Options A and D are not valid services, and DevOps Guru does not provide suggestions to improve or refactor code.

Chapter 2: Supporting Services from the AWS Stack

1. C. Custom containers on AWS Lambda are an excellent way to host models in a serverless way.

2. C. Kendra supports VPC endpoints.

3. A. Parallel state will let the customer call Batch Transform on SageMaker with multiple input options so that the jobs run in parallel. The number of jobs that can be run, however, is subject to a service limit.

4. D. The customer can use S3 for storing raw data files, Step Functions and Lambda for calling Textract and Comprehend, and DynamoDB for storing final outputs.

5. C. Amazon SageMaker RL works well with RoboMaker, which allows customers to replicate their workshop in a simulated environment and then use the same in reinforcement learning training runs.

6. C. FSx is a fast filesystem that enables sharing and reuse of data across different training runs.

7. C. Choice state allows you to add branching logic.

8. B. An interface endpoint is an elastic network interface with a private IP address from the IP address range of your subnet. It serves as an entry point for traffic destined to a supported AWS service or a VPC endpoint service. Interface endpoints are powered by AWS Private-Link. So option B is correct.

9. C. Bucket policies allow you to set additional controls that determine what principals can access objects in your buckets.

10. B. A Lambda layer is a zip archive that you can use to package code and share it among Lambda functions. So option B is correct.

11. B. Lambda functions do require initialization time, so option D is incorrect. However, you can pre-warm your instances using provisioned concurrency to get predictable startup times for latency-sensitive applications. Option B is the correct answer.

12. A. Since you want to trigger the Step Functions when new data is present, CodeCommit is not the right answer. You can use a Lambda function, which itself is triggered via S3, but that would be a complex solution. Instead, set up an EventBridge rule.

13. A. FSx for Lustre is a high-performance filesystem that you can attach to your computer to share data across nodes. In this case, you can share data across pods in your EKS architecture.

14. B. EFS is a shared filesystem that can be shared across Lambda functions.

Chapter 3: Business Understanding

1. D. The ML lifecycle starts with identifying the business problem.

2. A. Refer to the CRISP-DM diagram shown in Figure 3.1.

3. C. Since this is a simple pattern-matching problem, you do not need ML to solve this.

4. A, B. Option C is incorrect because, since the number of rules is small, they can be put on a single server and parallelized over multiple servers as the data grows instead of scaling up. Reinforcement learning is too complex a solution for this problem, so option D is incorrect as well. The correct answers are A and B.

5. D. Refer to the CRISP-DM diagram shown in Chapter 3, Figure 3.1.

6. A. Training ML models is only useful insofar as those models and use cases end up in production, unless the goal is for general training. For this, you need to train models on data relevant to your use cases, which in most cases is your first-party data. Note that labeling data is often expensive; if you have use cases where data is handy that is of strategic importance, focus on it first.

7. B. This is an ML problem, specifically image classification. However, training such a custom model will require high-quality labeled data.

8. A, C. Options B and D are incorrect since transfer learning is a great way to train ML models on custom datasets even when you don't have many images available. Similarly, automated labeling is another technique to speed up data labeling using ML.

Chapter 4: Framing a Machine Learning Problem

1. C. Option A is wrong since ML problems don't require labels, that is unsupervised learning. Option B is wrong because that approach will greatly delay her timeline to production. Option D is wrong because there are no labels available. Thus, C is the best option.

2. B. The correct steps are as follows: Business problem ➤ ML problem framing ➤ Data collection ➤ Data exploration ➤ Model training ➤ Model evaluation. Refer to the CRISP-DM diagram shown in Chapter 3 in Figure 3.1.

3. B. Entity recognition is an ML problem that requires labels, so options A and D are incorrect. Option C is incorrect because the data is custom to the business and the entities will not be found in a popular corpus like Wikipedia. You will need to factor in data labeling as part of the solution.

4. B. While options A, C, and D are valid answers, solution architects should avoid the temptation of jumping to the solution quickly but should ask more questions to qualify the use case further.

5. B, D. KYC can be an ML problem, so option A is incorrect. Option C is incorrect since the customer has labels on the transactions themselves and can use them to construct a score. Option D is always a good question to ask, because ML can be expensive and time consuming.

6. B. Option C is strictly speaking correct, but an architect should avoid finding solutions for the problem immediately without understanding the entire scope. Options A and D are incorrect, so option B is the right answer.

7. D. All the above questions are good questions to ask. You want to determine not just the inputs to a model but also how the outputs will be used for business outcomes and how success is measured.

8. D. All the above are good questions to ask. You want to determine not just the inputs to a model but also how the outputs will be used for business outcomes and how success is measured.

Chapter 5: Data Collection

1. B. The data is unstructured since it is not tabular. It is a time series because the sensor publishes data every second.

2. D. The data is unstructured since it is not tabular. It is textual data and the use case is streaming as social media feeds can directly stream data into AWS or news can be streamed in by calling the news APIs.

3. A. If you are trying to predict housing prices, then the house price column is the label.

4. B. The United States has a finite number of ZIP codes. And a ZIP code of 11002 is not "greater" than a ZIP code of "11000," so the ZIP code numbers do not have a well-defined mathematical relationship. This is a categorical feature, not a numerical one.

5. D. Your IT security is describing the need for a centralized data lake. AWS Lake Formation is a managed data lake solution that allows you to catalog your data in a centralized manner as well as establish fine-grained access controls.

6. B. Although option A might seem like a good answer, it does not achieve the result of converting the data formats. AWS Lake Formation is not an ETL service, so option D is incorrect, and the AWS DMS does not use Redshift as a data input, so option C is not correct.

7. B. Since you want to move data from one database to another, this is a heterogeneous database migration. You can use AWS DMS for this.

8. C. Option A does not work since you cannot run custom SQL queries or alarms on Kinesis Firehose. Option D does not work because this is a streaming data use case and S3 copy is not a good solution for ingesting streaming data into AWS. You can build a custom SQL-based database to write SQL queries on EC2, but that would be complex to build on incoming streaming data.

9. B. Since the data contains key/value pairs, which are structured, in addition to text fields, option B is correct.

10. D. Image data is unstructured.

11. C. Day_of_week is categorical since there are only seven and there isn't an ordinal relationship between them.

12. D. While SageMaker is a perfectly valid solution to train ML models, it will require considerable code management to set up SageMaker, EC2, or Lambda. Option D is the best choice.

Chapter 6: Data Preparation

1. B. SageMaker Ground Truth is the AWS data labeling service for ML.

2. C. Redshift Spectrum does not require data movement, and you already have a Redshift cluster up and running.

3. C. Although options B and D could work, they are much more complex solutions. SageMaker Ground Truth with automated labeling handles the heavy lifting of training the model to speed up the labeling process.

4. D. Since you want to run everything on EMR, option A is out. Options B and C don't apply because Pig and Hive are not suitable for distributed in-memory data processing. Therefore, Spark for distributed processing and Spark ML for ML is correct.

5. A. Jupyter Notebooks are an interactive web application to enable users to author code and text using Markdown.

6. D. Redshift ML provides direct integration between SQL and SageMaker for running ML inference on SQL queries.

7. A, D. Both options A and D are valid choices for serverless data processing, and the solution often comes down to customer preference and comfort level. For very large-scale workloads (TB+), we recommend using EMR or Glue over SageMaker Processing.

8. B. Glue Data Brew allows you to explore data directly from your data lake and inspect it visually, and it has over 250 built-in transformations to process data. You could use Sage-Maker Data Wrangler as well, but Glue Data Brew is a better choice since your ETL pipeline was built using Glue as well. Generally, it is a good idea to use fewer technologies if possible.

9. B. Of the options provided, only Apache Flink offers event-driven stateful stream processing.

10. D. As a customer facing SA, you are aware that the customer is under a tight deadline. Transforming the code to a container to run on SageMaker or to use a different framework altogether would be a waste of time without any clear customer benefit. However, you can directly use existing PySpark code to run training on EMR.

Chapter 7: Feature Engineering

1. C, D. SageMaker Data Wrangler and Glue Data Brew are two low-code tools for feature engineering.

2. B. While both SageMaker Data Wrangler and Glue Data Brew are two low-code tools for feature engineering, only Glue connects with Aurora.

3. D. Replacing with the most frequent value to reduce the bias and replacing with the mean will both introduce bias in the data. To avoid this, try training an ML model to predict the missing values.

4. A. Options C and D are not valid because the feature engineering has to be done both on training and test datasets or else the model will not return a result on the test set. The model inputs need to be identical for training and test sets. Option B is incorrect because it introduces data leakage. So A is the only valid method.

5. A, B, C. Option D does not make sense, because if you drop all the fraud examples, then you don't have an ML problem anymore because all the labels are the same.

6. A, C. Duplicating each image by converting the format from PNG to JPEG is not a feature engineering strategy, and stemming does not apply to images.

7. C. Data augmentation is a common way to quickly and cheaply generate more labeled data, particularly for image-based use cases.

8. D. Median imputation is better suited for non-normal distributions. SMOTE is not an imputation technique. Only consider dropping rows if there are very few missing values.

9. D. Normalizing before splitting the data can introduce leakage, which can cause the model to learn aspects of the test data. This is the most likely reason for the high model performance on the test set.

10. C. Linear models are typically sensitive to normalizing features whereas tree-based models are not. So options B and D are incorrect. Option A is incorrect because unsupervised algorithms like PCA are sensitive to feature normalization as well.

Chapter 8: Model Training

1. B. The tags can be used to classify videos.

2. C. Manual and random search may not get to the best answer with a limited cost budget, since information from previous searches is not used in subsequent searches. Bayesian optimization is a choice available on Amazon SageMaker that can help find the best training job by improving with every batch of training jobs you run.

3. D. Note that L1 regularization is a good way of removing redundant features and reducing the dimensionality of your feature space, because it strongly penalizes smaller weights compared to L2 or ElasticNet.

4. C, D. Option A is wrong since the XGBoost algorithm can handle missing values. Option B is wrong because it does not treat those values as NaNs.

5. A. Option B is wrong as you are not trying to classify the printer but rather determine the location. DeepAR is a time-series algorithm and Object2Vec is another classification algorithm, so neither applies here.

6. A, B. Both Amazon Forecast and DeepAR consist of time-series algorithms, which is the problem at hand. Amazon Personalize is used for recommendation systems, and AWS Lambda is not a machine learning algorithm.

7. B. Only option B applies here since the model does not fit in memory. Option A is not useful because the problem is the model size, not the data size.

8. C. Options A and B are wrong since SageMaker publishes logs to CloudWatch without any additional work from the user. Option D is incorrect—CloudTrail is not a logging service.

9. A. EventBridge monitors status changes to various SageMaker components, including training jobs.

10. B. SageMaker Summarizer is not a SageMaker algorithm, SageMaker NTM is used for topic modeling, and SageMaker BlazingText is used for document classification. Seq2Seq models are ideally suited for summarization tasks.

11. A. Since you are detecting objects in images using bounding boxes, option A is the only correct answer.

Chapter 9: Model Evaluation

1. A. Generally, list- APIs will provide you with a paginated list of training jobs, with unique job names identifying each training job. Using these names, you can then use the describe- APIs to obtain more information about the training jobs.

2. C, D. SageMaker Experiment management can be accessed using API calls as well as through a visual experience on SageMaker Studio. Additionally, the SageMaker Search APIs can also be used to filter and compare different trials.

3. B. Diverging loss curves for training and validation as shown in the graphic are indicative of overfitting.

4. A, B. RMSE and WQL are used for forecasting, whereas F1 score and recall are used typically for classification models.

5. C. FPR can be calculated as FP / (FP + TN).

6. C. Recall of 100 percent means that all patients who actually had cancer were correctly predicted by the model.

7. D. Neural networks (NNs) can be trained to obtain a nonlinear decision boundary in this case. Other methods can work as well, but the question is about whether NNs can work here.

8. A. An AUC graph will show the performance of the model at all classification thresholds, and it is useful in this case.

9. B. Except for the F1 score, all other metrics are not model metrics, but they may be useful to the company for reporting purposes.

10. B. A scatter plot with several colors is difficult to read since you may have hundreds of trials with slightly varying colors based on the validation accuracy values. A bubble chart can represent the float number of validation accuracy well. Line charts are not appropriate for this example. Creating one bar chart per trial can be very time-consuming and impractical for a case with hundreds of experiments and doesn't allow you to compare easily.

Chapter 10: Model Deployment and Inference

1. B. Amazon Kendra trains models that are hosted by the service. These models are not made available for self-hosting or hosting via Amazon SageMaker.

2. D. The easiest way to host this model trained on-prem is to use the model artifacts with one of SageMaker's built-in containers or use a custom container. There is no need to retrain the model, and hosting on EC2, though possible, is not the path of least resistance.

3. B. Personalize campaigns are models hosted on your behalf that can be used as an API endpoint by the engineers on this team.

4. B, C. Both larger instance types and autoscaling will work, but best practice is to set up autoscaling rather than scaling manually.

5. B. Canary testing will allow you to replicate a typical user flow to make sure multiple components of your system (including ML endpoints) work well.

6. A. Canary release allows you to test systems on a subset of users before rolling them out to all users in production.

7. C. Blue/green release consists of having a green model in production and a blue model in a staging or test environment. Once testing is complete, the traffic is switched over from one to the other.

8. D. All of the options are true of SageMaker hosting.

9. C, D. SageMaker handles the provisioning and deprovisioning of compute, so option B is incorrect. Only SageMaker online hosting supports autoscaling today.

10. A, B, D. The AI Services and Amazon SageMaker on AWS are designed to remove the undifferentiated work of managing compute from customers. The models are hosted in an AWS managed account, but with SageMaker, you have more control of the security, autoscaling policy, and the model artifact. With the AI services, those are all managed by AWS as well.

Chapter 11: Application Integration

1. C. Amazon SageMaker Neo allows customers to directly convert their models into the CoreML format, and in many cases, hosting on the cloud may not be an option.

2. B. AWS Amplify provides built-in NLU functionality for working with text.

3. A. Several companies do securely save and access sensitive data on AWS, but keeping the data on-prem may be an organizational decision and is a valid choice since the company has sensitive data. All other options force the customer to move this sensitive data onto AWS before using any AI/ML services.

4. B. Amazon EKS Anywhere helps you easily create and operate Kubernetes clusters on-prem. See the Amazon EKS Anywhere website to learn more about this option.

5. C. API Gateway to SageMaker is the simplest solution with the least number of components involved.

6. B. Option A does not exist, and option C is incorrect. You can export the SageMaker model artifact stored in S3. Edge Manager is not an inference service.

7. B. Use AWS Lambda functions to quickly preprocess client data and call the SageMaker model hosting the API.

8. C. Option D is incorrect as Lambda does not support GPU-based hosting today. Option A is incorrect as it will lead to high cost. Option B is also incorrect because although SageMaker multi-model hosting will lower costs, the models are loaded at runtime, adding latency. In order to meet both cost and latency requirements, consider EKS.

9. C, D. Both options C and D are good options. Option A will likely not work due to the high-throughput requirement while it will lower cost.

10. D. Options A and C are incorrect as Personalize only trains ML models; it does not handle communication to end customers. SQS is not an external email service. Although option B is a possible answer, you have to manage the custom messaging via Lambda. Pinpoint handles this for you.

Chapter 12: Operational Excellence Pillar for ML

1. C. Of the choices provided, only CloudFormation is an IaC tool.

2. D. Although both Step Functions and CodePipeline can be used to include manual human approval as part of the release process, only CodePipeline provides a simple step to build in manual approval, whereas with Step Functions, you have to build a custom Lambda function to handle this. Since the question asked for the simplest way, the answer is AWS CodePipeline.

3. A. Amazon ECR is used to store and version Docker containers but not build them. Only CodeBuild is a container build tool that you can use as part of your CI process.

4. C. Although option B is true, it does not solve the problem. Option C will let you diagnose when there is drift in your data. You can then decide whether to retrain your models. Option D is incorrect because every week may not be the right cadence for model retraining.

5. B. Option A is wrong because SageMaker Model Monitor needs a baseline to detect drift from. Option C is wrong because an endpoint that doesn't capture the incoming payload means there is nothing for SageMaker to monitor. Option D is wrong since it does not describe a model monitoring pipeline. Only option B is correct.

6. B. CloudFormation StackSets are the tool used to create, update, and delete stacks across multiple regions and accounts.

7. C. CDK uses programming languages to configure and create infrastructure templates that can be used to provision cloud applications.

8. A. Step Functions now integrates natively with over 200 AWS services and 9,000 API actions.

9. D. Condition Step lets you specify a condition and branching actions that execute depending on whether the step evaluates to the Boolean True or False.

10. B. CodeCommit is a source and version control tool for code.

Chapter 13: Security Pillar

1. A, B. As SageMaker is a managed service, options A and B are AWS's responsibility. Options C and D correspond to users' S3 buckets and users' networking in their AWS account and are therefore the customer's responsibility.

2. D. Only option D is under the customer's control because it deals with customer data. A major benefit of managed services is that the service handles a lot of the heavy lifting that you would otherwise have to do if you were building this on EC2 instances or on premises.

3. B. CloudWatch is the service you would use to publish metrics and measure the operational health of your applications on AWS.

4. D. CloudTrail logs all API calls made by IAM users or AWS services. Don't be confused here by the word "audit."

5. C. Option C is correct. By default, SageMaker uses an AWS-managed CMK, so options A and D are wrong. Option B is used to encrypt any model artifacts.

6. A. Option B is only true for hosting, not for model training. Options C and D are incorrect.

Chapter 14: Reliability Pillar

1. B. CloudWatch Metrics is used to monitor endpoints.

2. A, C. Although option B is a good security practice for least privilege, it will not on its own prevent model artifacts from being lost or deleted. Option D is a poor choice since the EBS volume is not a durable store for model artifacts. Options A and C are both correct.

3. B. Although option A is a good practice if the application needs to serve client traffic from different regions, an active-active configuration can be quite expensive. Options C and D are both incorrect. Only option B is the correct answer.

4. D. Only CloudFormation is an infrastructure-as-code service. However, CodePipeline is a pipeline-as-code tool for CI/CD.

5. B, C. Option A is wrong because AWS recommends separating these environments into their own accounts, and option D is incorrect because isolating production environments does not by itself help with disaster recovery.

6. C. There is no spot pricing for SageMaker deployments, so option A is out. Options B and D are both incorrect. Only option C is the correct answer.

7. D. All of the above are valuable and important metadata required to properly trace the model's lineage.

8.   B.   Generally, as a best practice, you want to use Jupyter notebooks for iterative development. Once data scientists are happy with the algorithm, they should try to convert the code to scripts and commit the code to a repo. Storing notebooks by themselves is not particularly useful unless the notebooks contain code for visualizations or debugging that may be useful. In general, you should limit writing production code in notebooks.

9.   A.   A/B testing is a way to measure functionality of new software with a subset of users against business KPIs. Rolling, blue/green, and canary are software release strategies and not testing strategies.

10.   C.   SageMaker outputs job logs to CloudWatch logs. SageMaker Studio and notebook instances are services that manage Jupyter notebooks. Although you can use the `aws logs` CLI to view, list, and `grep` logs in a notebook instance terminal, CloudWatch stores the logs automatically.

Chapter 15: Performance Efficiency Pillar for ML

1.   D.   Options B and C are wrong because they may affect the model quality, especially if you train with less data. Switching to a larger CPU may not improve your training times, either. You should switch to a P3 GPU instance. For more on how P3 instances can be used for optimizing machine learning training, please visit the AWS documentation page for P3 instances.

2.   A, B.   Although switching to CPUs can certainly lower the cost, it may come at a price to the performance and requires testing. Similarly, although AWS Lambda may lower costs, Lambda has other limitations such as the total memory available and the timeout limits that need to be considered when employing Lambda as a solution to inference. Options A and B are the best choices.

3.   C.   Option A will not save costs since these additional instances will always be on. Option B might meet the demand in traffic, but you will pay more for the larger compute instance type. Option D is a very complex solution and not recommended because SageMaker offers autoscaling for endpoints already.

4.   D.   Although option A is true, it is not a solution. TensorFlow is not inherently more performant than PyTorch. Although option C is a good choice, SageMaker recently released the Distributed Data Parallel library, which has better performance compared to PyTorch DDP.

5.   C.   Inference latency in the cloud (regardless of whether using AWS Lambda/SageMaker/EC2) will not meet your real-time, single-digit millisecond requirement, so options A, B, and D are incorrect.

6.   A. Options C and D don't apply as there is no indication that the model is deployed on a GPU. Although ModelLatency is a useful metric, the relevant one here is the number of invocations the model is able to serve per instance.

7.   B. ModelLatency is the key metric of relevance here since you have a service-level obligation to meet on the round-trip latency.

8.   C. Answer A is an option but will require some custom coding. Since the models are being trained on SageMaker already, Debugger is a good option. Model Monitor monitors production models for data/concept drift. So option C is correct.

9.   B, C, D. To build such a pipeline, you need a build pipelines-as-code. Options B, C, and D can all help you accomplish this.

10.   D. Since the customer is already familiar with and using Airflow, it is much better to not impose a new technology on them but rather use existing tools. SageMaker operators for Airflow allow you to build MLOps pipelines using SageMaker and Airflow and are the right option.

Chapter 16: Cost Optimization Pillar for ML

1.   C. Bayesian optimization can potentially find an accurate model using less training job runs compared to grid search.

2.   D. Although it is rare, training jobs that use spot instances may be interrupted, and checkpointing is essential to ensure that you don't lose progress in training.

3.   B. Auto-labeling using Active Learning can help reduce cost by labeling some images automatically with high confidence while sending lower-confidence data to Mechanical Turk for manual labeling.

4.   A. Given that you have low GPU utilization on a larger GPU instance, a smaller instance may increase the performance as well as reduce cost.

5.   C. Multimodel endpoints can help serve thousands of models, one for each ZIP code, on a single, appropriately sized instance type.

6.   D. Training using SageMaker spot instances requires the least amount of code change. Option C will dramatically increase training times. Option A is incorrect technically, and option B will require code change.

7.   B. While option D might lower cost, there is no indication in the question that SageMaker was used for inference. Option A is not guaranteed to provide better performance and requires code change. The customer has already verified that CPU-based instances are not performant for this workload, so option C won't work.

8. B. Answers C and D do not provide such an option, and the EC2-based approach would decrease the customer experience due to the longer instance startup times.

9. C. Answer D is wrong as SageMaker notebooks can be stopped. Both answers A and B are options, but A is manual and B shuts the notebook after a certain time of day. That is not the requirement.

10. D. Although option C will work, you will need to set up your own hosting infrastructure. Options A and B are currently not possible using Rekognition.

Index

Online Test Bank

Register to gain one year of FREE access after activation to the online inter-active test bank to help you study for your AWS Certified Machine Learning certification exam—included with your purchase of this book! All of the chapter review questions and the practice test in this book are included in the online test bank so you can practice in a timed and graded setting.

Register and Access the Online Test Bank

To register your book and get access to the online test bank, follow these steps:

1. Go to www.wiley.com/go/sybextestprep (this address is case sensitive)!
2. Select your book from the list.
3. Complete the required registration information, including answering the security verification to prove book ownership. You will be emailed a pin code.
4. Follow the directions in the email or go to www.wiley.com/go/sybextestprep.
5. Find your book on that page and click the "Register or Login" link with it. Then enter the pin code you received and click the "Activate PIN" button.
6. On the Create an Account or Login page, enter your username and password, and click Login or, if you don't have an account already, create a new account.
7. At this point, you should be in the test bank site with your new test bank listed at the top of the page. If you do not see it there, please refresh the page or log out and log back in.

SYBEX
A Wiley Brand